Politics in

ENGLAND

We live under a system of tacit understandings. But the understandings are not always understood.
          — Sidney Low, *The Governance of England*

The Little, Brown Series

in Comparative Politics

Under the Editorship of

GABRIEL A. ALMOND

JAMES S. COLEMAN

LUCIAN W. PYE

A COUNTRY STUDY

Politics in
ENGLAND

AN INTERPRETATION

Richard Rose
University of Manchester

Boston and Toronto
LITTLE, BROWN AND COMPANY

Published simultaneously in Canada
by Little, Brown & Company (Canada) Limited

PRINTED IN THE UNITED STATES OF AMERICA

Foreword

THE Little, Brown Series in Comparative Politics has three main objectives. First, it will meet the need of teachers to deal with both western and non-western countries in their introductory course offerings. Second, by following a common approach in the analysis of individual political systems, it will make it possible for teachers to compare these countries systematically and cumulatively. And third, it will contribute toward re-establishing the classic relationship between comparative politics and political theory, a relationship which has been neglected in recent decades. In brief, the series seeks to be global in scope, genuinely introductory and comparative in character, and concerned with broadening and deepening our understanding of the nature and variety of political systems.

The series has two parts: the Country Studies and the Analytic Studies. The Country Studies deal with a set of problems and processes deriving from a functional, as against a purely structural, approach to the study of political systems. We are gratified that the participants, all of them mature scholars with original insights of their own, were willing to organize their discussions around a common set of functional topics in the interest of furthering comparisons. At the same time, each author has been urged to adapt the common framework to the special problems of the country he is discussing and to express his own theoretical point of view.

An introductory book, *The Study of Comparative Poli-*

tics, written by Gabriel Almond, provides an analytic supplement to the Country Studies. It also will open our set of Analytic Studies, which will offer basic discussions of such topics as political change in the emerging nations, comparative analyses of interest groups, political socialization, political communication, political culture, and the like. We hope these books will prove to be useful and stimulating supplements to the country series as well as points of departure in more advanced courses.

Richard Rose's *Politics in England* suggests the usefulness of a method which asks functional as well as structural questions and which is informed by recent developments in social science theory and research. He treats the historical background and the social context of English politics perceptively and imaginatively. He introduces themes that have rarely if ever been discussed in texts on British government. Such are his discussions of political socialization and culture in England, political communication, and the characteristic methods of political legitimation. We are pleased that his is the first volume to appear in the Country Studies, since it demonstrates that a clearly written, basic text can also make an important scholarly contribution to the literature of comparative politics.

Gabriel A. Almond
James S. Coleman
Lucian W. Pye

Acknowledgments

THIS BOOK is an attempt to sum up the experience of a decade of studying politics while moving back and forth between America and England. As an American with an English wife and bi-national children, this experience has been personally congenial as well as professionally stimulating.

The debts acquired in writing a book are many, and all of them cannot be acknowledged. In writing successive drafts, I have specially benefited from the comments and criticisms of James Douglas and W. J. M. Mackenzie, both of whom read and reread manuscript with an attention to fundamentals and to detail far beyond the claims of friendship. Particularly helpful and pointed criticisms were also received from Gabriel Almond, A. H. Birch, David E. Butler, James B. Christoph, Leon D. Epstein, L. A. Gunn, H. J. Hanham, Anthony S. King, Allan Silver, and Peter Willmott. Unpublished research findings have been generously made available by Gabriel Almond and Sidney Verba, by the British Institute of Public Opinion (the Gallup Poll), and by Ian Budge. None of the persons mentioned necessarily endorses any particular point in this study. They share responsibility for merits, not demerits.

Richard Rose
Peel Hall, Manchester, England

TO MY FATHER

Table of Contents

ix

Politics in

ENGLAND

Only connect . . .
— E. M. Forster, *Howard's End*

Introduction

The Americans of 1787 thought they were copying the English Constitution, but they were contriving a contrast to it. [1]

M ANY SOCIETIES are in a state of political turmoil today; England is not. Violent breaks with the past are a common feature of 20th-century politics, in Europe as in the continents of the ex-colonial peoples. Yet for the past three centuries, England has avoided the bloodshed and stress of revolution, while developing from a feudal basis a strong, stable, and adaptable political system. In the study of comparative politics, England is important as a deviant case, deviant because of its success in coping with the many political problems of the modern world. Just as Alexis de Tocqueville traveled to America in 1831 to seek the secrets of democracy, so today one might travel to England in search of the secrets of stable representative government.

Because of a common language, Americans have easy access to the literature of English politics.[2] Perhaps because 19th-century England was a time of great

[1] The epigraphs in this book are taken from Walter Bagehot's *The English Constitution,* the classic study of politics in England.
[2] See Appendix, Section 1, "Notes on Further Reading."

1

social and political change, the period is rich in studies that examine fundamental questions concerning the relationship of politics and society. Walter Bagehot's *The English Constitution,* published in 1867, is outstanding among these works. Bagehot showed how the use of psychological and sociological insights can enrich the study of political institutions. His enduring classic is a fit counterpart to Tocqueville's *Democracy in America.* At the turn of this century, four major books were published, each of which dealt perceptively with some of Bagehot's themes. They were M. I. Ostrogorksi's *Democracy and the Organization of Political Parties,* Sidney Low's *The Governance of England,* A. L. Lowell's *The Government of England,* and Graham Wallas's *Human Nature in Politics.* Each remains interesting today because of the continuity between the past and present in English politics, and because the question each discusses — the relationship between English politics and English society — is of permanent significance.

The rise of the Labour Party after 1918 greatly affected the study of English politics. It seems as if the challenge of Socialism led Conservatives and Liberals to cease writing frankly about many important elitist presuppositions of the political system. It did not prevent them from acting upon these presuppositions. Furthermore, some Socialist academics between the wars were greatly influenced by Marxist thinking, although the Labour Party itself has never been Marxist.

Harold Laski of the London School of Economics was the leader of this group; his *Parliamentary Government in England,* published in 1938, its chief product. Laski's disdain for non-Marxist sociology led him to conclusions that events since 1945 have conclusively repudiated.[3] In reaction against this approach, Joseph Schumpeter, an Austrian economist teaching at Harvard, wrote *Capitalism, Socialism and Democracy.* Schumpeter developed a theory of democracy as popular choice between competing elites; in formulating this theory he drew heavily upon the experience of England. R. T. Mc-

[3] Cf. his later *Reflections on the Constitution* (Manchester: University Press, 1951) and R. T. McKenzie's review of it, *British Journal of Sociology* (London) III:3 (1952).

Kenzie has given further significance to this theory by applying it in his post-war study, *British Political Parties*. Schumpeter's book, first published in 1942, remains relevant today.

For the past two decades, most English students of politics
have concentrated upon the study of the formal institutions of
government. Sir Ivor Jennings is the elder statesman in this
field. His major works — *The Law and the Constitution, Cabinet Government* and *Parliament* — show a lawyer's careful
regard for historical precedent. The series of electoral studies
written at Nuffield College, Oxford, have made an important
contribution to the study of one institution, elections.[4] Some
English students of politics, however, have consciously avoided
investigating fundamental questions of politics. R. B. McCallum, the first Nuffield student of elections, has even defended
voting behavior from intensive analysis on the ground that the
ballot is "the great eleusinian mystery of the democratic
state." [5]

The object of this book is to analyze the political system of
England with full regard to the social and psychological influences at work therein. It is thus wider in scope and different in emphasis from conventional studies of political institutions such as Cabinet, Parliament, and the civil service.
Such books do not include chapters on political parties, pressure groups, or political processes, and often explicitly exclude
consideration of the society's effect upon politics. The concerns of this book more closely resemble the pre-1914 subjects
of political study. Since Bagehot's time, of course, great technical changes have occurred in the way in which people seek
answers to the enduring problems of social studies; most recently, great changes have begun to take place in the study of
comparative politics. To follow Bagehot in spirit today, one

[4] Studies of the British general elections of 1945, 1950, 1951, 1955, and
1959 have been written successively by R. B. McCallum and Alison Read-
man, H. G. Nicholas, D. E. Butler, and D. E. Butler and Richard Rose.

[5] "The Study of Psephology," *Parliamentary Affairs* (London) VIII:4
(1955) p. 509. See also Michael Oakeshott, *Political Education* (Cambridge:
Bowes & Bowes, 1951), and, most controversially, Andrew Hacker, "Political
Behaviour and Political Behavior," *Political Studies* (Oxford) VII:1 (1959).

cannot follow him in form — nor can one hope to imitate his gift for epigram and metaphor.

One advance since Bagehot's time has come from the development of quantitative techniques, especially in the form of sample surveys of political attitudes. In this book, findings from public-opinion polls and from academic surveys are quoted whenever available. The secondary analysis of surveys conducted for a variety of purposes presents difficulties, but it is absolutely necessary in any comprehensive analysis. Unfortunately, insufficient research has been done by political scientists in England concerning some problems of great interest. Thus, posing basic questions about the political system inevitably leads beyond available data. In these instances, the author has drawn upon his insight, theoretical literature, and research findings in other countries to suggest tentative answers.

Another advance since Bagehot's time has come from the development of common sets of concepts permitting comparisons between countries that differ in their formal institutions but have similarities in their fundamental political processes. The organizing concepts for this book have been developed from the framework outlined by Gabriel Almond.[6] This combines three distinct merits. First, it draws together politically relevant ideas from a wide range of social-science literature. Second, the social, psychological, and political concepts are so joined as to emphasize the active interchange of influence between parts of the political system and of society. Third, it describes processes common to a wide range of political systems, from England to Ethiopia. This permits comparisons across national boundaries, across continents, and across cultures.

Because of the complexities of the subject and the relative shortage of previous research, in a book of this scope one cannot hope or pretend to offer definitive answers to questions with which many have been wrestling for generations. As its subtitle indicates, this study is no more and no less than an in-

6 See his "Introduction" in Almond and James S. Coleman, *The Politics of the Developing Areas* (Princeton: University Press, 1960). References in the text and footnotes indicate other theorists to whom the author owes intellectual debts.

terpretation; it achieves comprehensiveness by the use of judgments that are tentative and subjective. *Politics in England* is only in part an attempt to sum up what is known about the theory and practice of politics in England today; it is also an attempt to explore what may be learned through further study tomorrow.

CHAPTER I

The Context of Politics

The first prerequisite of elective government is the mutual confidence of the electors.

THE GRANTING of parliamentary government to many English colonies since 1947 has strikingly illustrated the great effect that differing environments can have upon the working of political institutions. A study of politics in England must therefore begin with a consideration of the ways in which environment influences politics.

The boundaries between different parts of English society are not so clear as the boundaries between the academic disciplines that study them. Englishmen cannot be divided into citizens, consumers, and churchgoers with the same ease as professors are divided into political scientists, economists, and theologians. They are all these things in turn, and sometimes they play several roles simultaneously. As in America, an Englishman's political position is not necessarily identical with his economic position or social prestige; yet the three are often related. In studying politics in England, we do not need to study everything about English society; it is sufficient to be aware of social life generally only insofar as it directly or indirectly affects political behavior.

INSULARITY AND INVOLVEMENT

The island position of England is its most significant geographical feature; insularity is one of its most striking cultural characteristics. Bagehot's remark about his countrymen has not lost all its force: "Are they not above all nations divided from the rest of the world, insular both in situation and in mind, both for good and for evil?" [1] Although London is closer to France than it is to the center of England, the narrow strip of water called the English Channel separates the country from the Continent of Europe. English people do not consider themselves Europeans, although there is no other continent to which the island could conceivably be assigned. More meaningful politically is membership in the somewhat vaguely defined North Atlantic community, a community based upon military interdependence under American leadership. Close ties in all but a geographical sense with many members of the Commonwealth further blur the impact of physical geography. England can claim to be equally close to or distant from Europe, the North Atlantic triangle of America, Canada, and England, and a global Commonwealth.

Insularity is not to be confused with isolation. As an island with a strong seafaring tradition, the country has been, in the words of the late Sir Eyre Crowe, "a neighbor of every country accessible by sea." In this way England came to administer an Empire with outposts in all the continents of the world. Close political and economic ties were developed between nations as scattered and various as New Zealand, Ghana, Cyprus, India, and Canada. Gradually, Imperial colonies gained independence. With the granting of independence to Afro-Asian nations, the Commonwealth has come to be a unique meeting place for a great variety of independent member states. These states disagree upon many major political questions, but keep alive their historic ties by political consultation and special economic, social, and cultural contacts. The Commonwealth

---

[1] Walter Bagehot, *The English Constitution* (London: World's Classics edition, 1955) p. 185.

now belongs to all the members of the "club." It is no longer one nation's Empire.[2]

Isolation from the Continent has saved England from the heritage of war that has cost European countries dear. The last successful foreign invasion of England was the Norman Conquest of 1066; in France, it was the German invasion of 1940. In both the world wars of this century England has been saved from occupation and, unlike Germany, Poland, and other nations, has not had to face the task of building new political and social institutions in the midst of the havoc of war. The absence of land frontiers with foreign nations has meant that the country has not needed a large standing Army. Hence, the Army has not been a major social force in society. Furthermore, because Army officers were traditionally gentlemen, who put their social duties before a professional military code, no separate officer caste developed within society.[3] England's defense has rested in its sea power, and naval strength has contributed to its position as a maritime and trading nation. The development of aerial and missile warfare and of thermonuclear weapons has greatly reduced the strategic importance of England's insular situation, but it cannot cancel the great advantage of its heritage of impregnability.

Insulation from the great population movements of modern European history has helped to develop a remarkably strong sense of national identity in the English. Even the Norman Conquest, which provided a relatively strong, centralized government, might be said to have contributed to this feeling. Since medieval times, the English people have had a single national government to strengthen their solidarity, which is in marked contrast to the experience of Germans, Italians, Arabs, and other nationalities. Continuous involvement in Imperial and foreign affairs for the past century has further stimulated

[2] See, *e.g.*, A. P. Thornton, *The Imperial Idea and its Enemies* (London: Macmillan, 1959); J. D. B. Miller, *The Commonwealth in the World* (Cambridge, Mass.: Harvard University Press, 1958); Nicholas Mansergh, *A Survey of British Commonwealth Affairs* (New York: Oxford University Press, 1958).

[3] Cf. Simon Raven, "Perish by the Sword," in Hugh Thomas, editor, *The Establishment* (London: Blond, 1959).

solidarity in the face of common external concerns. Emigration from different parts of the country to the Commonwealth and to the United States historically served to remove some disaffected groups of citizens; today it is of no general consequence. The number of immigrants to England has been very small in comparison to America's experience. Since the population is 99 per cent white, there is no color problem by the standards of Southern Rhodesia or South Carolina. The sense of a secure national identity is shown in the use of the word "race" to distinguish persons of other nationalities, regardless of color.

Although all the inhabitants of the British Isles may appear equally foreign to Americans, there exist ethnic differences between the English, Welsh, Scots, and Irish that are usually noticeable in personal relationships. These differences are tokens of very different historical backgrounds. In land area, England constitutes 53 per cent of the country's territory, Scotland 32 per cent, Wales 9 per cent, and Northern Ireland 6 per cent. (The Republic of Ireland, or Eire, is politically independent although geographically an integral part of the British Isles.) The total land area of the whole country, however, is less than that of the state of Oregon. Population figures, however, give a very different emphasis, for the population of England at the 1961 census was 43,430,000, compared to a population of 5,178,000 in Scotland, 2,640,000 in Wales, and 1,423,000 in Northern Ireland. The resulting population density of 573 persons per square mile is ten times that of the United States.

The structure of government gives some recognition to these ethnic differences.[4] Northern Ireland has a separate and subordinate Parliament that sits in Belfast. Many aspects of domestic affairs are administered separately for Scotland, and are also sometimes the occasion of separate legislation; to a much lesser extent, special provision is made for Wales. All of the bodies so established are subject to the overriding authority of the central government in London. Technically, this government is the United Kingdom of Great Britain and Northern Ireland, more simply called Great Britain or Britain.

[4] See D. E. Butler and J. Freeman, *British Political Facts 1900-1960* (London: Macmillan, 1963) chapter 12.

The government itself has never adopted a consistent policy in differentiating the parts of the United Kingdom. Following customary usage leads to slight inconsistencies, but is necessary because of the way in which data are presented. For instance, election results include Northern Ireland, whereas sample surveys normally exclude Northern Ireland, and statistics on education exclude Scotland as well. Because the history and the social and political outlooks of the four ethnic groups are not identical, it is sometimes misleading to generalize about "British" society. Throughout this study English society is the center of focus for purposes of social analysis, because England is of overwhelming importance in the workings of government, and English attitudes toward politics are assimilated by the Scots, Welsh, and Northern Irish. But because the central government in London rules over all four parts of the United Kingdom, it is customary and correct to speak of British government in conjunction with English society.

Today politics in the United Kingdom is greatly simplified by the absence of major cleavages along the lines of ethnic groups, language, or religion. In earlier centuries, when religious feeling ran high, the government showed that it was ready to practice discrimination and repression against its own subjects. These problems have virtually disappeared since the granting of independence to the Roman Catholic parts of Ireland in 1922 after a generation of sabotage, guerilla war, and insurrection.[5] Although contemporary issues such as unemployment, transportation, and economic growth affect the parts of the United Kingdom differently, the major parties do not divide along ethnic lines, nor have the Irish Catholic immigrants to England formed a separate bloc within a major party, as in Australia. The unimportance of these differences in politics is demonstrated by the failure of Scottish and Welsh nationalist parties to maintain representation in Parliament with their handfuls of candidates at general elections.

[5] The unconstitutional aspects of the battle for Home Rule are discussed in, *inter alia*, George Dangerfield, *The Strange Death of Liberal England* (London: Constable, 1936) and C. L. Mowat, *Britain Between the Wars, 1918-1940* (London: Methuen, 1955) pp. 79-108.

The solidarity of the United Kingdom today may be due to fortuitous historical circumstances; it is nonetheless real and important.

In some respects there is a cleavage within English society between those living around London and those living in "the provinces"; that is, in the remainder of the country. This distinction conveys a sense of London's great pre-eminence, which it clearly enjoys in population, for, with more than 8,-000,000 residents it is seven times larger than the second largest English city, Birmingham; by itself, London contains nearly 20 per cent of the population of England. With the decline in the past century of a political aristocracy based upon landed estates in the country, the political pre-eminence of London has increased. Members of Parliament are more likely to have deep roots in London than in the constituency that elects them, for the majority of MPs have not been residents of their constituency before they are elected to Parliament. In London, politicians can easily meet the nation's leaders in many fields, because London, unlike Washington, New Delhi, Bonn, and many other capital cities, is simultaneously also a center of finance, of mass communications, and of the arts. As a result, the leaders in many aspects of English life tend to be geographically separated from the bulk of the population.

Within England, the various regions also have differing historical backgrounds, and today maintain differences in speech and life-styles. The government, however, is unitary, not federal, and even the councils of large cities are subject in their activities to the overriding authority of the central government in London. Thus, there is nothing directly analogous to the American problem of federal-state relationships. In party politics, the regions usually shift together in voting. Even when England is divided into 49 relatively small geographical areas, one finds that in the four general elections from 1950 to 1959, the areas have shown a swing of votes in the same direction 95 per cent of the time.[6] Differences in political allegiance be-

[6] As calculated by the author. See, *e.g.*, D. E. Butler and Richard Rose, *The British General Election of 1959* (London: Macmillan, 1960) pp. 208-214.

tween regions of England seem largely to reflect different proportions of manual and non-manual workers in the population there.[7] For instance, seaside resorts, such as Blackpool and
Brighton, evidence similarities in voting behavior though
they are in very different regions, because of similar socio-
economic characteristics. Thus, the social differences within
the British Isles between the English and other ethnic groups
is of very little *political* consequence today. Of greater political significance are the great differences perceived by English
people between their society and those of other nations. Constant involvement in international affairs has only emphasized
the extent of English insularity.

THE ECONOMY

Economically, England is vitally concerned with international affairs, since much of the food needed to feed its large
population is imported, as are vital raw materials needed to
keep industry alive. The nation stands at the center of a complex network of international trading relationships with the
area based on sterling as a currency, with America, and with
many other nations.[8] In 1962, the country imported £1,570,-
000,000 in basic foodstuffs and £1,435,000,000 of raw materials and petroleum. A total of £3,180,000,000 of manufactured
goods was exported from the factories and workshops of
Great Britain. Foreign exchange is also earned by "invisible"
exports such as banking services and insurance, centered in
"The City," the financial quarter of London and one of the
world's great financial centers. As Chancellors of the Exchequer (the Cabinet equivalent of the United States Secretary of
the Treasury) have repeatedly insisted, England must export
to live. Dependence upon exports means that economic and

[7] As calculated for the 1955 and 1959 general elections on the basis of
categories in Claus Moser and Wolf Scott, *British Towns* (Edinburgh and
London: Oliver & Boyd, 1961) p. 17. Cf. Jean Blondel, *Voters, Parties and
Leaders* (Harmondsworth: Penguin, 1963) pp. 61-65.

[8] The sterling currency of England has the following United States
values: One pound (£) equals $2.80. Twenty shillings (s) equal £1; one
shilling equals 14 cents. Twelve pennies (d) equal 1s; one penny equals 1.17
cent.

political changes in many parts of the world have a direct impact upon the political economy and the living standards of the English people. Since the end of the Second World War, the economy has been affected by the unanticipated recurrence of the following kinds of problems — a shortage of dollars, balance of payments deficits, sudden withdrawals of foreign capital from London, fluctuating demands for exports, shortages of vital imported raw materials, and a lagging rate of economic growth.

England has a long history of industrialism; the Industrial Revolution began there in the late 18th century, and by the middle of the 19th century England's industrial pre-eminence was world-renowned. As a consequence of intensive industrialization, the agricultural population has steadily declined in importance; today, only about 5 per cent of workers are in agriculture, many as laborers or tenants working for great landowners. There is not a significant peasant group; that is, farmers strongly attached to small and often uneconomic plots of land. In the North of England, the historic center of industrialism, rural areas are often dotted with coal mines and cotton or woolen mills. Notwithstanding the pervasiveness and importance of industrial achievement, industry and technology have never enjoyed the same prestige and importance in England as in America and some European nations. The leisured life of a country gentleman, or even making money in a bank in The City is a high-prestige occupation; making heavy engineering goods in an industrial city in the North is regarded as necessary, but far from prestigious. At the beginning of the 1960s opinion leaders began to voice concern about the way in which government and social leaders have for several generations tended to remain aloof from industry and technology.

The historic industrial strength of England means that it is a comparatively wealthy nation, with a per capita income of about £435. Economic and political disputes do not concern the bare necessities of life; there is sufficient national wealth to meet the costs of a modern welfare state. Nonetheless, in this century, the English people have not enjoyed economic abundance as it has been known in America.[9] For nearly the whole of this period the Conservative governments have concentrated upon efforts to maintain economic stability, rather than to promote increasing economic abundance. Living standards have risen slowly through this period, but there did not take place a similar rise in the economic expectations of the bulk of the population. Between the wars the continuous existence or threat of large-scale unemployment diffused a sense of scarcity and protectionism. The Second World War brought full employment, but it also brought rationing, which did not end entirely until 1954. The 1945-51 Labour government concentrated attention first of all upon measures to redistribute wealth rather than increase it; its welfare program was aimed primarily at achieving a national minimum of welfare services for all, rather than at raising the standards of the prosperous minority. The marked rise in consumer expenditure beginning in the middle of the 1950s still has not brought to the majority of English families such typically American "necessities" as an automobile, a refrigerator, and central heating.[10] And, as in America, poverty can still be found, particularly among old-age pensioners and unskilled workers with large families.[11] The political impact of this spurt in consumption is not entirely clear; at a minimum, it seems to be increasing electoral pressure upon the government to operate successfully as manager of the nation's economy.

The economic and the political systems have many points of contact. The economy is neither capitalist nor Socialist but mixed. The British government's expenditure of all kinds amounts to about 44 per cent of the gross national product. As an employer of civil servants, and through the state-owned nationalized industries, it is the country's largest single em-

9 See the use of this concept in David M. Potter, *People of Plenty* (Chicago: Phoenix, 1961).

10 See, *e.g.*, G. D. N. Worswick and P. H. Ady, *The British Economy in the Nineteen-Fifties* (Oxford: Clarendon Press, 1962); Ferdynand Zweig, *The Worker in an Affluent Society* (London: Heinemann, 1961).

11 See, *e.g.*, Barbara Wootton, "Is There a Welfare State?" *Political Science Quarterly* LXXVIII:2 (1963); Peter Townsend, "The Meaning of Poverty," *British Journal of Sociology* XIII:3 (1962).

ployer. Basic industries such as electricity, gas, the railways, and coal mining are owned by the state. Through its economic policies, the government directly or indirectly affects manufacturers, exporters, and retailers. The relative concentration of economic power in large corporations, national banks, and large trade unions facilitates coordinated economic planning, but, by the same token, it increases the strength of economic pressure groups opposed to the government of the day. The overlapping of economic and political systems is clearly recognized by the National Economic Development Council. This Council, the latest in a long series of government efforts to improve guidance of the economy, first began meeting in March, 1962. Its members consist of representatives of the government, of business and industry, of the trade unions, and economic planners. Its official aims are to seek agreement on economic plans and to recommend changes in the economy. In other words, the N.E.D.C. is intended to discharge responsibilities of the British government. Governments, whether Conservative or Labour, have repeatedly shown themselves willing to share with representatives of trade-union and business pressure groups the power of making decisions affecting the whole of the mixed economy.[12]

The links between economics and politics are strengthened by the structure of the political parties. The Labour Party, in the picturesque words of union leader Ernest Bevin, grew out of the bowels of the trade-union movement. It was founded in 1900 when trade-union leaders came to believe that they would need to gain political power in order to achieve their economic goals; these goals could not, they thought, be gained by collective bargaining alone. Gradually, the Socialists in the new Labour Party converted the great majority of these leaders to a belief in Socialism as the means to gain their major

---

[12] National Economic Development Council, *Conditions Favourable to Faster Growth* (London: Her Majesty's Stationery Office — henceforth, H.M.S.O., 1963) p. v. For an introduction to the literature on the mixed economy of Britain, see J. W. Grove, *Government and Industry in Britain* (London: Longmans, 1962) and W. A. Robson, *Nationalized Industry and Public Ownership* (London: Allen & Unwin, 2nd edition, 1962).

political-economic objectives. Today, the unions provide more than seven-eighths of the members of the Labour Party and more than three-quarters of its income. About 40 per cent of the 24,000,000 employed workers in Britain belong to a trade union, and trade-union workers are measurably more likely to vote Labour than are non-union manual workers. (An estimated 1,500,000 to 2,000,000 trade-union members — a large number though a small proportion — vote Conservative.) Notwithstanding the close ties between the Labour Party and the unions, the latter, individually and collectively in the Trades Union Congress, jealously preserve their autonomy from party politics in many areas of activity and do not hesitate to negotiate with Conservative governments. The Conservative Party does not permit corporate membership. Since its accounts are unpublished, there is no way of estimating how heavily the party is financed by business groups. The importance of nationalization as an issue, especially in steel and road transport, has served to bring businessmen and Conservatives to work closely together in a common opposition to the Labour Party — but it has not ensured full agreement between business pressure groups and Conservative governments.[13]

CLASS

The difficulty of measuring the impact of social class in English life is clearly brought out in T. H. Marshall's classic definition: "The essence of social class is the way a man is treated by his fellows (and, reciprocally, the way he treats them), not the qualities or the possessions which cause that treatment." [14] This view stresses the subjective nature of class evaluations, and the possibility of a variety of coexisting class relationships.

The idea of class plays a much more important part in English politics than it does in America. Since feudal times Englishmen have been accustomed to the existence of legally sanctioned differences in social rank, whereas Americans, without

13 Cf. S. E. Finer, "The Federation of British Industries," *Political Studies* (Oxford) IV:1 (1956); Martin Harrison, *Trade Unions and the Labour Party Since 1945* (London: Allen & Unwin, 1960).

14 *Citizenship and Social Class* (Cambridge: University Press, 1950) p. 92.

a feudal heritage, have especially valued the idea of social equality. The Labour Party, owing part of its origin to an explicit demand for working-class representation in politics, makes class relationships a political issue; Socialism is said to be about equality.[15] A horizontal division into categories based primarily upon occupation is more practical in England, because, unlike America, it does not have so many vertical divisions along the lines of race, religion, ethnic, and regional identity, lines that unite Americans who are divided on occupational grounds.

The concept "class" generates more dispute than agreement. Conservatives and Socialists both recognize class relationships, but disagree as to their nature. Some Socialists stress conflicts of interest between classes, though that is not official Labour Party doctrine. After the 1959 general election, 52 per cent of those interviewed by the British Institute of Public Opinion said that they believed there was a conflict of interests between classes. Many Conservatives recognize class differences, but regard class relationships as complementary, existing within the framework of a single, organically linked hierarchical society. A study of Banbury, a small Oxfordshire town, found that for some these organic ties still exist, even influencing voting behavior. But another system of ranking existed there as well, based not upon traditional, preindustrial ties, but upon relationships at the local aluminum factory. Two very different ranking systems were thus coexisting in one small town. In virtually single-class communities such as those of East London, differences within a given social class may be more salient than those between classes.[16]

[15] Cf. Asa Briggs, "The Language of 'Class' in Early 19th Century England" in A. Briggs and John Saville, editors, *Essays in Labour History* (London: Macmillan, 1960); Leon Epstein, "British Class Consciousness and the Labour Party," *Journal of British Studies* (Hartford) I (1962) pp. 136-150; C. A. R. Crosland, *The Future of Socialism* (New York: Macmillan, 1957) Part Four.

[16] Cf. Margaret Stacey, *Tradition and Change; a study of Banbury* (London: Oxford University Press, 1960) especially chapters 3, 8, 9; Michael Young and Peter Willmott, *Family and Kinship in East London* (Harmondsworth: Penguin, 1962) chapters 10, 11.

Social scientists working in England have failed to arrive at an accepted description of the determinants of class. F. M. Martin found in his study that the majority of people interviewed used occupation as the chief index in determining whether a person belonged to the middle class or the working class. But moral standards, such as "rough" and "respectable," or vague ones such as "everyone who works for a living," were also often employed. Style of life or a distinctive voice, whether Cockney or an Oxford accent, can also be used in placing people; George Bernard Shaw illustrated this point in his play *Pygmalion* (later adapted as the musical *My Fair Lady*). Elizabeth Bott found in a small number of very intensive interviews that persons whose social network was close-knit with only a limited number of social contacts separated people on the basis of economic and political power into two groups: Us and Them. Those with a wide variety of social experiences in childhood, the army, at work, and in clubs usually ranked people in a large number of separate categories, using general social prestige as their basis. Young and Willmott found in a small sample of East London manual workers that 22 of the 82 interviewed expressed Socialist attitudes in ranking people. This significant minority ranked a road sweeper above a lawyer and a company director; farm laborers and local medical officials outranked everyone. Socialist standards of usefulness, rather than monetary standards, were thus given explicit recognition.[17]

The most commonly used definition of class is that of occupation. Manual workers are assigned to the working class and non-manual workers to the middle class. Distinctions can be made within each of these two groups, separating skilled from unskilled manual workers, and lower-middle and middle-middle people from the upper-middle class. An upper class, consisting of families of the aristocracy and those who inherit

---

[17] See F. M. Martin, "Some Subjective Aspects of Social Stratification," in D. V. Glass, editor, *Social Mobility in Britain* (London: Routledge, 1954) pp. 58ff.; Elizabeth Bott, *Family and Social Network* (London: Tavistock, 1957) pp. 174ff.; M. Young and P. Willmott, "Social Grading by Manual Workers," *British Journal of Sociology* VII:4 (1957).

wealth, also exists. It shades imperceptibly into the upper-middle class. Defining class by occupation is relatively clear and straightforward. This definition will be used henceforth. It should be remembered, however, that class categories lump together people who may differ in many ways. Persons in the same class do not necessarily share a common outlook on life; at a minimum, they share only a common level of job.

On occupational grounds, approximately two-thirds of the nation can be classified as working-class. But surveys regularly conducted by the British Institute of Public Opinion since 1945 consistently find that slightly less than half of those interviewed place themselves in the working class. In a survey in 1960 only 46 per cent identified themselves as working class — and nearly one-third of those interviewed subjectively assigned themselves to a class different from that in which a sociologist would probably place them. The existence of social mobility — that is, individuals moving up or down the occupational ladder — may account for some of this confusion, especially if the findings of a Welsh study hold generally true: "The existence of this large culturally mobile group (36 per cent of persons interviewed) is perhaps the chief characteristic of contemporary class structure." [18] But much confusion also results from the inability of writers to develop definitions of class and class relationships that fit all the major aspects of English social life.

The existence of so many contradictory definitions means that it can be misleading to talk of a simple class structure in England. This gives to classes and class relationships a degree of stability and certitude that does not exist in actuality. Classes are only one of a number of groups with which individuals identify, and are identified with. Community studies in a variety of small British towns and villages emphasize the extent to which a multiplicity of standards may be employed in ranking people (even the same individuals) in differing

[18] C. C. Harris, "Who Are the People in Between?" *New Society* (London) November 29, 1962, p. 20. Cf. D. V. Glass, editor, *op. cit.* and Peter Willmott, *The Evolution of a Community* (London: Routledge, 1963) chapters 9, 10.

social contexts.[19] If only class did not have an observable relationship to political parties, to attitudes, and to voting behavior, it would not be necessary to be concerned with it here. (But it does. Cf. *infra,* Chapters III, IV, VII).

There is no reason why an individual's role in the political system should coincide with his role in a system of economic class relationships, or why either should correspond, say, to his role as a parent or as a music lover. Every individual occupies a multitude of differing roles in society. Incongruities are likely to exist, and may be politically significant. An extreme example is the bus driver who rides in a chauffeur-driven limousine while serving in the office of Lord Mayor of his city. Another example is the wealthy noble landowner who asks for the votes of farm workers at a general election. More usual are situations in which there appears to be *some* relationship between an individual's economic class and his political position, as in the nomination of a well-bred young gentleman to represent a safe Conservative constituency in the House of Commons, or of a veteran trade-union official to represent a mining constituency in the Commons. To analyze the political system as a system of class power (which some left-wing Socialists do) is to assume that which remains to be proven — or disproven. Only after completing the analysis of the political system can one judge the extent, if any, to which political roles and class positions are integrated.

RELIGION

The historical importance of religion as one basis of political conflict emphasizes the limitations of an analysis of English society couched solely in terms of economic class. In medieval times, the Church was a temporal power in its own right, closely associated with the King; the relationship was subject to frequent disputes. The hiving off of the Church of England from the Roman Catholic Church in the early 16th century under Henry VIII created a national church subservient to the

19 See D. E. G. Plowman, W. E. Minchinton, and M. Stacey, "Local Social Status in England and Wales," *Sociological Review* (Keele) X:2 (1962).

Monarchy. Differences between members of the royalist Church of England and various Protestant denominations played an important part in the English Civil War of the 1640s. The victory of the Church and Crown encouraged some Protestants, or dissenters, to emigrate to America. The rise of new classes of industrialists and manufacturers in the 19th century was linked to the rise in the political strength of Protestant denominations, especially in the Liberal Party. The refusal of some Protestants to accept Home Rule for a predominantly Catholic Ireland because of the alleged threat to the Protestant minority there split the Liberal Party in 1886 and caused unrest, including violence, up to 1922. (Occasional acts of political violence still occur in Northern Ireland.) The period since 1922 has been historically noteworthy because of the absence of religious controversy in politics.[20]

Religious differences are far fewer in England than in America. The chief distinction between the two countries is the existence of an officially supported state church. In England, this is the Church of England, an episcopal church (that is, one with bishops) claiming to be in the catholic tradition (that is, part of the universal church) as well as protesting against the authority of the Roman Catholic Pope. In Scotland, however, the state church is Presbyterian, and in the tradition of Protestants such as John Calvin and John Knox. Today, those who are not members of a state church do not suffer politically or economically for their failure to conform to the state religion. Unlike America, where the First Amendment restricts government intervention in religion, in England the government is free to intervene in religious matters, including the appointment of bishops. Notwithstanding its position as the Established Church, only 58 per cent of those interviewed in a Gallup survey in December, 1962 stated their religious preference as Anglican (that is, Church of England); another 6 per cent said they were Presbyterian (that is, Church of Scotland). Protestant denominations were named by 15 per

[20] See Robert Alford, *Party and Society* (Chicago: Rand, McNally, 1963) chapter 6.

cent; Roman Catholicism by 11 per cent, 4 per cent gave other responses, and 6 per cent said they had no religion.[21] There is thus an established major church — but more than one-third of the population stands outside it.

The impact of religion upon political attitudes is difficult to measure. Historically, the Church of England has been an Erastian church; that is, willing to accept the authority of the national government as superior to it. Clerics have tended to reinforce the authority of the government. Crusaders against the established political order have often come from the smaller Protestant denominations. Most Anglican bishops sit ex officio in the House of Lords. They are not trouble-makers on party matters. Bishops come from social strata closely associated with the Conservative Party leadership. Between 1942 and 1961, 54 of the 56 bishops appointed had attended socially exclusive public (that is, private boarding) schools.[22] It is possible that in the future the close attachment of many bishops to a traditionally established order may make them critics of an increasingly secular English society. But the Church of England has shown itself able throughout the centuries to conform to changing social conditions by adapting itself and its leadership.

By any comparative standards, the Church of England has been tolerant on doctrinal points. The religion of the Queen — Episcopal in England and Presbyterian in Scotland — symbolizes this tolerance. The break with the Roman Catholic Church and differences with Protestant bodies were settled with little bloodshed. Doctrinally, the Church of England, embracing High Church Anglo-Catholics, Low Church Protestants, and even Unitarians, represents a compromise. This spirit of religious compromise may well have nurtured a belief in political compromise and indirectly may even have affected

[21] See also Michael Argyle, *Religious Behaviour* (London: Routledge, 1958) especially chapter 2.

[22] See P. A. Bromhead, *The House of Lords and Contemporary Politics 1911-1957* (London: Routledge, 1958) pp. 53-67; Rev. Paul Welsby, "Ecclesiastical Appointments, 1942-1961," *Prism* (London) VI:5 (1962) p. 24.

the behavior of the Conservative Party, Anglican in leadership and strongly non-doctrinal in thinking.

The Protestant denominations (called "nonconformists") contributed disproportionately to the Liberal Party in the 19th century, and to the Labour Party in this century. In Victorian times, religious differences sometimes caused and sometimes intensified differences between Conservatives and Liberals. Working-class men, then denied the vote, could learn in their nonconformist chapels techniques of organization useful in trade unions and politics. Furthermore, they drew from religion a vision of society that led them, when confronted with Socialism, to give it a Christian rather than a Marxist interpretation, stressing brotherhood instead of class conflict. The first large group of Labour MPs returned to Parliament in 1906 reported in detail how the Bible and preaching had influenced their political views. John Bunyan's *Pilgrim's Progress* was mentioned more frequently than any Marxist book. Today, the Labour and Liberal parties still draw a disproportionate number of their parliamentary candidates from the nonconformist churches. A study of 110 Labour MPs in 1962 found that although religious reading was no longer as influential as books on social studies, 55 per cent of the MPs surveyed said that religious beliefs had been a significant influence upon their political attitudes. The testimony of one MP was: "I regard democratic Socialism as the political expression of Christianity." [23]

Studies in voting behavior have confirmed the importance of religion in party allegiance — even among members of the same economic class. In a study of the small town of Glossop, A. H. Birch found that active Anglicans in the working class voted nearly two-to-one Conservative, whereas workers who professed no religious affiliation voted nearly two-to-one Labour. Other community studies have found other religious

[23] See "The Labour Party and the Books that Helped to Make It," *Review of Reviews* (London) XXXIII:198 (1906); K. J. W. Alexander and Alexander Hobbs, "What Influences Labour MPs?" *New Society*, December 13, 1962; D. E. Butler and Richard Rose, *op. cit.*, p. 129.

differences in voting,[24] but not in a form suitable for generalization nationally.

Changes in society affect the churches, and have been contributing to a decline in their political influence. The rapid growth of large industrial cities in Victorian times created, as a by-product, large sections of the population remote from a Church rooted in agricultural England. Today, the Church of England has clergymen everywhere, but on Easter Day it will have only about 2,000,000 communicants, a figure representing little more than 6 per cent of the population of voting age. Activity in smaller denominations appears to be proportionately greater, but the majority of the population rarely attends church. The importance in this century of economic differences has apparently led some church groups to withdraw from social and political controversy so that their socially heterogeneous congregations will not divide along social and political lines.[25] Increasingly, religion is confined to specifically religious activities, and is not allowed a place in politics. A London bartender, an inactive Anglican, aptly summed up a point of view in a life-history[26] interview; religion, he thought, should play a part in national life "if not taken so far that it meant stopping people doing things."

The chief significance of religion for English politics today is its absence of influence. For centuries prior to 1914 religious differences tended to reinforce political differences in England. This broadened the area of political conflict, and in-

24 See A. H. Birch, *Small-Town Politics* (London: Oxford University Press, 1959) p. 112; M. Stacey, *op. cit.*, chapters 3, 4; R. S. Milne and H. C. Mackenzie, *Marginal Seat* (London: Hansard Society, 1958) pp. 64ff.

25 See Tom Brennan, E. W. Cooney, and H. Pollins, *Social Change in South-West Wales* (London: Watts, 1954) pp. 138ff.; F. Zweig, *op. cit.*, pp. 146-153; D. E. Butler and J. Freeman, *op. cit.*, chapter 16; G. Kitson Clark, *The Making of Victorian England* (Cambridge, Mass.: Harvard University Press, 1962) chapter 6.

26 The life-history interviews were collected in England by sample survey methods in preparation of *The Civic Culture* by Gabriel Almond and Sidney Verba (Princeton: University Press, 1963). Each of these open-ended interviews ranged widely over many politically relevant experiences during the whole of the subject's life. Quotations here and elsewhere in this text are drawn from the unpublished interview reports.

creased the emotion, the intensity, and the uncompromising tendencies of those involved in politics. The Church of England was not sufficiently powerful to cause a later anticlerical reaction, in part because the clergy itself was subject to political controls, and Anglican clergymen often shared the tolerant views of political leaders, as both came from a similar, tolerant social background. The Labour Party's Socialism has always drawn more inspiration from Christianity than from anticlerical secular and Marxist sources. Because of the small numbers of Roman Catholics and Jews in England, partisan appeals to these sectarian groups have never been practical. In these circumstances, the state Church can act in accord with Mathew Arnold's dictum: "Religion should have in it as little as possible of what divides us, and should be as much as possible a common public act." Americans familiar with the contemporary controversy in the United States about federal aid to parochial schools should have no difficulty in appreciating the advantages of a political system in which religious differences are not the source of intense political differences.

CHAPTER II

The Political Culture

It is the dull traditional habit of mankind that guides most men's actions and is the steady frame in which each new artist must set the picture that he paints.

THE POLITICAL culture of England — the values, beliefs and emotions of Englishmen — is not a tangible object like a written constitution or a book. Political values, *e.g.*, the importance attached in England to freedom of speech, are sometimes easily recognizable. Beliefs about what is politically possible or probable often overlap with values. For instance, if a man values the grant of self-government to Britain's African colonies then he is likely to believe that African nations are capable of self-government; his political opponent usually rejects both this value and the belief that Africans can now govern themselves. Political emotions may be aroused by symbols such as the Union Jack, the nation's flag. But emotional affect may also be important as one component of such formally rational activities as parliamentary debates or annual conferences of political parties.

Many basic political attitudes, such as those toward the Queen, Parliament, and politicians educated at Eton are expressed not so much in laws as they are in political behavior. These normative expectations are, in Sidney Low's phrase, "the tacit understandings" that are rarely made explicit because they are taken for granted.[1] The values and beliefs remain undiscussed until some deviant political group refuses to accept an "obvious" cultural norm and acts upon values and beliefs regarded within the culture as "unnatural," such as pacifism. The fact that many norms of the culture represent implicit expectations rather than explicit ones need not make them less important in influencing political behavior.[2]

Cultural attitudes concern basic features of the political system. Some relate to the territorial boundaries of the political community. Since the settlement of the Irish question, there has been virtual unanimity on the boundaries of the government of the United Kingdom. Norms focused on the regime deal with fundamental constitutional principles, such as the use of elections to choose governments and the legitimacy of competing political parties. No political group of any consequence has challenged the principles of the regime in England since 1926. Norms concerning political roles and officeholders affect which individuals expect and are expected to participate actively in politics, and which are expected to remain passive. Since the granting of the vote to women in 1918, there have been no significant legal inhibitions to political participation — but the unimportance of women in English politics today shows that the normative expectations concerning women in politics differ from those for men. Norms concerning the performance of government, its expected output, often undergo modification. For instance, before the Second World War the government was not expected to guarantee jobs for all; today it is. Sometimes the same norm is relevant on both sides of the boundaries dividing politics from nonpolitical parts of English society. The overlapping of boundaries was strikingly demonstrated during the trial of the publisher of D. H. Lawrence's *Lady Chatterley's Lover.* At one point the prosecutor asked the

[1] *The Governance of England* (London: Benn, revised edition, 1914) p. 12.
[2] Cf. M. Oakeshott, *op. cit.*

jury: "Is it a book that you would even wish your wife or your servants to read?" [3]

A high level of agreement, or consensus, on norms concerning these basic aspects of the political system — the community, the regime, roles, governmental performance, and political boundaries — is necessary for the English political system to endure without disruption by violence, civil war, or revolution. Consensus is not in itself good or bad. For instance, the American Revolution resulted from a breakdown in consensus about the community, the regime, and the role structure of the British Empire. In England today, those who challenge the basic norms of the political system are numerically insignificant, though their egregious political attitudes may give them some notoriety as eccentrics or crusaders, usually on the left.[4]

The existence of a high level of agreement on many basic cultural norms does not mean that all Englishmen share the same political outlook, especially on day-to-day political issues. Differences exist because the norms of the culture only concern broad, fundamental political questions, such as the rights and duties of the citizen; they do not determine specific positions on questions that are the basis of much party conflict, such as sharing out economic benefits. Controversy between and within parties continues peacefully just because those engaged in differing on specific issues agree in supporting the system by which their specific differences are resolved. Differences on day-to-day issues of English politics can be associated with *some* measure of difference in cultural orientations. Such differences can arise from particular individuals differing about one particular norm, or giving greater weight to norms concerning, say, social welfare, whereas others give greater weight to those concerning national defense. The possible

[3] C. H. Rolph, *The Trial of Lady Chatterley* (Harmondsworth: Penguin, 1961) p. 17. On general points in this paragraph, see David Easton, "An Approach to the Analysis of Political Systems," *World Politics* IX:3 (1957) and G. Almond and S. Verba, *op. cit.*, chapter 1.

[4] For the views of a tiny but articulate group of Socialist and Marxist intellectuals, see the files of the *New Left Review* (London), and Norman Birnbaum, editor, *Out of Apathy* (London: Stevens, 1960).

combinations of attitudes are numerous, because of individual differences in family background, in personality, and in political life histories. Some combinations often vary in relation to such recognizable political influences as party attachment, class, and role in the political system. When these combinations are particularly distinctive, one can speak of subcultures. In England, political subcultures are associated with complementary rather than conflicting patterns of behavior.

HISTORICAL BACKGROUND

The English are outstanding because of the continuity of their political development. Today, the political culture of England incorporates norms that have survived from preindustrial times. The process of incorporation and adaptation is itself of major importance if one is to understand the dynamic relationship between the culture, the system, and international social, economic, and political networks with which England is linked. What follows is only a sketch of the historical development of modern England, emphasizing certain themes of special contemporary relevance.[5]

Durable settlements of three great crises of cultural development were arrived at prior to the beginning of the upheavals of the Industrial Revolution from the end of the 18th century. A single, strong and centralized government was firmly established, the political community was clearly defined (Ireland was not then a cause of great unrest), and the settlement of the religious Reformation was beyond dispute. Furthermore, prior to the beginning of industrialization, England had shown cultural predispositions favoring modernization.[6] It had a thriving mercantile class, and the nobility and landed gentry were often prepared to invest part of their capital in

[5] There is no such thing as a good, brief introduction to England's many centuries of recorded history. For background to what follows, see especially Asa Briggs, *The Age of Improvement: 1783-1867* (London: Longmans, 1959), Elie Halévy, *A History of the English People in the Nineteenth Century* (London: Benn, six volumes, 1924-34); G. K. Clark, *op. cit.* and C. L. Mowat, *op. cit.*

[6] See, *e.g.*, R. K. Merton, "Puritanism, Pietism and Science" in *Social Theory and Social Structure* (Glencoe, Ill.: Free Press, revised edition, 1957).

new commercial enterprises. This situation strengthened ties with industrialists who, having gained wealth, sought social status as well. They could achieve status by leaving their factories and nonconformist chapels for the life of a landed Anglican squire. Tocqueville, writing in the 1830s, portrayed England as midway between America and France in the openness of its class structure. Unlike France, England had no rigid caste barriers preventing the assimilation into the traditional political leadership of aspiring, newly rich manufacturers and merchants.[7] The rise of this new industrial group did not immediately strengthen democratic tendencies, for the association of French democratic and revolutionary ideas with the military threat of Napoleon encouraged a reaction against ideas of great political innovation, led by Edmund Burke, the great philosopher of social conservatism. A monument to William Pitt, prime minister in this period, praised him because: "In an age when the contagion of ideas threatened to dissolve the forms of civil society, he rallied the loyal, the sober-minded and the good around the venerable structure of the English monarchy."

The existence in early industrial England of a politically and socially strong body of nobility and landowners placed restraints upon the diffusion of "new" ideas of laissez-faire liberal economists. The Poor Law Amendment Act of 1834 may be taken as the first step toward the regulation of the economy in changing industrial conditions. This act replaced the welfare system of agricultural England, but drew support from earlier values. A group of political radicals stimulated by Jeremy Bentham began at this time to influence the reform of government administration; reform was necessary for the government to operate effectively in an industrial society. The long-term influence of Benthamites on cultural attitudes appears to have been less important. The coexistence of differing cultural outlooks during the crisis of industrialization

7 Cf. *Journeys to England and Ireland* (London: Faber, 1958 edition) pp. 59ff.; W. L. Guttsman, *The British Political Elite* (London: MacGibbon & Kee, 1963); G. K. Clark, *op. cit.*, chapters 7, 8.

served to muffle the political impact of a great social and economic upheaval.[8]

The Reform Act of 1832, which recognized some claims of the rising middle class for political influence, marks the beginning of the gradual adaptation of political institutions in keeping with changes in society and in the political culture. The Whigs carried the bill, not because they believed in democracy, but because, in Briggs' words, "they believed that unless the privileged sections of the community were prepared to adapt and to 'improve,' waves of dangerous and uncontrollable innovation would completely drown the existing social order."[9] The object of this and of many later reforms was to adapt parts of the system in order to preserve the fundamental framework. By the 1860s, Conservative and Liberal leaders perceived that most English workingmen were not dangerous radicals, but potential supporters of the existing parties. To W. E. Gladstone, the Liberal leader, the cotton workers had shown their moral worth by siding with the American North during the Civil War, and against the South, with which they were bound by ties of economic interest. In 1867, another major franchise reform bill, this time on behalf of industrial workers, was carried by a Conservative government under Benjamin Disraeli. By the general election of 1885, the majority of adult men were enfranchised. Because, as Bagehot noted, each newly enfranchised group of voters still retained attitudes from the older political culture in which they had been raised, the impact of electoral reforms was not felt abruptly. The first manual worker did not enter the Cabinet until 1905, and the first Labour government was

[8] See particularly Karl Polanyi, *The Great Transformation* (Boston: Beacon Press, 1957 edition) Part II; A. V. Dicey, *The Relation Between Law and Public Opinion in England During the Nineteenth Century* (London: Macmillan, 1962 edition) pp. 62ff.; G. K. Clark, *op. cit.*, Stanley Rothman, "Modernity and Tradition in Britain," *Social Research* XXVIII:3 (1961).

[9] Asa Briggs, *The Age of Improvement,* pp. 238-239. See also W. Bagehot, *op. cit.*, pp. 259ff., and Charles Seymour, *Electoral Reform in England and Wales* (New Haven: Yale University Press, 1915).

not formed until 1924. The reforms undermined groups that had sought radical reform of the old regime and greatly increased popular support for the modified regime.

The rising importance of colonies and of the ideology of Imperialism in late 19th-century England provided a means of drawing together old aristocrats, industrialists, and workers in support of a common patriotic enterprise (an enterprise believed to be of economic benefit for all).[10] During the Boer War at the beginning of the 20th century, sections of the leadership of both the Liberals and the Fabian Socialists gave support to the South African adventure of a Conservative government. Intense disagreement about Home Rule for Ireland after 1885 united some Protestants of all classes in opposition to this measure, which further served to blur lines of class conflict.

From the middle of the 19th century a self-conscious Labour movement had begun to form. Trade unions, nonprofit retail co-operatives, and mutual-insurance societies provided means for manual workers to make collective provision for individual needs, in contrast to the ideology of rugged individualism. Significantly, some Socialists, notably William Morris, extolled medieval English society as superior to industrial capitalism because it too was based upon collectivist values. By the time that Marxist doctrines began to be propagated in England in the 1880s, working-class leaders had already begun to make some political headway, and, most important, to *believe* that they could make headway. They positively supported the parliamentary regime, and sought to make gains within it. Christian influences appear to have strengthened their commitment to the general culture, too. Due to their acquisition in youth of conventional political attitudes, many Labour leaders had much in common with members in other parties. The challenge of Labour on grounds of policy was rarely a challenge to basic cultural norms.[11]

10 See, *e.g.*, Bernard Semmel, *Imperialism and Social Reform* (London: Allen & Unwin, 1960).

11 See especially Egon Wertheimer, *Portrait of the Labour Party* (London: Putnam, 1929); Henry Pelling, *The Origins of the Labour Party 1880-*

Differences on basic aspects of the political system came to a head during a period of Liberal government from 1906 to 1914. The conflict concerned the relationship of Ireland to the political community, the place of the hereditary House of Lords in the regime, the political role of women, the government's responsibility for welfare, and the boundaries of economics and politics. At this period of English history, a generation of radical and Labour leaders and electors had come to take for granted the late 19th-century "democratization" of politics. Yet many Conservatives and some Liberals had not yet accepted the need to modify their older attitudes. The defenders of the older outlook were especially unwilling to adapt their general outlook at this time because change would have meant simultaneous acceptance of major substantive alterations in society. The result was a period of great political, economic, and social unrest, including violence and the threat of military disaffection in Ireland. The demagogic style of David Lloyd George, the Welsh leader of the radical wing of the Cabinet, accelerated changes and heightened tension. The outbreak of world war at the end of July, 1914, when the Irish question was reaching a new and graver crisis, provided an unexpected break from internal political strife.[12] During the 1914-18 War and its aftermath, a Coalition government under a mercurial, less radical Lloyd George, saw the country through most of its greatest immediate difficulties. During this period, the Liberal Party split and was broken as a major electoral force, and Labour became the second party in the nation.

From the First World War until the Second, England experienced heightened social, economic, and political unrest. The Labour Party, formed in 1900, adopted a Socialist program in 1918, and there were those — on the right and the left — who feared that party conflict might destroy previous

1900 (London: Macmillan, 1954); B. C. Roberts, *The Trades Union Congress 1868-1921* (London: Allen & Unwin, 1958); V. L. Allen, "The Ethics of Trade Union Leaders," *British Journal of Sociology* VII:4 (1956).

[12] Cf. G. Dangerfield, *op. cit.* and Elie Halévy, *The Rule of Democracy* (London: Benn, 1934).

agreement on cultural norms. The trade unions showed industrial militancy. In 1926 the trade unions called a general strike. It failed. When union leaders saw that their action had potential revolutionary implications, they disowned these implications and the strike, which was notable for its peacefulness, collapsed.[13] A weak Labour government under Ramsay MacDonald happened to be in office in 1931, when the full force of the world depression hit England. The problem was not met by a swing to political extremism, but by the formation of a National government of Labour, Conservative, and Liberal leaders. In the general election of October, 1931, this government received the largest popular and parliamentary majority in modern English history. Stanley Baldwin, who dominated the government for most of the 1930s, consciously saw his task as upholding an old Conservative ideal of lessening social and political tensions, rather than using his strength to pursue courses that would risk violent reactions. At a time when Germany, Italy, Spain, and France were subject to extreme conflicts involving the whole nature of society, and America was experiencing the turmoil of the New Deal, Communist and Fascist parties in England had only tiny followings in the electorate. The Marxist-oriented left wing of the Labour Party greatly influenced intellectuals at this time, but its national influence was slight. The moderates in both parties could rest content, for they held political power.[14]

After the fall of France to Germany in 1940, England faced its greatest military threat in nearly 150 years. In this time of common danger and common needs, great political changes took place, affecting both government policy and cultural norms. Labour leaders, having had a near-disastrous experience in a government coalition in the First World War, bargained for a full measure of authority before taking office in

[13] See Julian Symons, *The General Strike* (London: Cresset, 1957).

[14] Cf. G. M. Young *Stanley Baldwin* (London: Hart-Davis, 1952) pp. 110ff.; Alan Bullock, *The Life and Times of Ernest Bevin,* Volume I (London: Heinemann, 1960); Michael Foot, *Aneurin Bevan,* Volume I (London: MacGibbon & Kee, 1962), and J. M. Gaus, *Great Britain: a Study of Civic Loyalty* (Chicago: University Press, 1929).

Winston Churchill's National Coalition of 1940. The total war of modern technology, in Anthony Eden's words, exposed weaknesses in the nation's social life "ruthlessly and brutally." [15] National unity was sought not only through Churchillian exhortations but also through major policy changes intended to increase the positive allegiance of citizens to the political community and regime. Out of the Coalition emerged the Beveridge report on social welfare, the Keynesian Full Employment White Paper of 1944, and the Butler Education Act of 1944. These three measures — the first two named after Liberals, the third after a Conservative — remain major landmarks of the mixed-economy welfare state today. In wartime, politicians and administrators came to adopt new beliefs concerning welfare measures;[16] this change has been of great importance in eliminating the tendencies apparent between the wars toward basic cleavages within the culture.

The return for the first time of a Labour government by a large majority in July, 1945, had an impact upon the political system in some ways resembling that of Franklin D. Roosevelt's New Deal in America, although Labour's policies were more consciously to the left. In the domestic field, Clement Attlee's government nationalized coal mines, gas, electricity, the railways, road transport, and the steel industry, as well as establishing a national health service providing free medical care for all. In colonial affairs, Labour achieved the grant of independence to India, a milestone in the dissolution of the British Empire. In foreign policy, however, the Labour government disappointed advocates of a Socialist foreign policy. Under Ernest Bevin at the Foreign Office, it accepted balance-of-power politics, involving a close alliance with America to provide a counterweight to Russian influence in Europe. By 1950 the Labour government had nearly exhausted the list of innovations on which there was widespread agreement within

15 House of Commons *Debates* Vol. 355, Col. 757, December 6, 1939. (All references to *Debates* are to the 5th series.)

16 See R. M. Titmuss, *Problems of Social Policy* (London: H.M.S.O. and Longmans, 1950) *passim*, and "The World of Politics" (London: Mass-Observation typescript, c. 1949).

the party; it then chose to consolidate its legislative advances, thus precipitating a running conflict with its left wing, which has sought faster advancement toward the distant goal of Socialism. Even consolidation proved difficult, due to the limitations of the nation's resources. Following the third major economic crisis in six years, a weakened Labour government was defeated by a considerably reformed Conservative Party at a general election in October, 1951. Conservative governments headed by Winston Churchill, Anthony Eden, and Harold Macmillan, have accepted many of the innovations of their Labour predecessors, just as the Republicans under President Eisenhower accepted many of the innovations of the preceding twenty years in American politics. The past decade has been marked by a swing away from many Socialist attitudes — both in the public generally and in the Labour Party. Conservative governments, however, have not insisted upon the doctrines of free enterprise. The importance of economic differences has been muffled and blurred by a marked rise in consumer expenditure and the diffusion through society of living standards formerly thought the privilege of a relative few, or only of the middle class. The Conservatives, thanks in part to this prosperity, won general elections by unprecedented increasing majorities in 1955 and 1959.[17] In international affairs, England continued to move away from its historic great-power status. This was dramatically demonstrated in 1956, when England and France went to war with Egypt in order to control the Suez Canal. The two countries were forced to cease fire after the combined opposition of America and Russia.

Subsequent to the Conservative victory at the 1959 general election, political developments have taken new turns. Macmillan's effort to introduce fundamental changes in England's political and economic relationships by joining the European Common Market was frustrated by General de Gaulle's veto in January, 1963. Simultaneously, demands and fears concern-

17 On the period generally, see G. D. N. Worswick and P. H. Ady, *op. cit.;* F. Zweig, *op. cit.;* C. A. R. Crosland, *The Future of Socialism;* R. M. Titmuss, *Essays on "the Welfare State"* (London: Allen & Unwin, 1958) and D. E. Butler and Richard Rose, *op. cit.*

ing the need for fundamental structural changes in the economy have led the Conservative government to introduce a quasi-governmental National Economic Development Council to plan for economic growth. Labour has countered with arguments justifying Socialism as the basis for sustained economic growth. Educational reform, particularly of further education and scientific training, is being canvassed with renewed vigor in response to economic difficulties. Labour, under Hugh Gaitskell's leadership from 1955 to 1963, had been re-thinking its traditional attachment to Socialism. Following Gaitskell's unexpected death in January, 1963, the party elected one of his former opponents, Harold Wilson, to succeed him. In October, 1963, the Conservatives also changed leaders. Sir Alec Douglas-Home (formerly the 14th Earl of Home) succeeded Harold Macmillan. The extent to which the result of the 1964 general election will lead to an accelerated cycle of political and cultural change is an open question.

The political culture is in a continual state of evolution. One can see from a historical perspective that many different factors influence the development of the culture — the pattern of traditional norms, new historical processes such as industrialism and imperialism, the behavior of political leaders, international events, and purely fortuitous occurrences and conjunctions of circumstances. In the development of the political culture of modern England, many norms have been conserved, sometimes in modified or attenuated form, from generation to generation. At any given time, the things that have not changed are more numerous than the things that are changing. But the points at which change is taking place, or is imminent, are of special significance, because at these points political conflict is likely to be at its height; decisions taken there may influence future generations of Englishmen.

Because the political culture involves a mixture of attitudes developed in a mixture of historical periods, analysis is extremely difficult. The analysis here focuses on three major topics: the rights and duties of the citizen, the relationship of the state and society, and symbols evoking political emotions. It emphasizes the attitudes of the more politically conscious

members of English society. This group is of special importance in view of the value given leadership. The interpretation mixes information and ideas drawn from political philosophy, history, contemporary social surveys, and personal
observation of English political behavior.

THE INDIVIDUAL

Among the rights of Englishmen, liberty is pre-eminent. So
deeply inculcated in individuals is respect for the liberty to
speak, to act, and to travel as one pleases that there are few
statutory guarantees of liberty. In America, by contrast, liber-
tarian rights had to be written into the first ten amendments
of the Constitution, for fear that they would not otherwise be
observed. Allegations that the government has infringed individual liberties are less often heard in England than in
America. Even the security problems of the Cold War have
not challenged the absolute value of liberty, and Communists
continue to enjoy nearly all the civil liberties of other Englishmen, notwithstanding the uncovering from time to time of
Soviet penetration of the government's security barriers.[18]

The high value given to liberty is not matched by strong
support for norms concerning social equality: favorable attitudes toward inequality are important, and inequality has
much deeper and much stronger historical roots in the culture.
Traditionally, the government of England was not in the
hands of "the people" but rather in the hands of the Crown,
advised in its work by Parliaments controlled by small groups
of aristocrats and wealthy landowners. The vote was not only
restricted to a small proportion of the population, but also
granted in accord with anachronistic customs, and usually
determined by property. The law, the Church, and the large,
hereditary agricultural estates all emphasized differences in
rank. Virtue consisted in performing the duties appropriate to
one's station, whether high or low. Each man made a contribution and each drew benefits from society — but these

18 See E. A. Shils, *The Torment of Secrecy* (Glencoe, Ill.: Free Press,
1956) chapter 2. Cf. *Lord Denning's Report* (London: H.M.S.O., Cmnd.
2152, 1963).

were in no sense equal. The outlook is well summed up in the funeral monument of an 18th-century Oxford servant "who, by an exemplary life and behavior, and an honest attention to the duties of his station, deserved and obtained the approbation and esteem of the whole society." The gradual broadening of the franchise in the 19th century did not result in the adoption of the absolute principle of "one man, one vote" until 1948. Franchise reform has taken place in the context of a society in which political activity has been regarded as the duty of the few, and the majority have been regarded as unequal to the demands of public office.[19] In no society is equality fully achieved; in England, it is often not valued as a goal.

The Labour Party formally rejects inegalitarian attitudes, supporting as its ideal the classless society. Because of its electoral strength, its leaders have in the past generation made some headway in reducing some social inequalities. During the Second World War, the absolute shortage of goods and the importance of mobilizing the total civilian population for the war effort brought about a strict rationing scheme, based on a principle known as Fair Shares. The trade unions were represented as a major estate of the realm in the government. The postwar Labour government sought, by maintaining rationing and by taxation policies, to narrow income differentials; by controlling government, it raised the status of manual workers. It also created status insecurities among many middle-class Englishmen, and led to renewed insistence upon social inequality by some. Under Conservative governments of the 1950s, there has been an increase in observable evidence of social distinctions. Conservatives again feel free to emphasize that social inequality is both natural and desirable. For instance, Harold Macmillan, while Prime Minister, asserted:

> Human beings, widely various in their capacity, character, talent and ambition, tend to differentiate at all times and in all

[19] On the concept of "the people," see C. S. Emden, *The People and the Constitution* (Oxford: Clarendon Press, 1933) especially Appendix I. More generally, see L. S. Amery, *Thoughts on the Constitution* (London: Oxford University Press, 2nd edition, 1953) chapter 1; W. L. Guttsman, *op. cit.*

places. . . . To deny the bold, the strong, the prudent and the clever the rewards and privileges of exercising their qualities is to enthrone in society the worst and basest of human attributes: envy, jealousy and spite.[20]

The important thing about inequality in England is the attitude of Englishmen toward it. England, said Bagehot, writing a century ago, is a deferential nation. "Certain persons are by common consent agreed to be wiser than others, and their opinion is, by consent, to rank for much more than its numerical value. We may in these happy nations weigh votes as well as count them." [21] Instead of resenting the assumed superiority of a relative few, many Englishmen defer to those they regard as legitimately superior. The introduction of a democratic franchise has not eliminated deference from the political culture: it has altered both deferential and democratic norms.

Traditionally, the English have deferred to birth and wealth, criteria that have been challenged by liberal thinkers and by Socialist ones. Since the 1944 Education Act increased opportunities for university scholarships, discrimination on the grounds of educational achievement has also become an important basis of deference. This modification in the criteria for placing people in stations has not destroyed the fundamental hierarchical structure. Insofar as inequalities are now thought to represent fairly assessed intellectual differences, the support for hierarchical and deferential attitudes may be increasing. It is important to note that the private sector of education, which discriminates primarily on the bases of birth and wealth, remains a major influence upon recruitment into political offices. Thus it is possible for some members of society to show political deference on grounds of traditional attitudes, and for others to defer on the grounds that inequalities represent legitimate intellectual differences. Furthermore,

20 *The Middle Way: 20 Years After* (London: Conservative Political Center, 1958) p. 9. Cf. R. M. Titmuss, *Problems of Social Policy*, T. H. Marshall, *op. cit.*, and Roy Lewis and Angus Maude, *The English Middle Classes* (Harmondsworth: Penguin, 1953).

21 *Op. cit.*, p. 141.

new recruits to high political positions usually acquire some of the social characteristics and social advantages of traditional political leaders. As the Conservative MP Lord Balniel has pointed out, the English hierarchy is preserved "not so much by the conscious efforts of the well established, but by the zeal of those who have just won entry, and by the hopes of those who still aspire." [22] The traditional leaders simultaneously gain the advantage of the skills of their new associates. The current cultural attitude has been summed up by Lord Hailsham (who can be deferred to on the grounds of high birth and of educational achievement). Speaking as Conservative Minister for Science, he declared, "The democracy of the future . . . will be, as now, a society governed by its graduates." [23] Graduates constitute approximately 4 per cent of the nation's population.

Because of deferential norms, there is no support for the Jacksonian belief that all electors are capable of holding public office. Leaders in political life are expected to be uncommon men and enjoy deference on that basis. National politics is primarily for those who have been born to a high station in life, or have qualified for a high station by youthful educational achievement. (See Chapters III, IV.) Leaders are not expected to be friendly, back-slapping politicians, who mix well with ordinary people. A survey by Mark Abrams found that these traits were put at the bottom of the list, and the two most important ones were: "Strength" and "Strong enough to make unwelcome decisions." [24] The qualities that help qualify an Englishman for political office are diffuse, not specific to the political system. Birth, strength of character, and native intelligence can be demonstrated without political experience, and can constitute qualification for political appointments. The display of professional and tech-

[22] "The Upper Classes," *The Twentieth Century* (London) CLXVII:999 (1960) p. 432.

[23] *The Times* (London) report, November 24, 1962. See also Michael Young, *The Rise of the Meritocracy* (Harmondsworth: Penguin, 1961) Part One.

[24] Mark Abrams and Richard Rose, *Must Labour Lose?* (Harmondsworth: Penguin, 1960) p. 25.

nical expertise is often suspect. The devaluation of technical accomplishments is particularly marked in the recruitment of senior civil servants. In this process, Lord Macaulay's dictum of a century ago is still respected. Replying to the charge that ability in classical languages was not a substitute for technical knowledge in civil servants, he said: "If, instead of learning Greek, we learned the Cherokee, the man who understood the Cherokee best, who made the most correct and melodious Cherokee verses, who comprehended most accurately the effect of the Cherokee particles, would generally be a superior man to him who was destitute of those accomplishments." [25]

Leaders enjoy special advantages in English politics by virtue of cultural attitudes, but these same attitudes also reflect the expectation that leaders will pay heed to the needs and the desires of their own followers. Democratic elections, which may be dated from 1885, are the main institutional restraint upon leaders. Insofar as political leaders regulate their activities in anticipation of electoral advantages, the elections operate as a continuing restraint by followers upon leaders. As perceptive an observer as A. L. Lowell thought before 1914 that the Labour Party would never succeed because leaders of the Conservatives and Liberals would shift left in accord with electoral pressures, so great was the value they placed on winning.[26] Today, Conservative political leaders usually place much greater value upon electoral success than upon consistent adherence to programs and principles; Labour politicians disagree about priorities. The cultural role of a political leader, however, is to risk (temporary) unpopularity for his cause — and many have done so; most notably, Winston Churchill in the 1930s. Because elections occur infrequently and the governing party has the option of choosing any date within a five-year period as polling day, electoral pressures from followers upon leaders are not continuously important.

25 *The Life and Letters of Lord Macaulay*, Volume II (London: Longmans, 1923) pp. 585-586.

26 *The Government of England*, Volume II (New York: Macmillan, 1921 edition) p. 44.

A sense of trust is pervasive in the political culture. The ancient legal maxim, "The Queen can do no wrong," suggests the viewpoint that the government is not a menace to Englishmen. The Civic Culture survey found that English people are quite trusting in their general social relationships, and this trust is reflected in their political attitudes. At the level of government, trust is important between colleagues and partisan opponents because it reassures all that the particular group in office will not take advantage of the absence of constitutional restraints upon the powers of government. To do so would not be a violation of law, but of trust, and political leaders value their reputation for trustworthiness. The shock of the Profumo affair in 1963 was not that a government minister was committing adultery but that he would knowingly lie to the House of Commons in a personal statement, a statement involving his honor and the trust of his colleagues.[27]

Because there is trust in the good intentions of governors, it is possible for public officials to make public policy in considerable privacy. This privacy is strengthened by strong legal sanctions against those revealing unpublished government documents, and by strong cultural sanctions upholding the value of privacy in governmental deliberations. This privacy makes it extremely difficult for anyone not in personal contact with ministers, civil servants, MPs, journalists, and pressure-group spokesmen to keep informed of cross-currents in policy making, for the press is largely compelled to respect the privacy of public officials in their work. Those who value this privacy justify it on the grounds of its contribution to efficiency, just as those who dislike it believe it inefficient. Few impugn the trustworthiness of those who work so much in private. (See Chapter VIII.)

The ties between leaders and followers are strengthened by the support given values and beliefs concerning collective consultation. The importance of collectivist attitudes can be traced back in English history to the medieval guilds. Con-

[27] See G. Almond and S. Verba, *op. cit.*, chapter 10, and *Lord Denning's Report*.

servatives have retained throughout their history some collectivist views appropriate to an agricultural society; though
the party of businessmen, the Conservatives, have never been
thoroughgoing exponents of individualism, and nowhere in
England today does one find significant support for the individualist outlook of Barry Goldwater. The 19th-century
Liberal emphasis on political and economic individualism
was undergoing visible erosion well before Queen Victoria's
death in 1901. The rise of the Labour movement, based upon
the belief in collective action for individual ends, through
trade unions, co-operatives, and the Labour Party, did not
generate a conflict between individualist and collective outlooks, but only between contrasting conceptions of collec-
tivism.[28]

Not only are collective groups regarded as necessary and
desirable channels of political activity, but also there is a
strong belief in the right of these groups to be consulted by
government whenever the government is considering action
that would affect group interests. As Samuel Beer has shown,
the traditional belief that all with a material stake in society
have a right to share in government has a modern analogue
in the self-conscious accommodation of pressure groups by
British governments. The strength of support for collective
consultation is evidenced by the extent to which the government, formally highly centralized through the linkage of control of party, Parliament, and Cabinet, reduces its own authority and freedom of action by frequently appointing
committees of various kinds to advise it on policy. These committees include representatives of affected groups, and are a
chief channel of collective consultation. Through membership in pressure groups, individual Englishmen may indirectly
participate in the making of public policy. If the lone fron-
tiersman or the entrepreneur remains a valued symbol of in-

[28] See, *e.g.*, Lord Hugh Cecil, *Conservatism* (London: Williams & Nor-
gate, no date, c. 1912) pp. 169ff.; John S. Saloma, "British Conservatism
and the Welfare State" (Unpublished Ph.D. thesis: Harvard, 1961); Karl
Polanyi, *op. cit.*; and A. V. Dicey, *The Relation Between Law and Public
Opinion*.

dividualism in America, with the crusading Congressman his political counterpart, then the English equivalent would be the trade unionist and his trade-union leader, or the corporation president and his industrial trade association, pursuing collectively their individual wants.[29]

THE WORK OF GOVERNMENT

The great majority of English people believe that government has an impact upon their daily lives, and that it is beneficial. The Civic Culture survey found that 73 per cent of those interviewed saw some impact. Of these, more than three-quarters thought the government's activities were for the better; only 15 per cent thought they were sometimes for the worse, and only 3 per cent thought the impact generally harmful.[30] Such judgments are, of course, extremely broad and general. But the existence of broad approval for government is important in maintaining public support when governmental institutions are involved in particular difficulties.

One of the most important tasks of any government is to provide for the military defense of the country. Yet in England today there is deep disagreement about attitudes toward defense. A vociferous and well-organized group on the left rejects the belief that military strength and military alliances help to maintain peace. It favors unilateral nuclear disarmament by Britain, and includes many Cold-War neutralists and some pacifists. The group values peace whatever the diplomatic price, and includes those who believe that the renunciation of the use of force is more likely to reduce the risk of war than is the building up of large military establishments. Although cultural conflict today concerns nuclear weapons, members of the Campaign for Nuclear Disarmament and re-

[29] Note the importance of consultation in drafting legislation, as evidence in *The Times* annual survey of new bills, *e.g.,* September 19, 1963. Note also, *infra,* Chapter IX and Jean Blondel, *op. cit.,* chapters 6-8. For the historical background, see especially S. H. Beer, "The Representation of Interests in British Government," *American Political Science Review* LI:3 (1957).

[30] G. Almond and S. Verba, *op. cit.,* chapter 3.

lated bodies can trace their descent from political groups opposed to military action in the mid-19th century, in the Boer War at the turn of the century, and in the First World War.[31] Because defense involves the survival of the political community, those who value nuclear disarmament are prepared to act illegally since they reject the fundamental values of the country's foreign policy makers.

Cultural attitudes toward welfare services today reflect a very high level of consensus. Belief in community provision of basic necessities of welfare can be traced back to medieval times in England. The role of the Church as a provider of food, shelter, and care in old age survived the break with Rome. When England began industrialization there already existed a rudimentary national network of welfare services. Gradually these institutions have been modified. At no time, however, did believers in the economics of individual self-help dissipate entirely popular beliefs in the welfare responsibilities of British government. The Labour movement's contribution has been in widening the range of welfare services provided, and in attempting to raise the standard of services provided above the barest minimum.[32] The period of the 1940s was important primarily because the benefits were then widened to include employment, medical, and hospital care. At present, the chief controversy concerns whether university education should be provided as a welfare benefit for all who desire it, as medical services are, or whether what Americans, with their history of land-grant universities take for granted, should remain a restricted privilege. The contrasting English and American attitudes toward free higher education and free medical care reflect the extent to which values in England are

31 See, *e.g.*, J. A. Hobson, *Richard Cobden, The International Man* (London: Unwin, 1918); A. J. P. Taylor, *The Trouble-Makers* (London: Hamilton, 1957) and Richard Rose, "The Relation of Socialist Principles to Labour Foreign Policy" (Unpublished D. Phil. thesis, Oxford, 1959).

32 See, *e.g.*, Karl Polanyi, *op. cit.*; Asa Briggs, "The Welfare State in Historical Perspective," *European Journal of Sociology* (Paris) II:2 (1961) and David Roberts, *The Victorian Origins of the British Welfare State* (New Haven: Yale University Press, 1960) and Maurice Bruce, *The Coming of the Welfare State* (London: Batsford, 1961).

related to efforts to ensure against hardship, whereas in America greater emphasis is placed upon opportunities for advancement.

As well as expressing a positive valuation upon some activities of government, cultural attitudes also reflect values and beliefs limiting the activities of government in society. These boundary-maintaining norms are a part of the general cultural outlook. For example, religion today is thought to be an inappropriate area for continuous government intervention. Reciprocally, politics is believed to be an inappropriate area for clerical intervention. Both churchmen and government officials are expected to stay within jurisdictions reflecting prevailing values and beliefs about the boundaries of the religious and the political systems. In such ways, the scope of the government's impact upon society is restrained, without recourse to a written constitution. The precise definition of the limits of government action is often a matter of partisan controversy. Conservative values and beliefs emphasize the restricted role that government should play in social life. The importance of family, neighborhood, and religious claims are stressed against the importance of national politics. In the words of Lord Hailsham, all his life a Conservative politician, "The man who puts politics first is not fit to be called a civilized being, let alone a Christian." And many Conservatives even believe that party politics can be kept out of local government.[33] Left-wing members of the Labour Party reject the assumption that there are limits upon the impact of politics in society; their values and beliefs call for the transformation of England into a Socialist society by gaining political power. The leaders of the Labour Party, while favoring wider involvement of government in social life, do recognize limits upon its scope. For instance, the Labour Party favors reducing social differences by reducing the hierarchical differences between secondary schools, but party leaders have always been successful in rejecting the left-wing demand to prohibit, by

[33] Lord Hailsham, *The Conservative Case* (Harmondsworth: Penguin, 1959) p. 13; and, on local government, see F. Bealey and D. J. Bartholomew, "The Local Elections in Newcastle-under-Lyme: Part II," *British Journal of Sociology* XIII:4 (1962) p. 355.

Act of Parliament, parents from sending children to expensive, status-conferring public schools.

Widespread and conscious governmental intervention in society presupposes a reasoned case for such intervention, and a reasoned plan for proceeding. But the political culture supports skepticism about planning in politics, and intelligence is devalued. The term "clever" has been used as one of abuse by men as different as Lord Salisbury and Ernest Bevin. A party leader is not necessarily expected to be a clever man; Mark Abrams found in one survey that only 17 per cent of those interviewed thought it a desirable characteristic.[34] The Conservative Party has emphasized limits of rationalism since the days of Edmund Burke and before; it issues pamphlets that scorn those whose political policies are found "by the light of their naked intellect." [35] The Labour Party, in its Fabian Society branch, supports the application of reason to politics as the basis of piecemeal social engineering. The flights of the left wing of the Labour Party into the realm of grand Socialist theory have not devalued anti-intellectual norms; rather, they have tended to bring intellectuals into disrepute and to strengthen the intellectual conservatism of trade-union leaders as well as of those outside the Labour Party. Bagehot's remark still remains apt: "What we opprobriously call stupidity, though not an enlivening quality in common society, is Nature's favorite resource for preserving steadiness of conduct and consistency of opinion."

The positive side of this distrust of reason is shown in the support given to evolutionary change, instead of stand-pat conservatism or reaction. The process is colloquially described as "muddling through." Abrupt political change is associated with disaster or revolution or both. As the adaptation of the traditional political system in the past 150 years has shown, rigid opposition to all change is uncommon. English Conservatives appreciate that those who stand rigidly against all reform risk being swamped by social forces stronger than

34 Mark Abrams and Richard Rose, *op. cit.*, p. 25.
35 *Some Principles of Conservatism* (London: Conservative Political Centre, 1956) p. 8.

themselves. The Fabians, led by Beatrice and Sidney Webb, developed in late Victorian times their philosophy of the inevitability of gradualness, a distinctive contribution of England to European Socialism. The Fabian Society has as its emblem today a turtle, symbolizing the slow and steady advance of Socialism. Believers in evolutionary change have led both major parties for almost all of modern English history.

Belief in evolution, when combined with a skepticism concerning rational planning, can thereby produce a static political outlook. The preindustrial belief in the static character of society was undermined by the Industrial Revolution in England. But the 19th-century industrial and political eminence of the country gave Englishmen a vested interest in the *status quo*. Certainly, many of the country's major diplomatic and economic policies between the two world wars were designed to keep society static, a goal that seemed the more attractive in view of the collapse of many political regimes. Material standards of living have been rising throughout the century, but attitudes have not always supported change. The prevalence of static outlooks in the political system has been represented, for example, in the effort of successive Conservative Chancellors of the Exchequer in the 1950s to keep the economy in equilibrium, rather than rapidly expanding. This policy was discussed and endorsed at the 1959 general election.[36] Subsequently, the Conservative government has sought to encourage a more dynamic attitude toward the political economy; such an aim goes against much entrenched conservatism in both major parties, and in society as a whole.

Norms of gradual change may slow down innovation yet generate greater acceptance for innovations once introduced. The process of assimilation is complex and ambivalent. Assimilation involves the acceptance of change — but by accepting change, the possible chain-reaction effect of particular innovations may be muffled. Benjamin Disraeli, who saw the Conservative Party through the crucial developments of mid-Victorian England, expressed a still relevant outlook: "In a

[36] See D. E. Butler and Richard Rose, *op. cit.*, pp. 59-63, and C. A. R. Crosland, *The Conservative Enemy* (London: Cape, 1962).

progressive country, change is constant, and the great question is, not whether you should resist change which is inevitable, but whether that change should be carried out in deference to the manners, the customs, the laws and the traditions
of the people." Since 1945 the Conservative Party has shown
great skill in opposing Labour policies when first presented,
and then in accepting and sometimes expanding them later.
In this way the Conservatives have both altered their outlook
and retained control of office for more than a decade. In
a complementary fashion, the postwar Labour Party has in
its foreign policy assimilated pre-1914 balance-of-power ideas
as a consequence of experience in office, in spite of its traditional opposition to them. Its acceptance of the inevitability
of large-scale private enterprise in a mixed economy is further
evidence of its ability to assimilate existing norms. The alternation of control of an unrestrained Cabinet between competing political parties presupposes a willingness of each to assimilate the achievements of their immediate predecessors,
and a trust that those who succeed them will do likewise.

POLITICAL SYMBOLS

Bagehot provides the classic discussion of the part played
by emotion in the political culture of England. He distinguished between the dignified and the efficient parts of the
political system. The dignified parts "excite and preserve the
reverence of the population," they are the means by which
government gains authority. The efficient parts are those by
which the government carries out its work; they employ for
the sake of efficiency that homage created by the dignified
parts.[37] The same institutions can perform both dignified and
efficient functions. For instance, a general election is an efficient means of choosing a government; it is also an institution
that arouses emotions. Some parts of the political system primarily arouse emotions; these parts are usually political symbols. By concentrating attention upon symbolic sources of
emotions, one can gain precision in analysis. It should be re-

[37] *Op. cit.,* p. 4.

membered, however, that symbols are not the only source of political emotions.

Symbols can have both dignified and instrumentally efficient functions. For instance, the various hereditary titles and other honors conferred by the Queen, upon the advice of the Prime Minister, are symbolic awards. They carry no cash grants, and only those awarded peerages, a small proportion of persons honored, can sit in the House of Lords. Yet the anticipation of an honor, or the receipt of a knighthood or other award, may be a very efficient way to obtain the voluntary service of individuals on government committees, and to maintain discipline among the rebellious Conservative MPs.[38] The nominally efficient policy goals advanced by political parties may also have symbolic uses; some policy slogans are more efficient in arousing emotions than in giving guidance to a perplexed Cabinet. The activities of the Foreign Secretary may be intended to achieve great changes in international affairs. But because of England's reduced position in international affairs, these activities may have the equally important latent function of symbolizing great-power status for a nation that no longer has the substance to go with its symbolic status.

The Queen is the most prominent symbol in the political system. As head of state, the Queen performs many ceremonial functions that regularly involve her, though only as a figurehead, in the workings of government, and invest these workings with some of the monarchy's aura. Of special note is the sanction which royalty gives to party conflict. While one party forms Her Majesty's government, the chief competing party plays the equally honorable role of Her Majesty's Loyal Opposition. Opposing the government is given honor too. Through the Queen's dual position as head of state and de-

[38] Members of the hereditary peerage — Dukes, Marquesses, Earls, Viscounts, and Barons — are automatically qualified to sit in the House of Lords. Other honors, except for non-hereditary peerages, do not carry this or any other politically significant privilege. Knighthoods and baronetcies give the right to have the prefix "Sir" before one's name. Other honors are indicated by initials placed after the name, *e.g.*, T. S. Eliot, O.M. (Order of Merit).

fender of the faith, the government is linked to religion and
the sources of religious authority. The strength of emotional
attitudes toward the monarchy is indicated by the attacks
upon those who occasionally criticize the Queen — and also
by the rarity of criticism along republican lines.[39]

The sentiments and symbols of patriotism also provide
strong emotional support for the political system. The extent
to which English people, like Americans, give pride of place
to their political system is brought out clearly in Table II.1,

TABLE II.1   *Pride in National Attributes*

	(% Naming)				
Attribute	*Britain*	*America*	*Germany*	*Italy*	*Mexico*
Governmental, political institu-
tions	46	85	7	3	30
Social legislation	18	13	6	1	2
Characteristics of people	18	7	36	11	15
International position	11	5	5	2	3
Economic system	10	23	33	3	24
Geographical features	10	5	17	25	22
Contributions to science	7	3	12	3	1
Contributions to the arts	6	1	11	16	9
Spiritual values, religion	1	3	3	6	8
Other answers	11	9	3	21	14
Don't know, Nothing	10	4	15	27	16
Total mentions	148%	158%	148%	118%	144%

(Because of multiple responses, total mentions do not add up to 100%.)

Source: G. Almond and S. Verba, *op. cit.,* chapter 4.

which indicates marked differences from Germany and Italy.
The depth of this attachment to England and its political
system is indicated by the fact that when the Gallup Poll asks
individuals what country they would most like to live in if
not England, about three-quarters consistently name New
Zealand, Australia, or Canada, three nations perceived as
closely resembling England. The strong positive attachment

[39] See also Chapter X; W. Bagehot, *op. cit., passim;* and Lord Altrincham, *et. al., Is the Monarchy Perfect?* (London: Calder, 1958).

to the nation strengthens an individual Englishman's own sense of personal identity, for his own ego and self-esteem are involved in his orientation toward his society and its political system. Reciprocally, this secure sense of personal and national identity may enable the English to preserve political self-confidence even in the face of disasters such as the fall of France in 1940.

The past is ever present in England in the landscape, in social institutions, and in politics. Norms concerning the traditional English way of life may well be stronger than similar ones in America — if only because the American culture emphasizes dynamic change, whereas the English culture supports more strongly the maintenance of the *status quo*. Many Englishmen seem to approach politics with the belief that whatever was, is still right, and that whatever is now right, will continue to be correct in future.[40] Because norms concerning political behavior in the past do not involve fundamental conflicts (unlike France or the American South) this traditionalism is not a source of major political difficulty.

Parliament symbolizes a way of politics as well as serving as one branch of the institutions of government. (Parliament here is used as the English often use the word, to refer to the House of Commons, the elected branch of Parliament; the other chamber of Parliament, the House of Lords, is nonelective and cannot veto legislation endorsed by the House of Commons.) Emotional pride in the country's Parliament is stimulated in school, in the mass media, and by such bodies as the Hansard Society for Parliamentary Government. Pride in Parliament is not always equaled by an understanding of the greatly reduced and altered part that it plays in mid-20th century government. (Cf. Chapter IX.) When some politicians and journalists become conscious of the relative decline of Parliament, they jump to the conclusion that the political system is deteriorating; they have an emotional attachment to Parliament as the center of government, in an era when British government is Cabinet government. In some respects Parliament is more important today in its dignified contribu-

40 See the preference for everything "as it is," F. Zweig, *op. cit.* pp. 195ff.

tion to the work of British government, than for its efficient one.[41]

Political developments since the Second World War have reduced the utility of the word "Socialism" as a description of a tangible set of political principles or policies. The Labour Party is officially Socialist in principle, though not in name, and is a member of the Socialist International. Its program, however, is the hybrid product of the ideas of Socialists, trade-union officials, and reformers. Hence, major differences exist within the party about the meaning of "Socialism." (In this book the word is occasionally used in reference to the Labour Party in order to draw attention to features that have been greatly influenced by Socialist thinking.)[42] "Socialism" remains important as a symbol of the ideal society of some ardent Labour supporters. The existence within the Labour Party of those for whom Socialism is a sacred symbol and those who regard it as pragmatically limited in value gives controversies within the Labour Party some of the heat of a theological dispute. As Hugh Gaitskell learned in 1960 when he failed to have a symbolic pledge to achieve Socialism removed from Clause IV of the party constitution, the influence of the Labour Party leader cannot always hope to prevail against those partisans for whom Socialism remains an inspiring symbol. Socialism is also used as a symbol to stimulate political unity among opponents of the Labour Party who disagree about many things, but who share a deep revulsion to it. The electoral success of the Conservatives in the 1950s was in part due to their emphasis upon "anti-Socialism."

The country's historic status as a world power stirs strong emotions. England's position as a world power has been de-

41 Cf. Michael Foot, *Parliament in Danger!* (London: Pall Mall, 1959); Christopher Hollis, *Has Parliament a Future?* (London: Unservile State Papers No. 1, c. 1960), and "Torn Up Checks," *The Economist* (London) January 12, 1957, and J. P. Mackintosh, *The British Cabinet* (London: Stevens, 1962) Parts Four, Five.

42 The Labour Party has been staunchly anti-Communist ever since the formation of the Communist Party of Great Britain in 1920, and Labour Party members who associate with Communists or Communist-front groups are liable to expulsion.

clining since the First World War. The signing of the NATO agreement in 1949 marked the completion of its transition to the position of a country dependent upon the aid of another nation for its own defense. This decline has not been matched by a comparable decline in emotional involvement in world affairs. Today, both supporters and opponents of the country's H-bomb policy assume that England is a major world power. The unilateral disarmers think of the "power" of moral leadership which the nation could have if it disarmed and became neutralist; the advocates of possessing a thermonuclear deterrent independent of America stress its importance as literally a status symbol, *i.e.,* a token that England is still a world power. The extent to which this discussion involves symbols strong enough to obscure judgment is suggested by the fact that while the debate upon the H-bomb has been going on, the country's conventional military forces, its efficient military strength, have been deteriorating.

The use of old symbols to mask new relationships is particularly striking in the evolution of Empire into Commonwealth.[43] In late Victorian times, the Empire was regarded as one of the main foundations of England's international strength. Today, Commonwealth members may divide over the Cold War and over matters as crucial to England as the Suez War, but such disputes do not detract from the dignity and symbolism of Royal tours, Commonwealth political conferences in London, and the sending out of Governor-Generals, symbols of a vanished Imperial authority. In this way, Englishmen may continue to enjoy the emotional gratifications of great Imperial standing — even though the efficient authority has long since been lost. The significance of the Commonwealth as a symbol may alter greatly, however, in the next few years, because of the growing importance of colored ex-colonial nations in the Commonwealth, and the slowly growing number of emigrants from these nations to England. Opponents of the country's entry into the Common Market in 1962 found that "Commonwealth" was not a symbol

[43] See S. R. Mehrota, "On the Use of the Term 'Commonwealth,'" *Journal of Commonwealth Studies* II:1 (1963).

capable of arousing emotions as strong as those aroused by "Empire" in the debates on Indian independence prior to 1947. Labour politicians, however, have become increasingly pro-Commonwealth because it links England with new Afro-Asian states.

THE CULTURAL MIX

The political culture of England is a complex, not a simple thing. Theoretically, there are dozens of subcultural groups that could exist as the result of varying combinations of attitudes discussed above. What is most important in contemporary England is the amount of agreement on political values, beliefs, and emotions, despite the fact that many are derived

TABLE II.2 *Party Attitudes toward Cultural Norms and Symbols*

+: *Supports*　　　/: *Partially supports*　　　—: *Rejects*
(*More than one sign indicates sharp intra-party divisions.*)

Norms and Symbols	Conservatives	Labour	Liberals
Liberty	+	+	+
Universal suffrage	+	+	+
Deference	+	—, /	/
Equality	—	+	+
Leadership	+	+	+
Trust	+	+	+
Privacy	+	/	/
Collectivism	+, —	+	/, —
Consultation	+	+	+
Static society	+	/	/
Evolution/Assimilation	+	+	+
Government beneficence	/	+	+
Military defense	+	+, —	/
Welfare	/	+	+
Limits on government	+	/, —	+
Monarchy	+	+	+
Community	+	+	+
Past traditions	+	/	/
Parliament	+	+	+
Socialism	—	+	—
Empire/Commonwealth	+	+	+
World power	+	/	/

from partisan conflicts in previous generations. The extent of cultural integration can conveniently be depicted in a table, illustrating the position of the Conservatives, Liberals, and Labour toward major attitudes in the culture (Table II.2). The Liberals are included because Liberal ideas have been more important than the electoral weakness of the party in recent decades would suggest. Of course, such a table can only give a rough approximation of party attitudes, and what is generally true of a party or section within it will certainly not be true of every voter. A table can indicate the areas within the culture where there is consensus between the parties, and the points at which conflict occurs. There is clear conflict between Conservatives and Labour in only two areas — equality and Socialism. More often, the differences between the parties are matters of the degree to which norms are supported, or else, differences exist within parties. (Cf. Chapter VII.)

The political culture reflects a mixture of attitudes rooted in widely differing historical periods. For instance, universal suffrage is, in England, a 20th-century value, and in spite of its relative newness, it is so strongly supported that those who question it label themselves anachronisms. But the monarchy is a survival from a far older and different period, yet it is given equally strong and unquestioning support. Today, the largely hereditary House of Lords embodies in one chamber of Parliament values more appropriate to the 18th than the 20th century, whereas the existence of a strong Labour Party ensures simultaneously the presence of upwards of 100 trade unionists in the major chamber, the House of Commons. The two chambers of Parliament exemplify the importance of the mixture of 18th-century aristocratic attitudes and 20th-century collectivist attitudes in English politics. Less emphasis is given to attitudes characteristic of the 19th-century heyday of rugged individualism.

The present cultural mix is the product of a long historical process of development, in which support for various norms has altered, and the norms themselves have been altered, in the course of time. During the past two centuries, at least three

major emphases can be noted.[44] One is that of the social conservative, averse to change and strongly attached to the culture of a preindustrial and predemocratic society. Another
is that of the liberal reformer, concerned with removing the
barriers to individual and economic advancement. The third
is that of the trade unionist and Socialist, placing emphasis
upon the need for collective action to ensure equal treatment
for the needs of those who live by manual labor. The three
voices have different tones and have sounded different notes,
usually from different places in the choir. The product, in
spite of these differences, has usually been harmony. Accounting for this harmony is a major problem of historical sociology. One clue to an understanding would seem to be the
extent to which any given pattern of behavior is likely to persist in a culture from generation to generation. In England,
the persisting pattern is one embracing values and beliefs concerning the peaceful compromise of political differences, just
as in France it has been the persistence of a revolutionary tradition. The persistence of techniques of compromise is positively strengthened in England by the importance of norms
and emotions opposed to dynamic change. The great implicit
major premise of the English political culture appears to
be that all necessary and desirable changes can be assimilated into the existing political system; in the words of the
motto of Lord Hugh Cecil's study of Conservatism: "Even
when I changed, it should be to preserve." [45]

44 Cf. R. J. White, editor, *The Conservative Tradition* (London: Kaye,
1950); A. Bullock and M. Shock, editors, *The Liberal Tradition* (London:
Black, 1956); Henry Pelling, *The Challenge of Socialism* (London: Black,
1954).

45 *Op. cit.*, p. 243. Note that Buckingham Palace announced it would
conduct a time-and-motion study of its staff as a contribution to National
Productivity Year.

CHAPTER III

Political Socialization

People who learn slowly learn only what they must. The best security for a people doing their duty is, that they should not know anything else to do.

THE VALUES, beliefs, and emotions of the political culture are transmitted from generation to succeeding generation of Englishmen by such varied institutions of political socialization as the family, the school, and jobs. In this process, individual Englishmen are differentiated from one another, yet they are also integrated into a single political system. Differentiation begins in childhood, when from his family, playmates, and teachers a small child learns that some children are different from others, and that his society does not expect the same behavior from them all. Gradually, these differences become recognizable in politically salient contexts, and adolescents acquire attitudes toward a variety of roles with contrasting expectations of political activity or passivity. As an adolescent learns to identify these adult roles, he also begins to acquire, from his own self-evaluation and from others' evaluation of him, an idea of what roles he is expected to perform, or, in traditional language, what is his station in life. Most Englishmen gradually fit into social roles involving little expectation of political activity; a small minority are socialized for active participation in national politics. This political division of labor is largely completed by the time an Englishman is old enough to vote. Socialization facilitates social integration because in England there is a good fit between the political attitudes transmitted by the chief agencies of pre-adult socialization and adult roles of the political system. Adolescents who are predisposed by socialization to be active in public affairs find that adult society recognizes and approves early training. Undergraduate political activities at Oxford, for instance, can become national newspaper stories; very occasionally an Oxford undergraduate is elected to the House of Commons. The majority socialized for passive roles fit easily into the political system, because their expectations complement those of the leaders. Integration is also strengthened insofar as many cultural attitudes are common to all, such as affection for the community and for the parliamentary regime.

A young Englishman's socialization may begin with the acquisition of emotional attitudes; for instance, in early childhood his parents or teachers may teach him to stand in awe of the monarchy, or to respond positively to the manners of diffuse, gentlemanly leaders. Alternatively, he may begin to develop political awareness by forming beliefs; for instance, his playmates may teach him that authority, in the form of a policeman, can easily be disobeyed. Or initially an individual may learn political values, as in the case of a person who is taught from infancy that the British form of parliamentary government is the best in the world. Englishmen do not proceed inductively in politics, learning beliefs, then values, then emotions; any of these basic attitudes may in turn shape others.[1]

Political socialization does not determine adult political behavior. It creates predispositions that in later life may, and often are, influential upon behavior. But an Englishman's political actions will reflect a wide variety of influences, some of

[1] On this point, see Lewis Froman, "Learning Political Attitudes," *Western Political Quarterly* XV:2 (1962) pp. 306ff. More generally, see Herbert Hyman, *Political Socialization* (Glencoe, Ill.: Free Press, 1959).

which began operating in the political system long before his birth; others may be unique and contemporary. Individuals are always capable of learning new attitudes toward politics, or altering old ones, since political socialization occurs throughout an individual's lifetime; in many instances, however, what is freshly learned serves to reinforce what was learned previously.

FAMILY AND GENERATION

In the process of socialization, the family comes first in the time sequence. Political attitudes related to early family experiences may be influential because they are deeply rooted in primary family loyalties. Consider the instance of a widow, a small shopkeeper in Nottingham. She explained her present party loyalty in a life-history interview by referring to her childhood:

> We worked like blacks as youngsters and then we hadn't enough money to have holidays like the upper classes. It made me feel there was a law for the rich and a law for the poor. I didn't see why holidays should be only for the rich. I have always sided with Labour to get fairness for all.

This woman was giving lifetime support to Labour, even though she thought the Conservative Party had been correct in its approach to the major political problems of the past 25 years. But to have voted Conservative would have meant going against her childhood memories, and the politics of her father, who was "red-hot Labour." This she could not do. The persistence in adulthood of attitudes toward politics formed in childhood, clearly revealed in the life-history survey, is the more striking because the same pattern does not show up in attitudes toward religion. Many Englishmen who no longer go to church were brought up as church- or chapel-goers. They do not regard themselves as going back on their parents if they stop going to church — but they often appear to have emotional ties preventing them from shifting parties. Large national surveys consistently bear out this generalization. For instance, Mark Abrams found in 1960 that of those who had

fathers voting Conservative before the war, only 15 per cent
had become Labour supporters; of Labour supporters, only 28
per cent expressed a Conservative preference a generation
later.[2]

The persistence of party loyalties from generation to generation is strengthened by the extent to which Englishmen remain
in the same class as that of their parents. In a few cases, of
course, following directly in father's footsteps will lead into
politics. For instance, the eldest son of a peer is guaranteed a
seat in the House of Lords if he outlives his father. For Winston Churchill, entry into politics meant following his father's
career and even surpassing it. The same has happened to Roy
Jenkins, a Labour MP and the son of a trade-union MP. In
the Jenkins family, one can see social change at work; the
elder Jenkins entered Parliament after working in a coal mine
and as a trade-union official, whereas his son went to Oxford
and entered politics there.[3]

From infancy onward, a child becomes aware of authority,
as he is an object of parental discipline. (In a small but politically important section of the community, children may also
learn at an early age how to give orders to servants.) In the
Civic Culture study, Almond and Verba found statistical evidence suggesting that if an individual participates in making
decisions within his family, and later at school and at work, he
is more likely to feel able to influence government. The majority of the English respondents said that by the age of 16 they
had some influence upon family decisions.[4] The evidence is not
detailed enough to trace adult political activity to specific experiences in family discipline. It does indicate, however, that
the domineering father is not typical.

Within the home, children early become aware that sex differences are related to differences in adult behavior. At the

2 "Social Trends and Electoral Behavior," *British Journal of Sociology*
XIII:3 (1962) p. 238.

3 Cf. W. L. Guttsman, *op. cit.* pp. 158-163.

4 See *op. cit.*, chapter 12. Cf. F. Zweig, *op. cit.*, pp. 20ff.; Harry Eckstein,
A Theory of Stable Democracy (Princeton: Center of International Studies,
1961) pp. 10ff.

level of voting participation, women consistently show slight differences from men, more frequently abstaining and more frequently voting Conservative (Table III.1). In national political activity, a woman finds that her sex is a handicap, because national politics is not considered a woman's role. At the 1959 general election, only 25 women were returned for 630 parliamentary seats, although women are a majority of the electorate.[5]

TABLE III.1   *Sex Differences in Voting Behavior, 1959*

	Women %	Men %
Not voting	58	42
Conservative	55	45
Labour	49	51
Liberal	48	52
Other (N = 36)	42	58

Source: British Institute of Public Opinion post-election survey.

Changes in the historical experience of generations in turn influence family life. The improved status of the manual worker since the war, combined with the greater diffusion of decent housing and consumer goods, appears to be enabling the family to spend more time together as a unit. This turning inward to the family, in what Mark Abrams calls the "Home-Centered Society," may mean that the father of the house participates less in collective social activities that once reinforced his consciousness of working-class status. Simultaneously, women have more opportunity to move about outside the home, bearing fewer children and enjoying greater opportunities for employment. Some commentators have speculated that the apparently increasing autonomy of families, combined with greater income and a heightened sense of opportunity, will gradually produce major cultural changes by stimulating growing support for individualistic norms that have hitherto been

[5] D. E. Butler and Richard Rose, *op. cit.*, p. 126. See also J. F. S. Ross, "Women and Parliamentary Elections," *British Journal of Sociology* IV:1 (1953) p. 16.

of lesser significance. It would be premature to draw conclusions on this point.[6]

In discussing the politics of young people it is important to distinguish between features that persist for decades, and features that reflect the historical context in which one group comes of age. In England as in many other countries, teen-agers and those in their early twenties have persistently shown less political knowledge and participated less in politics than their elders. Among the minority who are active in politics, the largest single group are in the Young Conservatives, which claims to be the largest youth political organization outside the Communist bloc. The Labour Party's youth sections have historically been small, and though several times disbanded, have always suffered from Marxist infiltration. Most young people are similar to their elders in their political attitudes, according to sample surveys. The voting tendencies of young people are usually slightly in favor of Labour, but this tendency does not operate with equal intensity at each election.[7]

Old people constitute a time lag built into the political system, because their political outlook has been formed in very different historical conditions from those now prevailing. More than 10 per cent of today's electorate reached adulthood before the outbreak of the First World War in 1914, and about 20 per cent were first eligible to vote when the major competing parties were the Liberals and the Conservatives. Old people strengthen social conservatism in the political culture. Gradually, however, this group will come to consist of those who are conserving attitudes shaped during the more tense political period of the 1920s and 1930s, rather than during pre-1914 days. As this change occurs, old people may be important in conserving traditional pro-Labour rather than pro-Conservative norms.

6 For evidence and speculation see, *e.g.*, Mark Abrams, "The Home-Centered Society," *The Listener* (London), November 26, 1959; F. Zweig, *op. cit.*; J. H. Goldthorpe and David Lockwood, "Not So Bourgeois After All," *New Society*, October 18, 1962; G. M. Carstairs, *This Island Now* (London: Hogarth, 1963).

7 See D. E. Butler and Richard Rose, *op. cit.*, p. 193; *Youth Survey* (London: British Institute of Public Opinion 1959).

In terms of voting behavior, however, old people in England in the 1950s were politically volatile, contributing heavily to the floating vote. In 1950, those above the age of 65 voted Labour by a margin of about 4 to 3. In 1955, the group swung to the Conservatives by a margin of 5 to 4. In 1959, the same age group swung back to Labour by a margin of 8 to 7. In both 1950 and 1959, the group was swinging against the national trend. The chief reason for this shift is probably that many old people are entirely dependent for their income upon a small state old-age pension with a fluctuating rate subject to political influence.

SCHOOLING

English schools, like American schools, teach "life adjustment." They can hardly educate young people in ways that will make them social misfits. Schools help young people to adjust to adult life by giving explicit and implicit instruction in the norms and roles of the society, including those of the political system. The differences between English and American education reflect differences in the cultures to which young people are adjusted.

Overt political indoctrination is limited to a very few aspects of the political culture, especially those concerning the political community and the regime. Responses in life-history interviews indicate that before the Second World War, this instruction linked religion and patriotism. For example, a Banbury clerk reported that at his school no instruction was given in government, but that patriotism was taught "in the form of prayers and history." A Liverpool baker said that his school "always had the National Anthem on every occasion and scriptures and prayers. Told to love your own country. Always told our own country was the best and I still believe it."

Implicitly, the English[8] educational system transmits and emphasizes cultural norms concerning inequality. Inequality is presented as natural, and often as desirable. If the melting pot has been the symbol of American education, then the

[8] What follows specifically excludes Scotland and Wales, where the structure of education is different.

cream separator is appropriate for England. English governments have repeatedly upheld the cultural belief that the great
majority of the population is fit only for the most rudimentary
sort of education. Compulsory education was not introduced
until 1870, and free secondary education was not introduced
until 1944. University education remains the privilege of an
extremely small proportion of the population. There are still
more people in England who have left school at the age of 11
than there are persons who have attended universities. In 1962,
two-thirds of the youths left school at the age of 15, when they
first become legally able to do so. Only 8.6 per cent remained
at school at the age of 17, and only 3.3 per cent beyond the
age of 18. Metaphorically, one might speak of the English
educational system as a series of high steps, and of the American system as a sloping pyramid. In England, a young person
must jump up a step at the ages of 11, 16 and 18. If he fails
to do so by examination success at each stage, he is likely to
lose his chance for a higher education, and is given an inferior
educational status. In America, where there are fewer sharp
distinctions between parts of the educational system, one may
more easily move up or move across, and may gradually slide
off the pyramid without so clearly being said to have failed. In
recent years the Labour Party has begun to challenge the assumptions on which the educational system rests, but the
structure has as yet been little altered. The Conservatives felt
confident enough of support for the prevailing system to advertise at the 1959 general election: "Socialists take little account
of him [a schoolboy] as a person. They are far more concerned
with keeping people equal. That begins with children."

The inequalities recognized and emphasized by the educational system are politically important because they are directly
linked to differing social and political roles. Sir David Eccles,
when Minister of Education went so far as to state that English
schools are "one of the chief instruments which create the
social gulf in our society." Differences are impressed in a variety of ways. Expensive, private boarding schools (ironically
called "public schools") maintain a marked segregation of
pupils between those in the state system and those who are not.

Boarding schools also separate young people from children in their home neighborhood as well as from their parents. In local grammar schools — the chief academic secondary institution within the state system — the school heads may insist upon the maintenance of barriers between their pupils and those who attend the nonacademic secondary modern schools. These barriers can be maintained in sports and in social clubs, as well as during the school day. Uniforms — anachronistic in some public schools and simply distinctive in grammar schools — further differentiate teen-agers into separate and unequal communities. In the words of a grammar-school mistress, the uniform is "a reminder that each wearer of it is a member of a very special community." [9] The sense of inequality conveyed by such distinctions is illustrated in the responses of a group of 100 grammar-school pupils, writing an examination essay posing the question as to whether or not the bulk of the people is "a near-moronic mass." The majority accepted this description. The political implications were explicitly stated by the youth who wrote: "Fortunately, thinking people usually occupy high positions in our country and government." [10]

The schools discriminate on grounds of social status as well as intelligence. The public schools and their preparatory schools accept pupils of widely varying intellectual abilities. Their parents must usually evidence a preference for this form of education by the time a child is eight, as well as paying annual fees of approximately £500 ($1400). The state-run grammar schools discriminate primarily on grounds of measured intelligence. Indirectly, this practice gives an advantage to middle-class children, whose parents can more often provide opportunity for their children's intelligence to develop, but the favoritism is not intentional. There also exist a number of tax-supported, privately controlled direct-grant schools, which

[9] See Frances Stevens, *The Living Tradition; the social and educational assumptions of the grammar school* (London: Hutchinson, 1960) p. 93; Sir David Eccles' speech in *The Times,* February 9, 1962; "School Rules and Class Attitudes in State Education," *The Guardian* (London: formerly, the *Manchester Guardian*) February 5, 1963.

[10] Brian Jackson, "The Moronic Mass," *New Statesman* (London) November 3, 1961.

mix up fee-paying pupils and large numbers of pupils selected on academic grounds without regard to parental income. All of these secondary schools have university preparatory programs. The bias toward instruction in gentlemanly subjects such as Greek and Latin is declining in favor of science. Even today, however, Latin is virtually a compulsory requirement for entry to Oxford. The majority of young people attend secondary modern schools from the ages of 11 to 15, and then leave to go to work. These schools discriminate on the basis of intelligence, taking students judged to form the least intelligent three-quarters of the population; they thereby tend to have an inferior status. A small number of students attend comprehensive secondary schools; these are usually established under the auspices of Labour-controlled municipal authorities. These schools are intended to confer equal status upon all their pupils, and the divisions within the school into university preparatory and other programs are de-emphasized. Comprehensive schools contain children of all ranges of intelligence, and efforts are made to develop the abilities of those who would not have passed an entrance examination to an academic grammar school. Another small group attends secondary technical schools, with special facilities for vocational training. These schools have no clearly defined status; recruitment is influenced by youths' vocational preferences as well as by intelligence.

In theory, the secondary modern schools are meant only to be different, and not to be inferior. But in everyday speech, the majority of those who attend these schools are said to have "failed." In the words of a government pamphlet, many parents feel that if their children go there "they will not have a fair start in life." [11] More than three-quarters of the electorate were segregated in childhood in schools recognized as educationally and socially inferior. Since wartime reforms replaced parents' income in favor of measured intelligence as the chief

[11] *Secondary Education for All* (London: H.M.S.O., 1958, Cmnd. 604) paragraph 11. See also Olive Banks, *Parity and Prestige in English Secondary Education* (London: Routledge, 1955).

segregating factor,[12] the gulf between the secondary moderns and other schools may be greater, because it is thought to be fairer. Research indicates that attendance at secondary modern schools definitely decreases a young person's job expectations, regardless of his parents' social class. A similar effect appears to be exercised upon political expectations. The Civic Culture survey found in England, as in other countries, that those receiving more education were more likely to consider themselves capable of effective political action.[13] Young people attending secondary modern schools usually accept the politically passive roles implicitly stressed by the orientation of the schools.

Grammar schools accept students on the basis of measured intelligence shown on an examination taken at the age of 11 or 12, but once in the schools, children receive training overtly intended to build character as well as to develop the mind. Before the Second World War, this emphasis was often stressed in the hope of attracting parents who sought to purchase approved middle-class character values for their children. Today, shaping character is still important. One master summed up his view with the remark, "Though the grammar school like the public school cares very much for brains, in the last resort character counts more." [14] The character training in the grammar schools is one that accustoms pupils to hierarchical authority. They are expected to look up to their masters (the symbolically significant name for teachers) and those among the older pupils who exercise some authority by delegation as school prefects. This training in followership is complemented by the implicit assumption that all in this selective category will assume the responsibilities of leadership *vis à vis* those in secondary modern schools. Problems may develop within the small group of pupils from working-class families

[12] But, on the persisting influence of class in selection, see, *e.g.*, J. E. Floud, A. H. Halsey, and F. M. Martin, *Social Class and Educational Opportunity* (London: Heinemann, 1956), and the Crowther Report, *15 to 18* (London: H.M.S.O., 1960), especially Volume II.

[13] See, *e.g.*, W. Liversidge, "Life Chances," *Sociological Review* X:1 (1962); G. Almond and S. Verba, *op. cit.*, chapter 12.

[14] F. Stevens, *op. cit.*, p. 216. See also Diagram IX, p. 286.

who like the educational advantages of a grammar school but reject the middle-class and hierarchical bias of its subculture.[15] This group, though noteworthy, is statistically small.

The public schools were developed from medieval foundations in Victorian times to provide an education and character training suitable for the sons of gentlemen and for those who aspired that their sons become gentlemen, though they were not of such status themselves. At that time, this status was accepted as a prime qualification for holding public office. Particularly by the late 19th-century reform of the civil service, the government sought to encourage public service as a career for gentlemen university graduates. These historical influences remain important today (see Chapter IV). The public schools, which educate less than one-twentieth of the population, very disproportionately supply recruits to the Cabinet, the civil service, and Parliament. Hence, the character-training biases of the public schools are specially important insofar as these schools are formative influences upon the behavior of national political leaders. Public schools normally stress group solidarity within the school, and exclusiveness in relation to those outside the school. The curriculum emphasizes language, history, and literature, on the grounds that such general liberal education develops the mind better, and better prepares a person to handle any job well, than would a more highly specialized and scientific curriculum. The pattern of authority within the school prepares boys to obey authority as well as to give commands, and to act as leaders.[16] A few public schools, such as Eton and Winchester, appear to give special emphasis to leadership in public service, in party politics, in the civil service, in the armed forces, and formerly in the Empire. This tendency, complemented by the increasing commercial and industrial bias of the majority of those at the minor public

15 See, *e.g.*, Brian Jackson and Dennis Marsden, *Education and the Working Class* (London: Routledge, 1962) and, for an autobiographical specimen, Dennis Potter, *The Glittering Coffin* (London: Gollancz, 1960).

16 Note the long-established preference of the Army for selecting officers from those who have attended public schools. Evidence is summarized in Anthony Sampson, *The Anatomy of Britain* (London: Hodder & Stoughton, 1962) pp. 258ff.

schools, makes for a marked difference in political socialization even within the confines of the public-school section of society.[17] The public schools do not create differences in political roles, which antedate the rise of these schools. But they are important in maintaining the existence, into the middle of the 20th century, of a pattern of differentiated attitudes toward political roles that has its roots in predemocratic times.[18]

Of particular significance for the political culture is the fact that nearly all the schools, within their own school community, stress a hierarchical system of authority, training youths for different but complementary roles of leader and follower. This system, in the words of Professor W. A. Robson, a supporter of the Labour Party, "produces a sense of responsibility and of leadership on the part of boys and girls who hold these offices or aspire to them; while the other pupils absorb the notion of authority being exercised by some of 'us' as well as by 'them' [*i.e.*, the teachers]." [19]

The universities play a small part in the political socialization of the great majority of the population, since more than 95 per cent of English people have not entered a university. For the small group who do attend universities, this experience appears to have an important effect in breaking them loose from attitudes inculcated by their secondary schooling and by their families, regardless of their nature. A survey of student attitudes at Manchester University in 1963 found that the majority of students expressed a large measure of dissatisfaction with many norms in the political culture — even though, as individuals, each expressed strong satisfaction with life as a student and with general expectations of an adult career.[20] There appear, however, to be marked differences in socializa-

[17] See the author's "Old School Tie-Up," *The Economist*, May 25, 1963.
[18] See, *e.g.*, Rupert Wilkinson, "Political Leadership and the Late Victorian Public School," *British Journal of Sociology* XIII:4 (1962); the Fleming Committee Report, *The Public Schools* (London: H.M.S.O., 1944).

[19] "Education and Democracy," *Political Quarterly* XXX:1 (1959) p. 73. See also the Fleming Committee Report, *op. cit.*, paragraph 106.

[20] See the author's "How Much Education Makes a Tory?" *New Society*, November 1, 1962, and *Students in Society* (Manchester: University Union, 1963).

tion between universities. Oxford and Cambridge students (collectively called Oxbridge men) have a national political career held up as a model, and contacts are made there that may later help individuals to realize such expectations.

WORK

Most English people spend the important adolescent years between the ages of 15 to 21 at work and not at school. Thus, the potential influence of employment upon political socialization is increased by the shortness of the school life, as well as by the daily importance of work to almost all members of the adult electorate. Because of the consistent correlation between parents' job, education, and an individual's own job,[21] experience at work tends to confirm and strengthen political attitudes developed in the family and at school. A minority of the population do undergo upward or downward social mobility through their jobs. The more rapid expansion of industry and commerce in relation to further education has provided middle-class and upper-middle class jobs and incomes for many individuals with minimal educational qualifications. Among those who because of their jobs rank in the top 4 per cent of the nation, 73 per cent left school by the age of 18. Of those who rank in the next 11 per cent of the nation by job, 45 per cent left school by the age of 15, and 85 per cent by the age of 18.[22] Individuals who are occupationally mobile in their working careers rarely became prominent as national political leaders, except for trade-union officials.[23] A very small number become occupationally mobile through election as MPs, but the economic rewards of British politics are not so great as to attract people on monetary grounds.

Because of the links between occupational class and party politics, an individual's experience at work influences political

21 See, *e.g.*, D. V. Glass, editor, *op. cit.*, and the ideas and data set forth in A. H. Halsey, Jean Floud, and C. Arnold Anderson, *Education, Economy and Society* (New York: The Free Press, 1961).

22 Calculated by the author from Mark Abrams, *Education, Social Class and Newspaper Reading* (London: Institute of Practitioners in Advertising, 1963) Tables 2, 3.

23 See W. L. Guttsman, *op. cit.*, pp. 173ff., 201ff.

attitudes and voting behavior. A survey conducted some years ago by F. M. Martin came to the conclusion that English people expect class differences to have more influence upon political attitudes than upon a variety of other social orientations. A comparative study by Robert Alford of the relationship between class and voting behavior in Britain, America, Canada, and Australia demonstrates that Britain has the highest level of class voting of these four countries, and that this class influence is constant (see Table III.2).[24]

TABLE III.2   *Socio-Economic Class and Voting, 1945, 1950, 1959*

% Sample 1959	Socio-economic class*	% Conservative			% Labour		
		1945	1950	1959	1945	1950	1959
4	Average plus	76	79	79	14	9	15
21	Average	61.5	68	66	22	15	14
62	Average minus*	30.5	35.5	34	54	53.5	46
13	Very poor		24.5	19		64	51

* The socio-economic classification employed here reduces the figures for working-class Labour voting because some persons with lower middle-class jobs are placed in the Average Minus category.

Source: British Institute of Public Opinion.

The minorities who behave differently from most in their class may at times be decisive in general elections. But they have this effect only because of the partisan stability of the majority of middle-class and working-class Englishmen. Middle-class voters show more class solidarity than do working-class voters.

Job differences can also exist within the same broad classification, and these lateral differences can also affect political attitudes. A manual worker employed by the government, or by a nationalized industry, may develop a political outlook different from that of a person doing the same job in private employment. A manual worker on a factory assembly line or a coal miner in the pits may feel more solidarity with his co-workers

[24] See F. M. Martin, "Social Status and Electoral Choice in Two Constituencies," *British Journal of Sociology* III:3 (1952); Robert Alford, *op. cit.*

than a self-employed truck driver or a plumber. In the Civic Culture survey, Almond and Verba found in England and elsewhere that individuals who felt that they could influence conditions at their place of work were more likely to feel that they could also exercise political influence than those who did not, even within the same occupational class.[25] Since an individual's chance to influence his working conditions will be related to trade-union membership and, in the case of a nationalized industry, to government policy as well, politics and economics here closely affect each other. In the extreme case of the coal industry, the miners used their collective political power to alter working conditions fundamentally, by helping to elect a Labour government that displaced their employers by nationalizing the coal industry.

POLITICAL PARTIES

The stress placed upon nonpolitical agencies of socialization is not meant to denigrate political parties as agencies capable of influencing the outlook of their members and supporters. Political parties gain adherents through the influence of other agencies of socialization upon potential recruits. The parties are limited in the extent to which they may influence basic cultural attitudes toward the monarchy, Parliament, and the community because of the deep attachment to these norms already developed in members by pre-adult socialization. But at the level of government policy, and in resolving conflicts between norms, or creating them, parties may be important influences upon individuals. Though their members are a small proportion of the electorate, they include a large segment of those in active political roles.

In the Civic Culture study, Almond and Verba found that, potentially, party members were more likely to be opinion leaders in their face-to-face contacts. Of party members, 81 per cent said that they talked politics, compared to 62 per cent of those who were not party members. Furthermore, 70 per cent of party members showed definite views about policy on a set of six attitude questions, compared to only 46 per cent of non-

[25] *Op. cit.,* chapter 12.

members. Of special importance is the finding that these differences did not represent the indirect influence of educational differences between party members and nonmembers. Party membership can substitute for education as a means of developing an informed interest in politics.[26]

At the level of the general electorate, however, parties have shown a striking failure to develop among their voters a coherent set of attitudes toward matters of public policy. For instance, in a study of a parliamentary constituency in Bristol, R. S. Milne and H. C. Mackenzie asked respondents their views on four major issues on which the Conservative and Labour parties clearly differed in their national programs. Among Labour voters, only a third could be classified as pro-Labour on these issues, and 39 per cent were classified as pro-Conservative. Among Conservative voters, only 4 per cent were classified as pro-Labour, but only 38 per cent expressed support for official party policy on at least three of the main issues.[27]

Although party programs and the preferences of party voters are far from identical, it does not follow that political parties cannot influence the attitudes of voters. As established social institutions linked with class, jobs, schooling, and family background, political parties can draw upon emotional loyalty as well as policy preferences. In Graham Wallas's words, "Something is required, simpler and more permanent, something which can be loved and trusted, and which can be recognized at successive elections as being the same thing that was loved and trusted before; and a party is such a thing." [28] Such loyalty and trust can affect attitudes. The Gallup Poll consistently finds that respondents are more likely to endorse a policy if it is identified as the policy of their party than if it is not. In other words, they will take policies and actions on trust if they come from a trustworthy source — the party leadership. The loyalty to the party is usually a diffuse loyalty, and is not rooted in approval of specific policies. Because loyalties are diffuse, party

[26] *Op. cit.*, chapter 11.

[27] *Op. cit.*, p. 119. See also Jean Blondel, *op. cit.*, pp. 75-79.

[28] *Human Nature in Politics* (London: Constable, 4th edition, 1948) p. 83.

leaders enjoy considerable leeway in framing policies, particularly in the Conservative Party. In the Labour Party, emotional loyalties can be developed, at least among active party workers, to such policies as nationalization.

Party leaders have long recognized the importance of cultivating the emotional loyalties of party sympathizers. A notable late 19th-century innovation in this respect was the Primrose League, founded in 1883 to strengthen the Conservative Party by mobilizing politically the personal loyalties of newly enfranchised voters to Conservatives of wealth and high status. Since 1957, the major parties have shown a fresh awareness of the possibility of exploiting emotions by means of advertising techniques. In that year the Conservative Party began a lengthy national campaign that emphasized emotionally appealing slogans and symbols of home, family, and children, rather than overtly political themes customarily stressed in party literature. In 1963, the Labour Party began to follow with its own national advertising campaign, in which party strategists have been particularly concerned with making an emotional impact upon prospective voters, in contrast to the former emphasis upon policy in Labour propaganda.[29]

THE CUMULATIVE IMPACT

Life-history interviews illustrate clearly how political socialization involves an accumulation of experiences reaching across the generations. For instance, Mrs. Blue, now an elderly widow living in a middle-class London suburb, was born into a middle-class Conservative family. Her mother was "a very hot Conservative" though she did not have a vote. Mrs. Blue went to an Anglican school in a cathedral town; there she joined the Young Primrose League, a Conservative auxiliary organization. Upon leaving school in 1906 she became a governess and shortly thereafter married a builder. When asked if any events

[29] See J. H. Robb, *The Primrose League, 1883-1906* (New York: Columbia University Press, 1942); M. I. Ostrogorski, *Democracy and the Organization of Political Parties* (London: Macmillan, 1902) Volume I, *passim,* D. E. Butler and Richard Rose, *op. cit.,* Chapter 3 and illustrations, and Mark Abrams, "Why the Parties Advertise," *New Society,* June 6, 1963.

particularly influenced her political outlook, Mrs. Blue replied, "No I've always been the same." The First World War has left little impression on her political memory. The General Strike of 1926 was simply an occasion when "we had to walk everywhere. Fortunately, it was the summer time." Of the interwar depression she remarked, "I don't think everyone should blame the government for anything that goes wrong. Nobody can work miracles." The Second World War caused anxiety about her son in the Army, but had no impact on her political outlook. "Same as I say before, you can't blame the government." Mrs. Blue could recall nothing of the postwar innovations of the Labour government. She considers herself a Conservative because "they've done the most good." The Labour Party, which she confuses with the Liberals (the opposition party of her youth), is regarded as for "the majority of working men, who can't think for themselves." Of her two children, both have been to public schools. One is an Army Lieutenant-Colonel. The other, her daughter, is an active Conservative, and her son-in-law is a past chairman of the local Conservative Party branch.

Mr. Red's life as a Lancashire coal miner is very different from that of Mrs. Blue, but it similarly shows how the socialization experiences of a lifetime accumulate. Mr. Red was born in a mining village in 1914. His father was a miner, and in childhood, his family was sometimes short of money. This was a period of great industrial and political unrest in the industry. When he was 14 he left school and shortly thereafter went down into the mines, where he has worked ever since, rising to a supervisory position underground. No political event is particularly memorable. When asked explicitly about various things, he could only recall the sunny weather during the General Strike, cigarette shortages during the Second World War, the Labour government's introduction of a national health service, and the British invasion of Suez, of which he approved. Mr. Red thought of himself and his council-house neighbors, mostly miners, as members of the working class. In spite of a limited political interest, his party attachment is deep-rooted. Mr. Red is a lifelong Labour supporter because "My Dad worked in the pit all his life and it was nothing but slavery in the pit. And it's only since the Education Act came into force that people have been educated and therefore they can think for themselves. It was the Conservatives in when the Education Act was passed. This was the silliest thing they did against their own party."

These two case studies illustrate the coherence of the political outlook of many Englishmen. The outlooks of Mr. Red and Mrs. Blue have remained consistent throughout their lives. What they expect of politics, and what is expected of them, has also remained clear. As individuals and as members of the political system, they have a clearly defined political identity. Furthermore, this identity is linked with a conception of their general social identity. These people can take their politics for granted, and decision makers know what to expect from them. There is a security and stability in politics that cannot be enjoyed by, say, a first-generation American, with ties to both the Old Country and his new home, or a Burmese civil servant, with ties to both a traditional Buddhist culture and to a modern, technological one.[30] An Englishman can take his Englishness for granted, and has no doubts about what it means to be English. Individual politicians may be accused of being incompetent, but not of being un-English. Their loyalty is taken for granted. So secure are Englishmen in their personal and national identity that ineptness does not stimulate a fear of national disintegration, a fear facing many newly formed nation-states: "there will always be an England." This calmness may, of course, lead to unjustified self-assurance in the face of unprecedented developments, as in the case of the government's policy toward Hitler Germany in the 1930s.

The segregation of people in adolescence by means of the educational system helps a maturing Englishman to identify himself with one of the varied political roles. As Erik Erikson has written, at this age a young person must develop an aware-

---

[30] Cf., *e.g.*, Daniel Bell, editor, *The New American Right* (New York: Criterion, 1955); Lucian Pye, *Politics, Personality and Nation-Building* (New Haven: Yale University Press, 1962).

ness of "what he has come to see in himself and what his sharp-ened awareness tells him others judge and expect him to be." [31] Membership in a school community aids him in recognizing his station in life — in politics as well as in the economy. By the time English youths reach the voting age of 21, about 97 per cent are working full time, and the majority have already been at work for six years. The educational system may create a crisis of identity for a minority, especially when children from working-class homes win places at middle-class secondary schools. Some resolve this crisis by identifying completely with middle-class roles; only a few appear to be disturbed.[32]

The most outstanding characteristic of political socialization in England is that it is homogeneous; that is, the differing agencies of socialization to which a young person is exposed tend to strengthen his early political outlook. There is not the sort of built-in conflict that may occur in America. The ab-sence of important differences of race, religion, language, and ethnic group in England results in fewer primary socializing influences, and also reduces the possibilities for conflicting pressures. Furthermore, the stability of society does not en-courage sharp discontinuities in an individual's life experi-ence. For instance, in a survey of an older London suburb, a total of 73 per cent of those interviewed had the same occupa-tional class as their parents and also an education appropriate to that class. The three chief influences upon political social-ization — family background, education, and adult employ-ment — were homogeneous. Only 7 per cent had a socialization history that showed marked discontinuities. The remaining 20 per cent had been born in working-class families and had stepped up to a middle-class job either after years of work, or else through education.[33] This homogeneity is important in stabilizing political behavior from one generation to the next. Mrs. Blue's life history illustrates this point in an extreme

[31] *Young Man Luther* (London: Faber, 1959) p. 12.

[32] See Brian Jackson and D. Marsden, *op. cit.*

[33] Calculated by the author from data supplied by Ian Budge; from a random sample of 143 persons.

form, because she clearly links across three generations attitudes extending back to a time before the introduction of the democratic franchise.

Political socialization is a stabilizing influence, but not a stagnating one. The agencies of socialization themselves change. Family life in the full-employment welfare state, with rising incomes and more women working is different today from family life in the childhood of many adults. Education is far more widely available and distributed far less on grounds of family wealth than it was before 1914. Religion is no longer so important in political socialization. The disturbances of two world wars have affected the lives of millions of people in unanticipated ways. The political parties themselves have changed, for until 1922, the Liberals, not Labour, were the chief alternative to the Conservatives.

Differential exposure to agencies of political socialization helps maintain political variety. Of particular note are those adults who were little exposed to political socialization in childhood and youth, or who were exposed to conflicting sets of political attitudes. For instance, an individual might have parents who disagreed strongly in their politics or avoided political discussion. Major social changes operate differentially within society. Between the wars unemployment was widespread, but the majority held jobs. Life-history interviews show that the reactions to mass unemployment of those who remained at work were often very different from those of the people directly affected.

Socialization is a continuous process. Potentially, individuals remain open to changing their political attitudes at any time in their adult lives. In practice, the majority do not. Their steadiness, whether it is attributed to apathy, common sense, or prejudice, is shown by the ability of people to interpret new political occurrences in such a way as to fit them into pre-existing outlooks. For those who wish to change their political roles and outlooks, opportunities exist. The positive approval given to assimilating new ideas and individual outsiders into the political system is of special importance in preventing the formation of politically active groups feeling alienated from the existing regime or community. The educational system is always ready to "sponsor" the upward mobility of very able persons from humble backgrounds, and these individuals may forge ahead in politics. The sponsorship system, requiring a mobile person to shape up to the standards of those who determine his future, may contribute more to changes in the sponsored recruits than it does to changes in the political system.[34]

Of particular importance at the level of national political activity is "role socialization"; that is, the acquisition of attitudes specific to particular kinds of political roles. For instance, an individual who is elected to the House of Commons when his party is in Opposition becomes, through contact with his fellow MPs and experience in the House, socialized into the role of Opposition MP. He learns how to criticize and harass those responsible for the administration of government. But when his party becomes the majority party and forms a government, the same individual must then learn how to conduct himself in a responsible, administratively efficient manner, and must abandon the obstructionist outlook characteristic of Opposition. Of course, some MPs cannot learn the norms appropriate to the role of government minister, and remain perpetually opposition-minded. But the socialization agencies of English society place so much emphasis upon sensitivity to group expectations that many are quick to learn attitudes appropriate to new political roles, even after years in active politics — provided that there is strong incentive. The majority of English people do not undergo intensive political socialization in adulthood, of course, because their involvement in politics is relatively slight.

It would be a mistake to think of many agencies of political socialization as consciously attempting political indoctrination. Instead, this process seems to take place as a by-product of other functions. It is intimately linked with the family, schooling, early friends, and experiences at work. The result may be

[34] See the development of this point, R. H. Turner, "Sponsored and Contest Mobility and the School System," and the exchange between Turner and A. H. Halsey, *American Sociological Review* XXV:5 (1960); XXVI:3 (1961).

a political outlook that appears illogical or uninformed when judged by a political philosopher. But it is also an outlook that is strongly held, stable, and regarded by individuals as natural, just because it is rooted so deeply in their whole experience of English life.

CHAPTER IV

Participation in Politics

The principle of popular government is that the supreme power, the determining efficacy in matters political, resides in the people — not necessarily or commonly in the whole people, in the numerical majority, but in a chosen people, a picked and selected people. It is so in England.

THE STUDY of who does and who does not participate in politics can broaden understanding of the relationship between English politics and society. Furthermore, the delineation of who are the politicians helps to illuminate the structure of politics.

There are, broadly speaking, four levels of political roles in England. At one extreme are national leadership roles, taken by individuals participating in the making of policy decisions, with ready access to other policy makers. The national leaders include members of the Cabinet, the most senior civil servants, important expert advisors who may or may not hold public appointments, and spokesmen for major pressure groups in industry, the trade unions, and the social-welfare field. Working closely with people in leadership roles are those in the roles of political auxiliaries, often holding formal appointments as deputies or assistants to national leaders. Sometimes auxiliaries act as intermediaries between national leaders and local political activists, as in the case of a regional secretary of a national political party. At other times, auxiliaries may act as intermediaries between leaders, as in the case of a prominent journalist. Because of the close contact between those in national leadership and auxiliary roles, they can usually be grouped together as national political roles; individuals frequently taking such roles can be termed national politicians.

In England, national politicians are usually clearly distinguished from those in local activists' roles whose political influence tends to be confined within a single community. Typical local activists' roles are those of town councillor, branch secretary of a trade union, or voluntary leader of a social-service group. Sometimes, of course, local activists may be intimately involved in the administration of central government policy, as are those concerned with a town's educational system, a system that operates within a framework determined by the central government. The largest portion of the population have strictly peripheral political roles, whether nominally involved in politics as members of a pressure group or party, or outside the boundaries of organized political activity, participating at most by casting an occasional vote. The members of what may be called the peripheral public are indirectly linked to national politics by the local activists.

The political role of an individual is not identical with the functions implied by a constitutional description of an office held. Roles are generalized patterns of expected political behavior that reflect actual relationships in the political process, whether or not these relationships are based upon officeholding. For instance, a pressure-group official is unlikely to hold a public office. Yet he may take a national political role, if he expects to be consulted when government policy is made in a certain area, and if Cabinet ministers expect to consult him. Stratifying the political system into four main kinds of roles "unites into groups people who differ from one another." [1] Elected officials, appointed officials, and individuals

[1] A phrase used to describe social class by T. H. Marshall, *op. cit.*, p. 114. Cf. Chapter I. See also, Heinz Eulau, *The Behavioral Persuasion in Politics* (New York: Random House, 1963) chapter 2.

without formal office interact politically. For instance, Cabinet ministers, very senior civil servants, and outside experts in the department's field, though differing in institutional positions, can see each other daily and work together. It is this frequency of interaction arising from the working relationships of the political process that helps to define the different levels of roles. The structure is very complex.

THE PERIPHERY

Participants at the level of the local activists and of the peripheral public can be grouped together. Both usually have only a part-time involvement in politics, and work at a distance from central government. This group constitutes the great majority of the population, as in all large nations, where size makes it impossible for large numbers of people to participate directly in national politics. In England, nonparticipation is also supported by traditional predemocratic norms in the culture.

The political role that the majority of the population takes is that of voter at a general election. Turnout at the polls on election day has been consistently high since 1885. In the four general elections of the 1950s it averaged 80 per cent. Of the minority who do not vote, many are prevented from doing so by circumstances beyond their control. Nonvoters are not disaffected from the political system. The Gallup Poll found in a survey just after the 1959 general election that a very small percentage gave dislike of all parties or lack of interest as their reason for staying away from the polls. Because national elections are usually held about once in four years, and because only one office is at stake in each constituency — that of Member of the House of Commons — voting represents minimal participation in politics. A vote for many English people is the by-product of experiences in other aspects of social life.[2]

Responses in the Civic Culture survey concerning the meaning to the individual of his vote indicate the shallowness of

[2] See the author's contribution in Mark Abrams and Richard Rose, *op. cit.*, pp. 67ff.; R. S. Milne and H. C. Mackenzie, *op. cit.*

this form of political participation. Only 43 per cent of those interviewed said that they had a feeling of satisfaction when voting, compared to 71 per cent in America.[3] Others indicated low involvement, reporting that when voting they were thinking "nothing special" or "it was a waste of time." But a surprising minority responded in words that suggested voting caused unpleasant anxiety, giving replies such as: "I hate going into them cubicles. Felt rotten. Was thinking 'they're like a lot of sheep, all following one another.' Would have got out of it if I could," or "I hope I'm not doing the wrong thing."

English people show a firm attachment to parties, almost certainly because party allegiances are an integral part of other social allegiances. Socialization links an individual's party identification with his conception of himself and his place in society. In Gallup Poll surveys, approximately four-fifths of respondents are always ready to identify themselves with one of the three major parties; in 1958, only 7 per cent of those interviewed classified themselves as independents, and 14 per cent as uncertain about their party identification. But partisanship is not so strong as to involve strong dislike of partisans of the opposition party. Almond and Verba found that only 14 per cent of their English sample were intensely partisan in nonpolitical social contacts.[4]

Another minimal index of political participation is self-expressed interest in politics. A striking feature of responses to a direct question about political interest is the relatively small number of persons who report that they are very interested or not at all interested in politics (Table IV.1). The small but important section who describe themselves as "very interested" appear to be distinguished as much by their sex as by their education or economic class. The pattern of responses in the life-history interviews suggests that many people were overestimating their consistent interest in politics in order to gain esteem in an interview situation. Perhaps the most meaningful feature of Table IV.1 is that 85 per cent of the sample are not "very interested" in politics.

[3] G. Almond and S. Verba, *op. cit.*, chapter 5.
[4] *Ibid.*, p. 155.

TABLE IV.1   *Self-Assessed Interest in Politics*

	Total (N—1496)	Men	Women	Middle class	Working class	Left school Under 16	16 or over
	%	%	%	%	%	16	over
Very interested	15	21	8	17	14	14	19
Interested	37	39	35	52	30	32	53
Not really interested	33	29	38	22	38	37	22
Not at all interested	15	11	19	9	18	17	6

Source: Mark Abrams, "Social Trends and Electoral Behavior," p. 233.

The limited interest of the majority of people in politics is emphasized by their lack of political information. In England, as in America, "don't knows" always form a sizable proportion of those replying to a question about public policy. There are, in addition, many who have opinions on an issue, but are un-informed about the details of the problem, or even about the broad differences between alternatives. The names of leading national politicians are also unfamiliar, despite the years of publicity they have had. Mark Abrams found in one survey that the median respondent could only name three national party politicians. Only 5 per cent could name three Conserva-tives, three Labour, and one Liberal Party MP, out of the 630 members of the House of Commons.[5]

Indirectly, individuals may participate in politics by holding membership or office in organizations that consistently or in-termittently act as political pressure groups. In the Civic Cul-ture survey, 47 per cent of people interviewed said that they belonged to at least one social organization — most frequently, a trade union. But studies of trade unions indicate to what a large extent formal membership is the limit of an individual's participation in the affairs of nis pressure group.[6] The Civic Culture study found that 70 per cent of those who belonged to an organization had never held any office in it. Furthermore,

[5] Mark Abrams, "Social Trends and Electoral Behavior," p. 234.
[6] See, *e.g.,* Martin Harrison, *op. cit.;* B. C. Roberts, *Trade Union Gov-ernment and Administration* (Cambridge, Mass.: Harvard University Press, 1956) chapter 4.

organizational officials were not typical of the population. Those with higher education were proportionately much more likely to have held office than those with only an elementary education. The relationship between education and office was stronger in England than in America, Germany, Italy, or Mexico.[7]

Party organizations show a similar pattern of active and passive participation. The number of party members is large in proportion to the electorate. In 1963, the Labour Party reported 6,325,000 members, slightly more than half its total poll in the 1959 general election. This figure is misleading, however, because less than 12 per cent have joined as individuals; the rest join, or are joined, by their trade unions. The Conservative Party keeps no systematic membership records, but estimates that it has between 2,000,000 and 2,500,000 members; that is, individuals who pay more-or-less annually a minimum subscription of 35 cents to a local constituency party. In 1962, the Liberals estimated their membership at 275,000 on a similar basis. The majority of dues-paying party members are *only* members. Payment of dues represents the maximum amount of involvement in the party organization.

The party organizations, divided into constituency groups, and within that, ward groups, make available to every Englishman facilities for participating in politics. The parties welcome into membership all who are prepared to pledge support to it, without regard to race, religion, or other social characteristics. Constituency party organizations nominate candidates at parliamentary elections, and they can submit resolutions to national party conferences, though these may be treated with short shrift. The party organizations provide better opportunities than their American counterparts do for individual part-time participation in politics, but only a few hundred thousand people are active in them. Nor are the activists necessarily concerned with national party politics, for these organizations also deal with local and parochial matters, and in some cases may make a point of building up membership through social

[7] Calculated by the author from data in G. Almond and S. Verba, *op. cit.,* chapter 11.

clubs, or lotteries on athletic events. (In the author's constituency, the Labour Party has a large membership because it provides pubs and entertainment in an area short of both, offering a better platform to rock and roll singers than to aspiring MPs.) An analysis of the resolutions forwarded to national party conferences indicates that local activists are not especially partisan or extremist in their national political views.[8]

Many Englishmen maintain a shallow, intermittent participation in politics; few are inclined to sustained participation (Table IV.2). If one defines sustained participation as indi-

TABLE IV.2 *Political Participation in Britain*[a]

	Estimated number	Estimated % electorate
Electorate, 1959	35,400,000	100%
Party identifiers	27,950,000 [b]	79%
Voters, 1959	27,850,000	79%
Organization members	16,650,000 [b]	47%
Party members, all categories	8,850,000	22%
Informed (named 6 politicians)	5,650,000 [b]	16%
Very interested in politics	5,300,000 [b]	15%
Organization officers (past, present)	4,950,000 [b]	14%
Individual party members	3,225,000	9%
Local party activists	138,000 [c]	0.5%

[a] United Kingdom figures and estimates.

[b] These numbers derived by projecting survey findings.

[c] Estimated at 125 in each Conservative and Labour party and 50 in each of 400 Liberal constituency parties.

Sources: See text, *supra.* Cf. estimates in A. H. Birch, "Citizen Participation in England & Wales," *International Social Science Journal* (Paris) XII:1 (1960).

cated by the self-assessment "very interested" in politics, then the figure is 15 per cent of the electorate. If one takes active participation in a local party organization as the appropriate indication of participation in politics, if only on a part-time

[8] See Richard Rose, "The Political Ideas of English Party Activists," *American Political Science Review* LVI:2 (1962), the articles referred to in its footnotes, and Jean Blondel, *op. cit.,* chapter 4.

basis, then the proportion is something like one in every 200 members of the electorate. It is possible that the proportion of the adult population actively participating in politics in England today is the same as (or even lower than) it was before the passage of the great 19th-century democratic franchise reforms.

NATIONAL ROLES

Studies of political participation in England show a fairly sharp division between participation in politics at the local level and participation nationally, except for the few who function as intermediaries. Englishmen seeking careers in national politics are not expected to start at the bottom and gradually work their way up from the equivalent of a precinct captain. In this century, only two national leaders, Neville Chamberlain and Herbert Morrison, built national political careers on local foundations. In the North of England and Scotland, where the practice of sending local activists to Parliament is often still strong, these groups are under-represented in leading positions, because ex-local activists are rarely chosen as Cabinet ministers.[9]

Those in national political roles, excepting many spokesmen for pressure groups, usually enter national politics as young men, and spend their lives accumulating experience and seniority at this level, rather than working their way up from one level to the next. The centralization of politics in London facilitates this way of life, and permits a politician to spend a working lifetime in one city, accumulating experience all the time, rather than moving from state to national levels and back, as often happens in America. The absence of residence requirements for MPs means that many in Parliament have no roots in the constituencies that nominate them. For instance, in 1959, 69 per cent of Conservative MPs returned in solidly Conservative seats could claim no local connection at all with their constituents.

[9] This represents an important qualification to data in W. J. M. Mackenzie, "Local Government in Parliament," *Public Administration* (London) XXXII (Winter, 1954).

There is a fairly clear distinction between those whose political roles represent career commitments, part-time involvement, and intermittent involvement. For instance, the administrative-class civil servant makes a full-time career of public employment, and can look forward to a pension at the end. Many, though not all, MPs devote most of their time to their jobs in the House, and come to regard the job as a career. By contrast, pressure-group spokesmen can only be involved part of the time; they must also perform duties within their organization, if they are to remain effective group spokesmen to government. Political participation for such men is not a career, but a by-product of a career in an organization. Intermittent involvement, either full-time or part-time, characterized men who went temporarily into public employment during the Second World War, from careers in industry, the universities, and elsewhere. Today, it particularly characterizes men who take up voluntary or paid appointments as heads of a great variety of public commissions, committees, and boards. Recruitment studies, partly as a matter of convenience and partly because of methodological biases, concentrate almost exclusively upon holders of public offices. In the following section public offices will be used as the point of departure in discussing roles, because of the wealth of data available in this form; national politicians who do not hold office as MPs or administrative-class civil servants are discussed separately, for convenience's sake.

The small group of men who have been either Prime Minister, Foreign Secretary, or Chancellor of the Exchequer since 1900 may be regarded as ex officio national leaders. As for social origins, the group is dominated by men drawn from very small and select strata of the population. Nearly half were educated at one of three public schools — Eton, Harrow, or Winchester. Only six of the 40 received the ordinary education provided in state schools. Of the total, 15 were professional politicians and all of this category except one inherited both money and family connections, facilitating a professional political career.[10] In the 1945-51 Labour government, four of the six

[10] Calculations by the author. Cf. W. L. Guttsman, *op. cit.*, pp. 78ff.

men who held these offices had been at major public schools, and only one, Ernest Bevin, had ever been a manual worker.

Entry into the Cabinet, which is ex officio a national politician's role, tends to be confined to narrow social strata. It is possible to distinguish between those with hereditary aristocratic connections and those who are "only" upper-middle class by background; together, the groups form about 5 per cent of the population. Those with high social status can gain entry into the House of Commons at an early age. This is an important advantage because of the degree to which promotion to the Cabinet requires the accumulation of experience. Those who wish high office usually spend a long apprenticeship in the lower ranks of the hierarchy of government ministers; a sprinkling of experts and new men are included in the Cabinet, but except in wartime they have been of limited significance. A Prime Minister has on the average served 26 years in Parliament before taking that office. Unlike America, where newly appointed Cabinet ministers may be strangers to the President, in England Cabinet ministers form a group of select individuals who have worked together for a decade or more.[11]

Recruitment into the Cabinet is a reflection of recruitment into the House of Commons. The Conservative Party in Parliament has for more than a century largely consisted of men drawn from the top 5 per cent of the nation's social structure. Alteration in the social origins of MPs has come about through the rise of the Labour Party. Today, a system of trade-union nominations in many safe seats provides approximately 90 ex-manual workers in a House of Commons of 630. By comparison with the United States Congress, Parliament contains more upper-class and more working-class members.[12] Although the

[11] See especially W. L. Guttsman, *op. cit.*, pp. 199ff.; Philip W. Buck, *Amateurs and Professionals in British Politics, 1918-59* (Chicago: University Press, 1963) p. 118, and Richard Rose, "The Emergence of Leaders," *New Society*, October 17, 1963.

[12] Cf. J. A. Thomas, *The House of Commons, 1906-11* (Cardiff: University of Wales Press, 1958); J. F. S. Ross, *Parliamentary Representation* (London: Eyre & Spottiswoode, 2nd edition, 1948); D. E. Butler and Richard Rose, *op. cit.*, chapter 10; Andrew Hacker, "The Elected and the Anointed," *American Political Science Review LV: 3 (1961)*.

bulk of the members of the House of Lords have inherited their qualifications for membership, much of the actual work done in this legislative chamber is carried on by individuals who have received peerages themselves for public services, often in the House of Commons and the Cabinet.[13]

Once an individual becomes a Member of the House of Commons, he finds that there are a wide variety of recognized roles he can take, ranging from aspiring minister to parliamentary jester. Social origins will greatly influence an individual's chances of entering Parliament, but they do not appear to affect greatly his choice of political roles. For instance, some Conservatives from Eton are prominent in the Cabinet, whereas others are insignificant as back-benchers with more interest in fox-hunting than in affairs of state. Parliament works well because many of its members are not interested in reaching national office. The odds were about one in 40 for a Conservative MP reaching the Cabinet, and one in 25 for a Labour MP in the period 1918-59.[14] Many MPs are content with the role of a national auxiliary, quietly supporting the party line in each division, or undertaking an unglamorous junior ministerial post. These MPs provide ballast; their inactivity and lack of initiative contributes to the stability and predictability of parliamentary life. By the same token, when trade-union MPs in the Labour Party or the "knights of the shires" in the Conservative Party begin to express disquiet, party leaders are alerted to the seriousness of a political situation. Some MPs, of course, pay limited attention to parliamentary affairs, using their position to advance themselves outside Parliament in their employment, or in their social status. All MPs do not share the same conception of their role in Parliament, or their role in relation to ministers, to pressure groups, and to their constituents. There are several dozen combinations of roles for MPs to choose from.[15]

[13] See P. A. Bromhead, *op. cit.*, chapter 3.

[14] See P. W. Buck, *op. cit.*, p. 74.

[15] Cf. the variety of ideas expressed in House of Commons *Debates*, Vol. 673, Cols. 1715-1819, March 15, 1963. See also P. G. Richards, *Honourable Members* (London: Faber, 1959).

A small proportion of the more than 600,000 nonindustrial civil servants take national leadership or auxiliary roles in politics. The officially defined "highest ranks of the civil service" includes about 170 men, and the "higher civil service," 2800.[16] Together they constitute a large and important phalanx within the strata of national politicians, outnumbering ministers and MPs. The largest single section of this civil-service group is the administrative class, divided into the Home Civil Service and the Foreign Service. The higher and highest ranks also include an admixture of scientific, legal, medical, and other specialists.

Civil servants in high political roles, like many elected politicians, have been recruited in youth without any technical or specialized skills. The traditional ideal was expressed by Lord Macaulay in 1854: "We believe that men who have been engaged up to twenty-one or twenty-two in studies which have no immediate connection with the business of any profession, and of which the effect is merely to open, to invigorate and to enrich the mind, will generally be found in the business of every profession superior to men who have, at eighteen or nineteen, devoted themselves to the special studies of their calling." [17] Postwar figures on direct entry to the Home Civil Service show that 171 successful candidates studied history, and 110 Greek and Latin. These were the two largest groups. Twelve majored in mathematics and six in science and technology. Of 149 successful competitors for the Foreign Service, one had studied mathematics and another was a scientist.[18] Because of this bias toward "good generalists" or "amateurs," scientists and economists have strongly criticized the workings of the

16 See W. J. M. Mackenzie and J. W. Grove, *Central Administration in Britain* (London: Longmans, 1957) chapter 3, especially Table IX.

17 Quoted in A. Sampson, *op. cit.*, pp. 222-223. See also the famous Northcote-Trevelyan Report of 1854, reprinted in *Public Administration* XXXII (Spring, 1954).

18 *Recruitment to the Administrative Class* (London: H.M.S.O., Cmnd. 232, 1957) p. 27. See also *Change or Decay* (London: Conservative Political Center, 1963) pp. 18ff.

civil service in their own fields.[19] Generalists argue, and they have the English tradition on their side though not the French, that the skills of the generalist are valuable at the top of government because those without specialist biases can best fit together contributions of experts in many areas. Today, the civil servants in leading political roles include some recruited for specialist skills, and also civil servants who have acquired specialist knowledge by long service in a single department. Occasionally, politicians with expert knowledge of an area of public policy will be put in charge as ministers. For instance, since the war two Chancellors of the Exchequer, both Labour, have been former university lecturers in economics.

The recruitment of leading civil servants not only provides a strong generalist or amateur bias to national politics, but also reinforces the bias toward participation by those in the highest social strata. Between 1948 and 1956, the top 3 per cent of the population by occupation supplied 38 per cent of successful candidates for the Home Civil Service and 63 per cent for the Foreign Service. Families ranked in the "bottom" 80 per cent of the population supplied only 22 per cent and 9 per cent of young men and women recruited for the two services. (Somewhat offsetting the social bias caused by recruiting among university graduates is the promotion upward of those in the executive class of the civil service into the administrative class).[20] The Civil Service Commission makes a special effort to recruit young men and women who have not been to public schools or Oxbridge. It also makes special efforts to recruit

[19] See, *e.g.*, C. P. Snow, *Science and Government* (London: Oxford University Press, 1961) especially pp. 66ff.; P. D. Henderson, "Government and Industry" in G. D. N. Worswick and P. H. Ady, *op. cit.;* Thomas Balogh, "The Apotheosis of the Dilettante," in *The Establishment.* Cf. Z. M. T. Tarkowski and Avice V. Turnbull, "Scientists versus Administrators," *Public Administration* XXXVII (Autumn, 1959).

[20] Cf. *Recruitment to the Administrative Class;* House of Commons *Debates,* Vol. 674 Cols. 371-372 (March 20, 1963), R. K. Kelsall, *Higher Civil Servants in Britain* (London: Routledge, 1955) and a review of it by Kenneth Robinson in *Public Administration,* XXXIII (Winter, 1955). Those promoted from executive to administrative class rarely attain the highest administrative positions.

scientists and technologists. Measures are taken in marking the competitive examinations to guard against class bias. (Of course, nothing can be done about any biases created by the educational system or by the distribution of natural ability in the population.) In spite of these efforts, public-school products and Oxbridge graduates are consistently over-represented in recruitment to the civil service. Pre-adult socialization leads Oxbridge men to expect to win places in the administrative-class civil service. Students at other universities do not expect to be recruited into the top positions in the civil service and are less inclined to compete. The expectation that the administrative-class civil service is for Oxbridge men who are arts graduates thus tends to be self-justifying.[21]

More important than pre-recruitment socialization is the "role socialization" of aspiring national politicians while in the civil service. Upon entering the civil service young recruits, whether their fathers were coal miners or members of the aristocracy, are shown what happens and are expected to learn what should be done by imitating the civil servants senior to them, who will rule on their promotion. In this way there can develop an excellent *esprit de corps,* and great procedural stability.

S. E. Finer asserts that "the most powerful cement in the whole executive structure" is the civil servants' common outlook developed by "the long-term cumulative effect of informal collaboration — ringing up, chatting at lunch, dropping in to see." [22] This process of on-the-job socialization creates what may be regarded as the typical administrator — although it should not be overlooked that there are always some atypical administrators who try to fight the system.

Some men have national political roles thrust on them, because they are officials in pressure groups and other organiza-

21 Cf. "The Same Ruling Classes," *The Economist,* December 9, 1961. This article neglects to note that non-Oxbridge graduates are disproportionately scientists or technologists, as well as from families with lower social status.

22 *A Primer of Public Administration* (London: Muller, 1950) p. 68. See also C. H. Sisson, *The Spirit of British Administration* (London: Faber, 1959) pp. 35, 37. Notice how Sisson echoes Michael Oakeshott, *op. cit.*

tions that require representations to be made to government, or they take up quasi-official part-time appointments on government committees. A trade-union official or an officer of an industrial association will hardly be able to avoid contact with national politicians and auxiliaries — and becoming one, part-time, himself. Others gain entry to these levels because they are experts, or opinion leaders within a chosen profession. Scientists, economists, and a host of other experts will find their views solicited by government officials, or will try to influence government in order to advance their professional goals. J. M. Keynes, for instance, could enjoy a national political role because of his standing as an economist. Others become national politicians, often in the role of committee chairman, because they are not experts; in Bentham's phrase, they are "lay gents," useful because they can approach controversial problems free from the prior commitments of experts and pressure-group representatives.[23] The Treasury appears to keep a special list of men useful because of this diffuse skill. Some individuals become national politicians because of personal connections with important men in government and remain important while they stay in favor. Lloyd George and Winston Churchill were both renowned for short-circuiting established channels by relying upon personal advisors. F. A. Lindemann, later Lord Cherwell, an Oxford physicist, was the most renowned (or notorious) of those around Churchill.[24] Some in national political roles, especially in Conservative Cabinets, have relied upon inherited family connections or marriage for recruitment into leading political positions. Kinship ties can also serve to bring closer together some who are full-time politicians and some who hold important posts in other parts of the social system. In appointing relatives to high office, a man such as Harold Macmillan was not suddenly elevating men

[23] Cf. Political and Economic Planning, *Advisory Committees in British Government* (London: Allen & Unwin, 1960) chapter 3; K. C. Wheare, *Government by Committee* (Oxford: Clarendon Press, 1955) pp. 15ff.

[24] See, *e.g.*, J. P. Mackintosh, *op. cit.*, pp. 353ff., 433-434; A. Sampson, *op. cit.*, pp. 336-337; Sir Roy Harrod, *The Prof* (London: Macmillan, 1959); Earl of Birkenhead, *The Prof in Two Worlds* (London: Collins, 1961); C. P. Snow, *op. cit.*

without any training in politics; he was favoring those who in youth have been through socialization for national political roles.[25]

No estimate of the number of national politicians can include everyone who, at some time in his life, acts as a national political leader or auxiliary, even if only part-time. The number who have taken such roles without holding either elective office or a full-time civil-service appointment is greater than the number of career politicians — if only because the ranks of career politicians are small, including at any one time only a few thousand people in a nation of 52,000,000. It is not difficult to reach sums larger than this by reckoning businessmen, financiers, trade-union leaders, professional spokesmen, scientists, and educators, and others who from time to time are active in national politics.[26] The varied forms of participation in politics can best be made clear by describing the life histories of several men who take national political roles, though neither candidates at election nor civil servants recruited in the ordinary way.

Sir Harry Pilkington. Born 1905 into a family of glass manufacturers. Educated at a major public school, Rugby, and at Cambridge. Chairman of Pilkington's, a glass manufacturing firm with interests on five continents. President, Federation of British Industries, 1953-55. Chairman, Committee on Payment of Doctors and Dentists, Committee on Broadcasting, and National Advisory Council for Education for Industry and Commerce. Director, Bank of England. Knighted for public services, 1953.

Sir John Wolfenden. Born 1906. Educated at Wakefield School and at Oxford. Oxford fellow, 1929-34; headmaster of Uppingham, then Shrewsbury public schools. Chairman, Ministry of Education's Youth Advisory Council, 1942-45; Chairman, Headmasters' Conference 1945, 46, 48, 49; Chairman of Committees on Homosexuality and Prostitution, Social Services, and Sport. Member of various other government, educational, and

---

[25] See especially C. S. Wilson and T. Lupton, "The Social Background and Connections of Top Decision-Makers," *The Manchester School* (Manchester) XXVII:1 (1959).

[26] Cf. the tables in W. L. Guttsman, *op. cit.*, pp. 196, 328.

philanthropic committees. Vice-Chancellor of Reading University, 1950-63. Now chairman of the University Grants Committee, which deals with the financing of university education. Knighted in 1956 for public services.

George Woodcock. Born 1904. Educated at elementary school. Cotton weaver, age 12 to 23. Adult scholarship to Oxford, graduating 1933. Civil Servant, 1934-36. Staff member of the Trades Union Congress since 1936. Member of Royal Commission on Taxation, British Guiana Constitutional Commission, Committee on the Monetary System, BBC General Advisory Committee, and National Economic Development Council. General Secretary of the Trades Union Congress since 1960.

There are dozens of men dispersed throughout English society with as varied an experience of public life as Sir Harry Pilkington, Sir John Wolfenden, and George Woodcock.[27] Their career patterns illustrate the extent to which a national political role can be combined with other leadership roles in the social system.

CONSEQUENCES

Participation in politics is clearly influenced by pre-adult socialization. Success in national politics, like success in polo, is ultimately due to skill and timing. But the opportunity to develop such skill and the predisposition to play the game depend only in part upon natural aptitude; in part they depend upon social influences. A critic of the socially biased pattern of political recruitment has charged that the system has changed so little that recent political leaders such as Anthony Eden, Harold Macmillan, Clement Attlee, and Hugh Gaitskell would all have been at home in any Parliament since 1832.[28] This criticism misses the point that for more than a century national political roles have been open to a mixture of persons from the middle and upper classes. For instance,

[27] The point can easily be substantiated by browsing through *Who's Who* (London: Black, annually). A. Sampson, *op. cit.,* provides a journalistic tour of this world.

[28] Hugh Thomas, in *The Establishment,* p. 17. Cf. W. L. Guttsman, *op. cit.*

Benjamin Disraeli, born of a Jewish family at a time when Jews were denied the vote, became the most important leader of the mid-Victorian Conservative Party. Openness to middle-class participation in Victorian times (and the aspirations of middle-class politicians to penetrate, rather than transform, the structure of leadership) has provided durable support for the maintenance of many traditional criteria even up to the present, as the emergence of Sir Alec Douglas-Home as Prime Minister illustrates.

The slow, limited changes in recruitment into national politics have made it easy to transmit informal norms of political behavior from generation to generation. Career politicians can spend years being socialized for leadership roles while serving apprenticeships as auxiliaries, since recruitment begins at a relatively early age (*e.g.*, 21 to 23 for an administrative-class civil servant). This stability of personnel encourages informality and assurance; it helps to make the routine work of the political system flow with ease, though it may be a handicap when unfamiliar problems arise requiring major innovations.

Most national politicians come from socially atypical backgrounds. This factor distinguishes them, in dress, in speech accent, and in their everyday routine from the majority of the peripheral public. This is in accord with the norms of the political culture, which support deference to public-school manners and to unusual educational merit. Politicians are not expected to be "of the people" or to mix readily with them, rather, they are there to exercise their judgment and give leadership (cf. Chapters II, VIII). Correspondingly, working-class people, rarely involved in national politics, are heavily involved in a complex network of social institutions that they manage themselves, such as trade unions, co-operative societies, working mens' clubs, etc. Within these organizations, they take leadership roles. By means of offices in the more important of these organizations, some manual workers are sure of achieving, ex officio, the status of national politicians. Working-class politicians are not expected to compete with middle- and upper-class politicians for many offices; they have a virtual monopoly over some important posts in the economic and political system, because of organizations exclusive to one class.[29]

The contrast between the egalitarian basis of the electoral franchise and the deferential basis of recruitment to public offices may serve in one way to lessen rather than exacerbate class tension. Just because political leaders are conspicuously drawn from narrow social strata, they must be wary of appealing to those numerically small social groups that could stimulate the numerically predominant working class to stand against them.[30] Bagehot foresaw this restraint, but he did not foresee that working-class leaders socialized to respect traditional deferential norms might feel insecure when challenging these norms. As a consequence of this insecurity, many early Labour leaders attempted to demonstrate their worthiness to socially superior colleagues in national politics by playing down issues stimulating class antagonisms or otherwise threatening to break down or transform the political system. A major object of the two interwar Labour governments under Ramsay MacDonald was to demonstrate the "moderateness" and social acceptability of Labour leaders, rather than to emphasize political conflict.[31]

The *relative* homogeneity in social origins displayed by most participants in national politics is far from conclusive evidence about the making of policy or the distribution of power in English society, although it is sometimes assumed to be proof. Similarities in social background do not necessarily guarantee similarities in all phases of political activity. For instance, until a half-century ago, national political offices were so much the monopoly of narrow strata of society that there was, in H. R. G. Greaves' phrase, "class nepotism." [32] But this homogeneous social group differed as much in policy as did Ameri-

[29] For the theoretical implications of working-class autonomy, see William Kornhauser, *The Politics of Mass Society* (London: Routledge, 1960).

[30] See W. Bagehot, *op. cit.*, p. 272.

[31] See, *e.g.*, Egon Wertheimer, *op. cit.*, V. L. Allen, *op. cit.*, and Beatrice Webb, *Diaries, 1924-32* (London: Longmans, 1956).

[32] *The British Constitution* (London: Allen and Unwin, 2nd edition, 1948) p. 164.

can politicians of the same period. Only a viewpoint so broad, vague, and distant that it can ignore differences between parties, between government departments, and between quarreling individuals could assume that homogeneous social origins of policy makers guarantee a homogeneity of interests and preferences.

In a sense, all national politicians form a homogeneous group because they have chosen a political career (except for some involved ex officio through pressure-group offices). Such a choice has been taken in contrast to the non-political choices of the majority with whom they underwent pre-adult political socialization — whether working in a coal mine or studying at Eton.[33] Unexplored psychological factors would appear to be at work in influencing those who select for themselves a political role. The number of political organizations in England, and the perennial problem of securing volunteer workers provide opportunities for the majority of the population to participate in politics as local activists if they so choose. But they do not choose to do so.

The extent to which national politicians form a socially homogeneous group is, however, often exaggerated, because holders of public offices are assumed to constitute the majority, or the totality, of those who take national political roles. In practice, public office provides only one means of entry into national politics. Pressure groups, academic institutions, technical knowledge, personal friendship, and social status all provide alternative routes to participation in national politics. The social biases resulting from recruitment into governmental offices must be set off against the biases arising from the varied leadership characteristics of those who participate in policy making (cf. Chapters V, IX). The recruitment process is not simply democratic, meritocratic, fortuitous, or the embodiment of class nepotism — it is all these things in turn and simultaneously.

[33] No study exists explaining why only a minority of those who undergo pre-adult socialization suitable for political leadership actually attempt to take a role in national politics.

CHAPTER V

The Political System
and the Social System

The order of nobility is of great use too, not only in what it creates, but in what it prevents. It prevents the rule of wealth — the religion of gold. This is the obvious and natural idol of the Anglo-Saxon.

THE ENGLISH political system does not exist in a social vacuum. It consists of all kinds of social institutions insofar as they have political functions, in addition to explicitly political institutions such as Parliament and political parties.[1] A major problem is defining the boundaries between the system of politics and other systems in English society. Definition requires studying the power relationships between these systems (technically but awkwardly, each is a subsystem in the English social system). It would be of little point to study the workings of the Cabinet without also considering whether, or in what circumstances, decisions made in the name of the Cabinet might be taken or greatly influenced by bankers, by trade unionists, or by those of superior social status outside government. The continued existence of close personal and

[1] See G. Almond, "Introduction," G. Almond and J. S. Coleman, *op. cit.*, pp. 5ff.

family connections between some in national roles in government, in economics, and in the social-status hierarchy has made
the question perennially important to English students of politics. Bagehot, writing a century ago, stressed the importance of
integrating the status and the political systems, so that deference to those of high social status could be used to offset what
he thought were the ill effects of extending the franchise. Sidney Low, writing at the turn of this century, emphasized the
extent to which "politics has always been a kind of adjunct to
society." After 1918, the spread of Socialist and Marxist ideas
prompted interpretations stressing the threat that economic
power allegedly held for political democracy. Harold Laski was
foremost in outlining the possibilities of civil war through a
power conflict between a Socialist government and capitalists
in the economic system.[2] In the past decade there has been concern with the political influence of those with high social
status, loosely termed "The Establishment." This renewed concern has resulted from the ability of status-conferring institutions such as the public schools to survive through six years of
a Labour government, and to benefit from the economic prosperity of the 1950s.[3] A small group of left-wing Socialists, receiving inspiration from Marx and technical assistance from
America, in the form of C. Wright Mills' *The Power Elite,*
have stressed the alleged domination of capitalists in the political system. They devote special attention to the web of personal, family, and school links between the Conservative Party
and leaders in economics and social prestige.[4] All of these in-
terpreters have been strongly criticized by the main body of
political scientists in England.[5]

[2] Cf. W. Bagehot, *op. cit.;* S. Low, *op. cit.,* pp. 177ff.; H. J. Laski, *Parliamentary Government in England* (London: Allen & Unwin, 1938).

[3] See, *e.g., The Establishment;* Philip Toynbee, "The Governing Class,"
The Twentieth Century CLXII:968 (1957).

[4] See, *e.g., Out of Apathy.* The orthodox Communist viewpoint is contained in J. Harvey and K. Hood, *The British State* (London: Lawrence &
Wishart, 1958).

[5] A variety of journalistic views are briefly and stimulatingly set out in
"Who Governs Britain?" a special number of *The Twentieth Century,*

The difficulties in studying the relationship of the political system to other parts of the English social system are great. Marxists are not likely to accept the findings of non-Marxists. Nor are sociologists likely to accept the assertion of lawyers that a dictum about the sovereignty of Parliament describes or explains the distribution of power in society. The very limited quantity of relevant research (and the obstacles that constitutional conventions place in the way of case studies) creates more problems. Perhaps the greatest difficulty has been the failure of students of social power in England to specify clearly the various relationships possible between the political system and other systems, and to consider what sort of information is needed to establish the validity of any conclusion. This chapter is intended to discuss the most meaningful questions to ask, and also to suggest tentatively some answers.

PATTERNS OF AUTHORITY

Authority exists in many forms.[6] Each pattern has distinctive values, interests, and social institutions. There are many different patterns of authority, in politics, economics, the arts, sports, etc. Almost all of these patterns have a recognized place in society, though all are not expected to have political functions. Every individual has many roles, involving him in a variety of authority patterns.[7] Theoretically, any one pattern of authority could dominate the political system. For instance, the Marylebone Cricket Club, by virtue of its pre-eminence in this national sport, might hold the Cabinet subservient to it. In practice, studies in England concentrate almost exclusively upon the extent to which those exercising authority within the eco-

---

CLXII:968 (1957). See also A. Sampson, *op. cit.*, chapter 39, and Jean Blondel, *op cit.*, chapter 9.

[6] See the discussion in Max Weber, *The Theory of Social and Economic Organization* (Glencoe, Ill.: Free Press, 1947) pp. 152ff., 324ff.

[7] For theoretical discussion of this approach, see especially Max Weber, *op. cit.*, Part Three; H. D. Lasswell and A. Kaplan, *Power and Society* (New Haven: Yale, 1950); Robert Dahl, "The Concept of Power," *Behavioral Science* II (1957), and Harry Eckstein, *A Theory of Stable Democracy.*

nomic and status systems can thereby dominate the political system.

Within these patterns of authority, there are important distinctions to be made about the direction of authority, the channels, the weight and the scope. For instance, Englishmen expect that the electors should determine which party shall govern, and the party in government should determine what new laws the electorate must obey, in a reciprocal flow of influence. Channels through which authority is exercised may be more or less institutionalized. For instance, a popular singer affects the behavior of popular-music fans and of other singers through the institutions of the entertainment industry. These institutions are very different from those employed by the Archbishop of Canterbury, as head of the Church of England. The weight of authority varies, too. A banker's authority is highly tangible, and readily assessed in the economic system. Money does not have the same weight in politics as in business, because though in business it may purchase goods, it cannot be used in politics to purchase votes. The scope of authority is the area in which a particular pattern is relevant. For instance, painters exercise authority within a very narrow scope, whereas bank directors and Cabinet ministers usually have much wider and less well-defined scopes within which they try to exercise authority.

Each of the chief systems of English society contains a variety of patterns of authority; there is no single set of values, interests, and institutions that completely commands allegiance within the economic, the social, or the political systems. Differences *within* these systems must be examined first, and then relationships *between* these systems and their parts. Only after this examination can we hope to arrive at some tentative assessment of the distribution of authority within English society today.

Viewed from a sufficiently great distance, the economic system may appear to involve a single pattern of authority. But enormous differences are institutionalized within the interdependent parts of the economic system. The trade-union segment of the economy is based upon values and beliefs con-

cerning collective action by employees for their mutual benefit; such action brings unions regularly into conflict with employers, be they private or government. The widespread acceptance of the Socialist case against capitalists sharpens this
conflict, and can lead to demands for the nationalization of
the employers with whom the unions bargain.[8] Co-operative
societies, among the very largest retailing organizations in the
country, do not pay profits to shareholders, but return profits
earned to members in proportion to their purchases. Formally,
they are dedicated to serving the consumer; in practice, the
co-operatives suffer from value conflicts within their organization, and their share of a growing consumers' market is in
many places declining.[9] They remain separate from ordinary
retailers. The government-owned nationalized industries are
subject to the overriding authority of the Cabinet rather than
of company directors or shareholders. In some respects they
resemble large private firms, but they are operated without
special regard for profit seeking.[10] The financial segment of
the economy, The City (cf. "Wall Street") deals in capital
and credit, both within England and internationally. Because
it concentrates upon lending, The City is particularly sensitive
to conditions that increase or depress confidence in sterling.
This reaction can bring it into conflict with those who bor-
row money from it and those who deposit large sums in London from outside the sterling area.[11] Industrial manufacturers
are profit seeking; their profits are determined by such factors

[8] See, *e.g.*, Allan Flanders and Hugh Clegg, editors, *The System of In-
dustrial Relations in Great Britain* (Oxford: Blackwell, 1954); *The Trade
Union Situation in the United Kingdom* (Geneva: International Labour
Office, 1961).

[9] See especially *Co-operative Independent Commission Report* (Manchester: Co-operative Union, 1958).

[10] Contrast, *e.g.*, W. A. Robson, *Nationalized Industries and Public Ownership;* Michael Shanks, editor, *The Lessons of Public Enterprise* (London:
Cape, 1963); R. Kelf-Cohen, *Nationalization in Britain* (London: Macmillan, 2nd edition, 1961).

[11] Cf. The Radcliffe Report, *The Working of the Monetary System* (Lon-
don: H.M.S.O., Cmnd. 827, 1959); Andrew Shonfield, *British Economic
Policy Since the War* (Harmondsworth: Penguin, 1958); *The Bank Rate
Tribunal* (London: H.M.S.O., 1958).

as technological and production skills, and the state of the import and export markets. Retailing firms, by contrast, are less concerned with manufacturing processes and with exports; they are oriented to consumer behavior. Marked differences exist in the retailing field between firms operating large numbers of chain stores and small family shops.[12] Agriculture is an industry of limited economic importance in England, where many basic foodstuffs are imported. Agricultural interests are very well organized, however, and, since the Second World War, have been extremely successful politically, in spite of their highly marginal position.[13] The segmentation of the economy is so great that it is not difficult to find economic groups in opposition to each other. This situation was made particularly clear in the dispute as to whether or not the country should enter the European Common Market in 1961-62. This proposal to alter basic economic arrangements brought out major divisions within categories such as the trade unions.[14]

Each of these segments of the economy has its own leaders; each has its own pattern of authority. Leaders in industry, The City, and retailing are sometimes subjected to nominal control by their shareholders. Such a statement greatly oversimplifies the actual position of skilled managers in highly complex organizations in which shares are widely dispersed. In fact, managers enjoy a large measure of autonomy. They can be judged by criteria of performance — long-term profitability and long-term economic expansion, though neither seems to be valued so highly in England as in America. Trade unions and Socialists sometimes criticize highly profitable firms, and firms whose expansion has threatened with unem-

12 See, *e.g.*, R. S. Edwards and H. Townsend, *Business Enterprise* (London: Macmillan, 1958); B. S. Yamey, *Resale Price Maintenance* and *Shoppers' Choice* (London: Institute of Economic Affairs, 1960); P. W. S. Andrews and F. A. Friday, *Fair Trade* (London: Macmillan, 1960).

13 See J. Roland Pennock, "Agricultural Subsidies in England and the United States," *American Political Science Review* LVI:3 (1962), and Peter Self and Herbert Storing, *The State and the Farmer* (London: Allen & Unwin, 1962).

14 See, *e.g.*, *Report of the Sixty-First Annual Conference of the Labour Party* (London: Labour Party, 1962) pp. 154-194.

ployment men with traditional and obsolescent skills. Some retailers are particularly vulnerable to short-term fluctuations in consumer preferences and spending, which can operate as an external check upon their actions. Co-operative societies are less affected by short-term consumer preferences, because of control by boards elected by small proportions of the membership.[15] Trade-union leaders are set apart from other economic leaders by being recruited from the shop floor. Wages and working conditions negotiated by the union leaders provide tangible criteria for their followers to judge them by. Members can reject their leaders by leaving unions, by organizing wildcat strikes, and by ignoring contractual arrangements. The existence of elected national executive committees in each of the unions institutionalizes competition between oligarchies for greater rank-and-file support. The relative weakness of leaders vis à vis members has been demonstrated by the failure to maintain wage restraint in 1950, and again by the cautious approach to the subject in the early 1960s.[16] The nationalized industries are different again, because the board members, appointed by the government from within and without the industry, need to bear in mind the concerns of several groups. For instance, the coal nationalization act charged the National Coal Board first with looking after the welfare of coal miners, then with gaining co-operation from the miners, and only third with covering the costs of operation "on an average of good and bad years." The employees of a nationalized industry, the Cabinet, and the customers of the industry can each make conflicting demands upon the nominal leaders on the boards.[17] In most instances, the authority of economic

[15] See, *e.g.*, Geoffrey Ostergaard, "Parties in Co-operative Government," *Political Studies*, VI:3 (1958); J. A. Banks and G. Ostergaard, *Co-operative Democracy* (Loughborough: Co-operative Union, 1955).

[16] For a case study, see Graham Wootton, "Parties in Union Government: the AESD," *Political Studies* IX:2 (1961). Cf. B. C. Roberts, editor, *Industrial Relations* (London: Methuen, 1962); B. C. Roberts, *National Wages Policy in War and Peace* (London: Allen & Unwin, 1958).

[17] See, *e.g.*, A. H. Hanson, *Parliament and Public Ownership* (London: Cassell, 1961) and *The Financial and Economic Obligations of the Nationalized Industries* (London: H.M.S.O., Cmnd. 1337, 1961).

leaders over employees is specific, not diffuse; it governs activities during working hours but not extramural activities. For instance, few employers of large numbers of manual workers would find a majority of their workers voting as they do; voting behavior is more influenced by class divisions than it is by employment in a given firm or industry.

Within the economic system, the operations of different patterns of authority work to constrain each other. As constraints upon controllers of capital, Anthony Crosland lists "strong trade unions, a seller's market for labor due to full employment, a growing consumer movement, the countervailing power of nationalized industries and large distributive organizations, the fear of a Labour Government, and an intense sensitivity to their public image in the light of an altered climate of opinion." [18] Manufacturers and retailers usually have autocratic control over their own companies, though from time to time boardroom differences erupt in spectacular take-over bid battles for company control, as in the case of British Aluminium and Courtaulds.[19] Few could claim control over their competitors, their unionized employees, consumer preferences, and the general economic climate. Trade-union leaders often enjoy pronounced autonomy in fields unrelated to wages and working conditions. For instance, they may use the union's influence within the Labour Party in accord with their personal preferences,[20] though even Frank Cousins, head of the mammoth Transport & General Workers Union and Sir William Carron of the huge Amalgamated Engineering Union, have suffered setbacks in attempts to wield influence. In bargaining on behalf of their members, trade-union leaders are confronted with permanently opposed groups of employers. The co-operative societies are restrained by the competition of private retailing firms, most notably today by rapidly expanding chains of cut-price supermarkets. Cliques of customers,

[18] *The Conservative Enemy,* p. 56.

[19] See Stephen Hatch and M. Fortes, "The Struggle for British Aluminium," *Political Quarterly* XXXI:4 (1960); on Courtaulds, articles by Roy Jenkins in *The Observer* (London) March 18, 25, April 1, 1962.

[20] See the analysis in M. Harrison, *op. cit.,* chapter 4.

trade unions, and in some cases co-operative suppliers may also restrain co-operative retailing societies more than private-enterprise counterparts. The operation of nationalized industries is subject to the formal restraints of Acts of Parliament. These restraints are vague in many respects; they are supplemented by informal pressure from Cabinet ministers, as well as by the same market forces that affect other businesses.

The economic system may have a unity from the vantage point of the economist or the grand theorist of society. But, when viewed more closely the unity disappears. Different segments of the economic system seem to be differentiated in at least two important ways: differences in values and goals, and differences in the authority relationships of leaders and followers.

The status system is based upon the value of prestige; it is much more heterogeneous than the economic system, where pecuniary standards loom so large. In England there is no longer, as there was in the 18th century, a large measure of consensus concerning the criteria for allocating prestige.[21] In some ways, the preindustrial criteria of title, gentle birth, and gentlemanly upbringing are still significant, but these values are no longer heavily dominant. The range of prestige standards existing today is strikingly illustrated by a Gallup Poll of people 15 to 19 years of age. The persons most admired, in order, were Winston Churchill, Elvis Presley, "My mother," the Queen, and Tommy Steele, a popular singer.[22] This list of five persons employs three quite separate status criteria.

To designate those at the top of a particular prestige hierarchy as status leaders is in a sense misleading; it presupposes that the leaders have clearly defined followers. In some cases, the answer is simple, because the status is extremely specific. A respected designer of women's hats may exercise influence over wealthy women, by means of fashion shows and a small number of exclusive retail shops. But this individual may not exercise leadership in the styling of men's hats, and certainly does not in regard to politics, religion, or education. Some

[21] See especially the case study of Margaret Stacey, *op. cit.*
[22] *Youth Survey*, p. 5.

kinds of status may exist whether or not others show respect. A lord remains a lord whether or not anyone defers to his lordship, as in the case of the Earl of Buckinghamshire, who decided, after inheriting his title in 1962, that he would prefer to work and live as a gardener rather than as an Earl. In some instances, prestige follows appointment to an office that confers political influence — such as the Prime Ministership. No matter how humble his birth, a retired Prime Minister can always, if he wishes, claim an hereditary earldom.

Because high status rarely provides clearly defined groups of followers, individuals with inherited high status must translate this prestige into positions in other parts of the social system if they wish to exercise authority. The incentives for translating their status into a political position appeal to some, but hardly the majority, of this group. Politics does not attract men on the grounds of financial rewards. Public offices do not carry high salaries, for it is still assumed that those in national politics have sufficient private incomes so that they need not live on their public salaries. Many who inherit great wealth do not regard politics as an attractive pursuit. For instance, the great majority of hereditary peers, men with lifetime seats in the House of Lords, do not participate actively in Parliament.[23] Persons of high status but without great incomes may be compelled to go into businesses in which their status is commercially valuable, as in the case of the advertiser in *The Times:* "The Earl of X would be interested to hear from industrial or another responsible organization who might use his connections and flair for sales or relations &c." [24]

The divisions of values and institutions in the political system are also wide. The existence of two political parties, each of which maintains a more distinctive set of political principles than those held by American parties, provides one division within the system. Another is found between those whose posi-

[23] See Gerald Kaufman, "A Time and Motion Study of the House of Lords," *Time and Tide*, March 1, 1962; W. L. Guttsman, *op. cit.*, pp. 135-137.

[24] December 11, 1961. In late Victorian times, marriage to an American heiress might have substituted for public relations as a source of income.

tion rests upon electoral success — the party leaders — and those whose position rests upon the demands of specialized pressure groups. The values of senior civil servants are not the same as those of most party politicians. Civil servants are less likely to be partisan in outlook; their views on policy questions may reflect personal, professional, or departmental values, or may arise from some vague conception of the national interest (cf. Chapters VI, VII, IX).

The authority patterns within the political system combine extremes. On the one hand, the leaders of the governing party may be abruptly dismissed by the electorate at a general election. On the other, this ultimate sanction is often years away, and the relationship between any particular decision and an election result is faint or nonexistent. In between elections, ministers are subject to influences from pressure groups of many different sorts, yet they can influence these groups as well. Civil servants are in an anomalous position, for they are formally subordinate to ministers, yet the exigencies of departmental operations result in ministers delegating to them extensive discretionary authority.[25] The Opposition party's leadership does not exercise direct influence upon policy; its influence lies chiefly in its potential for replacing the governing party after a general election. People who have national political roles without holding public office work in many differing patterns of authority, from that of the secretary of a trade union to that of the expert in nuclear physics. It is particularly important to note that a national political leader usually must accept restraints, and must show a willingness to accommodate his own views to those of others.

The distinctions discussed above are hardly exhaustive: they simply illustrate the complexities of social influence obscured by loose talk of "elites." A unity of sorts may be imposed upon men as different as Lord Cromer (a banker), Frank Cousins (a trade unionist), and Lord Rootes (a self-made auto millionaire); but each performs different tasks in different ways

[25] See especially comments on Sir Henry Tizard and Lord Cherwell by C. P. Snow, in *A Postscript to Science and Government* (London: Oxford University Press, 1962).

toward differing ends within the economic system. The same sort of unity can be given to J. H. Sparrow, (the Warden of All Souls College, Oxford), Arnold Wesker (a left-wing playwright), and Cliff Michelmore (a television personality) or to Sir Alec Douglas-Home (Prime Minister), Harold Wilson (Leader of the Opposition), and Sir Solly Zuckerman (Chief Scientific Advisor, Ministry of Defence). But within each part of the social system, the differences appear to be at least as important as the similarities.

RELATIONSHIPS BETWEEN SYSTEMS

In studying the relationships between authority patterns in different parts of English society, one must determine what aspects of relationships are to be studied. One convenient way to study the interchange of authority is to trace the movement of personnel from one system to another. Economic and political leaders move very little, either within segments of their system or between systems. A study of industrial managers concludes, "All in all, top managers have not had marked experience outside industry, outside their own firm, or outside their own line of work. Specialization, whether trained early to a high pitch or gained by long experience, is the hallmark of most careers." [26] This statement covers equally well the trade-union world, co-operative societies, The City, and retailing, though it is less applicable to nationalized industries. The few individuals in The City who do hold many directorships may well diminish their influence by spreading their involvement.[27] Within the political system there is even less movement from one segment to another — be it into or out of the civil service, or across party lines. With few exceptions, those who are party leaders or leading civil servants have devoted their adult lives

[26] R. V. Clements, *Managers* (London: Allen & Unwin, 1958) p. 151. See also Rosemary Stewart, *Management Succession* (London: Acton Society Trust, 1956) pp. 9ff.

[27] See C. A. R. Crosland, *The Conservative Enemy, passim.* Cf. *The Insiders* (London: Universities and Left Review, 1957) and A. A. Rogow, *The Labour Government and British Industry, 1945-51* (Ithaca, N.Y.: Cornell University Press, 1955).

to activity as professional politicians, and within only one segment of the political system.[28]

Movement from economic leadership posts into leading political offices is limited, and appears to be declining. Since 1900, only seven businessmen and two trade unionists have been among the 40 men holding office as Prime Minister, Chancellor of the Exchequer, or Foreign Secretary. In the original Cabinet of Sir Alec Douglas-Home, only three of the 23 ministers had been full-time businessmen before entering politics; the majority are best described as professional politicians. No leader from the business world was in the Cabinet; the businessmen were simply ordinary money-makers. In the Labour Cabinets of Clement Attlee, businessmen were few, and so were prominent trade unionists. In any future Labour government, it will be the atypical Cabinet minister who will also have sat with leading general secretaries of the Trades Union Congress.[29] Only in the exceptional circumstances of wartime has there been a noticeable influx of economic leaders into government; such individuals are now fast dying out. Today, many unions even have rules barring national officers from sitting as MPs; large industrial firms are also loath to see their full-time leaders remain indefinitely away from the job in order to participate in politics.[30]

The interchange between status leaders and the political system is very noticeable in certain segments. The Conservative Party recruits about three-quarters of its MPs from those who enjoy the status resulting from a public-school education. The Conservative Party is notable because only among its back-bench MPs can one easily find some in national political roles who have gained their position primarily by their diffuse social prestige, without any academic or professional achievements. However, civil servants recruited from those with high

[28] On a new trend of civil servants to leave their posts for the sake of business jobs, see House of Commons *Debates*, Vol. 669, Cols. 570-573, December 13, 1962.

[29] Cf. W. L. Guttsman, *op. cit.*, pp. 102-107; M. Harrison, *op. cit.*, p. 269.

[30] See, *e.g.*, the experience of Viscount Chandos, *Memoirs* (London: Bodley Head, 1962) pp. 331ff.; pp. 431ff.

social prestige have to pass a stiff competitive examination, and those in national political roles without public office, such as specialists in missiles or experts on pensions, depend upon their expert knowledge for both status and political position. The "lay gents" who chair government committees often may be more gentlemanly than expert, but those who are repeatedly appointed to such posts can usually claim to be experts in committee work, and in observing the norms concerning the chairman's role.

The status system does provide a useful means of facilitating the movement of individuals out of active participation in national politics. Individuals can be "kicked upstairs" to the House of Lords and rewarded with a peerage to ease the pain of enforced retirement or dismissal from office. This happens more often with Conservatives than with Labour MPs. Leading Conservatives also may find that high political office helps them to acquire company directorships when they have had their fill of politics, or when, as in the case of seven of Macmillan's Cabinet ministers in July, 1962, they are sacked from office. Labour MPs, especially ex-trade-union officials, are more likely to hang on in the House of Commons after their career prospects are blighted, because of an inability to obtain alternative employment. After the setback of the Labour Party at the 1959 general election, however, a number of abler MPs left Parliament to take other jobs, rather than suffer more frustration in Opposition. Some of these jobs, such as head of the National Coal Board or the Director-General of the Royal Institute of International Affairs, allowed the individuals concerned to remain within the political system.

A very few simultaneously have leading roles in the political system and outside of it. Elite theorists assume that an individual may easily transfer the values inherent in one role to the performance of quite different roles in very different structures — that is, a man who is once an Etonian or a businessman maintains this outlook in all his subsequent social activities. But social psychologists emphasize how readily an individual adjusts his behavior to the situation. The Prime Minister provides the most notable example of a man with many differing roles — chief partisan, head of a policy faction within his party, symbol of party unity, chief executive, leader of public opinion, supplicant for votes, bargainer with pressure groups, subordinate leader in NATO, etc.[31] Whether or not a political, economic, or social leader enjoys adjusting his behavior when he changes roles is beside the point. He is compelled to alter his behavior when he has varied roles within very different patterns of authority.

The lack of movement of personnel between systems gives some indication of social differentiation. But contacts between different parts of the social system are also important. Elite writers usually allege that the authority patterns of English society form a single and integrated pyramid. But in theory at least four different relationships could exist simultaneously between the political, economic, and status systems.[32] Certain writers assume that the parts are hierarchically related; a constitutional lawyer would place Parliament at the top of the *hierarchy,* just as a Marxist would place financiers in The City at the top. A second relationship is *bargaining.* Bargaining can take place when the co-operation of several different groups, each with differing sources of strength and differing needs, is required for the attainment of an object of government policy, such as the increase of production, or exports. Another relationship is *autonomy.* There is, after all, no necessary reason why those whose status rests upon knowledge of medieval literature should automatically be involved with those concerned with politics; each can function autonomously. Last but not least, some relationships involve *democracy;* that is, decisions taken to favor the largest number of persons. The condemnation of private property to provide land for a public highway or park illustrates this point.

If one can risk a generalization about a subject so complex as the relationship of economics with politics in England, one

---

[31] See Richard Rose, "Complexities of Party Leadership," *Parliamentary Affairs* XVI:3 (1963) pp. 267ff.

[32] This paragraph condenses and slightly modifies certain concepts in Robert Dahl and Charles Lindblom, *Politics, Economics and Welfare* (New York: Harper, 1953). Cf. *infra*, pp. 218ff.

might stress the importance of autonomy and of bargaining.[33] Autonomy results from the contrasting values of the economic system and of politics. A businessman or a trade unionist concentrates first of all upon the details of his own organization, and upon its economic welfare. Questions of foreign policy, of criminal law, or of hospital facilities are not likely to impinge directly upon his activities. Reciprocally, Cabinet ministers are not likely to spend much time concerning themselves with spring fashions in the garment industry, or with the manufacture of do-it-yourself household supplies. In some instances autonomy can lead to a derogation of government's power, as in 1962, when the Chancellor of the Exchequer was publicly pursuing a policy of wage restraint, but was incapable of influencing trade unions and employers jealously guarding their autonomy in wage negotiations. Bargaining is specially important between the party in government and pressure groups. (See Chapters VI, IX.) The great scope of government legislation means that many policy and administrative activities affect economic groups.[34] The economic responsibilities placed upon government, however, cannot be fully achieved without bargaining with various segments of the economy.

The relationship between the social-status system and the political system seems best characterized as autonomy and integration. There are few necessary points of contact between those with high status and those in politics. The power of the government today to award peerages, knighthoods, and lesser honors is no longer as important as it once was — though the Conservative Party apparently still finds these honors useful as recognition for party services.[35] Awareness of the niceties of distinction between Upper Class and non-Upper Class speech (*e.g.*, saying "looking-glass" instead of "mirror") may make one acceptable at stately homes — but it has little to do

---

[33] In addition to books cited above, see especially S. E. Finer, "The Political Power of Private Capital," *Sociological Review* III:2 (1955), and *Private Industry and Political Power* (London: Pall Mall, 1958).

[34] J. W. Grove, *op. cit.*

[35] See, *e.g., Honours and Awards* (London: Daily Mirror, c. 1955).

today with political leadership.[36] The public offices for which high social status is virtually a prerequisite, such as Lord Lieutenant of a County, or Lord Chamberlain, are not themselves of significance in national politics; they are chiefly concerned with ceremony. The House of Lords is today very definitely a minor chamber of Parliament, and little political influence is gained simply by membership. Active members of the House of Commons such as Anthony Wedgwood Benn show a preference to renounce inherited titles rather than accept ennoblement and banishment to the second chamber. On the other hand, though high social status may not raise one higher in politics than the position of back-bench Conservative MP, it can, when added to other qualifications, facilitate promotion and give some added influence to those who have the aura of social leaders. The selection of the 14th Earl of Home as Prime Minister in October, 1963, illustrates the way in which a skillful politician who enjoys high social status can capitalize politically — at least, in the Conservative Party. Even the Earl of Home, however, had to renounce his earldom and translate himself into a "mere" knight (Sir Alec Douglas-Home) to become Prime Minister. Furthermore, when Foreign Secretary, he was unique among the 178 earls in the House of Lords because he was the only one in the Cabinet.[37]

The integration of some born with high social status into some major roles as national politicians does not produce the harmony necessary to prove a conspiracy theory of rule by a well-born "elite." Despite the extraordinary social homogeneity of the Conservative Party in government, and its difference in background from the nation as a whole, disputes about politics within this socially homogeneous group are quite frequent.[38]

36 The symposium on this topic is notable for the way in which politics is avoided. See Nancy Mitford, editor, *Noblesse Oblige* (Harmondsworth: Penguin, 1959).

37 See his responses when interviewed by Kenneth Harris, *The Observer*, September 16, 23, 1962, and *The Observer* profile of October 20, 1963.

38 See R. T. McKenzie, *British Political Parties* (London: Heinemann, 1955) chapter 3.

Sharing the experience of an Eton education may help a man get into the Cabinet; Harold Macmillan, an Old Etonian himself, thought that deference remained widespread enough to boast during the 1959 general election: "There were three Old Etonians in Mr. Attlee's Cabinet; I have six. Things have been twice as good under the Conservatives." [39] But it did not ensure him their loyalty. In 1957, the Macmillan government was rocked by the resignation of three Old Etonians. The three replacements were also Old Etonians.

The government of the day is superior to those with inherited status, because it can create new peers and distribute honors at will, without regard to the views of those who already enjoy that status. But the enormous slowness of House of Lords reform suggests that in some respects those with high status may in *limited* areas exercise veto or delaying power. For instance, it took from 1856 to 1958 to secure admission to the Lords of individuals whose peerages would be non-hereditary, held only for life.[40] And the assumption that appears in almost all discussions on educational reform except on the Labour left, that the status-conferring public-school system cannot be abolished, indicates that traditional deference and liberal political norms can combine to protect the position of those of high status in society.[41]

One might speculate that the integration of many of high social status in the Conservative Party gives that party a special attachment to national symbols of world status, such as Empire and military strength. Since 1957, for instance, the government has concentrated upon nuclear weapons, often explicitly referred to as symbols of world power, at the expense of more useful conventional forces. For families accustomed to provide diplomats, Governors-General of colonies, and Army generals, admission of England's lowered international status also

[39] Quoted in D. E. Butler and Richard Rose, *op. cit.*, p. 130. Sir Alec Douglas-Home appointed ten Etonians to his Cabinet.

[40] See P. A. Bromhead, *op. cit.*, pp. 245-249.

[41] See the debate at which the Labour Party rejected a proposal to abolish public schools, contained in *Report of the Fifty-Seventh Annual Conference of the Labour Party* (London: Labour Party, 1958) pp. 90-113.

means admitting to a lower group status. Since the measurements are intangible, it is possible for Conservatives to continue to assert the high status of the nation in world affairs.[42]

AUTONOMY AND CONSTRAINT

Against the historical background of close ties between status, economic, and political leaders, the most striking feature of English society today, in the opinion of the writer, is the degree of autonomy of these major subsystems.[43] This autonomy provides both freedom in decision-making and constraints.

Autonomy results from the diversity of values, interests, and institutions in English society. The general socialization processes intensify these differences. Young people are usually taught goals that are within their grasp. For the Etonian, the goal may be going into politics; for a boy at a local secondary modern school, becoming an apprentice engineer in a motorcar factory. Such individuals usually do not compete with one another for advancement in society: they do not meet. The rewards gained by a successful politician are not purchased at the expense of a prosperous automobile salesman. Politicians and students of politics may feel that political leaders are superior to economic leaders — but businessmen, economists, and trade unionists may feel the opposite. Those with inherited social status may feel so superior to both as never to be involved in politics or industry. Survey data indicate that the great majority of Englishmen are satisfied in their work (see Chapter XI). The process of socialization makes it possible for many aspirants to win success. "Many" refers to the proportion who succeed in comparison to those taught to strive for success. By inculcating aspirations for success in a relative few, the number who think of themselves as failures is

[42] See the comments in the English press from December 11, 1962 about Dean Acheson's remark that England no longer is a first-rank world power.

[43] Cf. Anthony Sampson's conclusion, *op. cit.*, p. 632, "My own fear is not that the 'Establishment' in Britain is too close, but that it is not close enough, that the circles are overlapping less and less, and that one half of the ring has very little contact with the other half" with that of W. L. Guttsman, *op. cit.* chapters 11-12.

decreased.[44] Though many may have prizes, the prizes sought and awarded differ greatly. Political, economic, and status leaders may each be amazed that the others regard their rewards as worth seeking.

Leaders in the political system are constrained insofar as cultural norms inhibit them from influencing activities in other parts of society. By the same measure, however, they enjoy autonomy insofar as taboos inhibit leaders in other systems of society from interfering with the politicians' exercise of political power. In the past twenty-five years, the change in cultural attitudes toward the responsibilities of government for the economy and for welfare have greatly enlarged the government's involvement in society. Today, for example, English political leaders are legitimately able to interfere in the operations of the national economy much more than is possible for an American president. But the enlargement of governmental responsibilities has also created constraints, since the government can only fully meet its responsibilities by bargaining successfully with leaders in other parts of the social system (see Chapter IX).

There is thus no simple or single pyramid of influence in English politics. The distribution of power in English society appears to share characteristics elucidated by Robert Dahl in his study of New Haven, Connecticut.

"1. Many different kinds of resources for influencing officials are available to different citizens.

2. With few exceptions, these resources are unequally distributed.

3. Individuals best off in their access to one kind of resource are often badly off with respect to many other resources.

4. No one influence resource dominates all the others in all or even in most key decisions.

5. With some exceptions, an influence resource is effective in some issue-areas or in some specific decisions, but not in all.

6. Virtually no one and certainly no group of more than a few individuals is entirely lacking in some influence resources." [45]

44 Cf. R. K. Merton, *op. cit.*, chapters 4, 5.

45 *Who Governs?* (New Haven: Yale University Press, 1961) p. 228. See also W. L. Burn, "Who Does Not Govern?" *The Twentieth Century*

These statements describe what Dahl calls the politics of "dispersed inequalities." In analyzing politics in England, it is easy to note the existence of marked inequalities in society and in the distribution of political influence. Equally important, however, is the fact that the holders of political influence are not concentrated in one part of the political or social system; they are widely dispersed.

CLXII:968 (1957) and D. C. Miller, "Decision-Making Cliques in Community Power Structures," *American Journal of Sociology* LXIV:3 (1958) pp. 308-309.

CHAPTER VI

Pressure Groups

*The unsectional Parliament should know what each section
in the nation thought before it gave the national decision.*

PRESSURE GROUPS and parties work at the boundaries of the
political system; they are the chief institutions managing
the flow of influence between government and society.
Pressure groups and parties both articulate and aggregate
policy demands arising from the interests and principles of
their supporters. They also receive and transmit influence
from the government to their supporters.[1]

The conventional clear-cut distinction between parties
and pressure groups cannot always be maintained in England, because of the interpenetration of the two kinds of
institutions. This running together is particularly marked
in the Labour Party, which regards itself as simply one
wing of the Labour movement. The movement consists of
the party, the great majority of the unions affiliated with
the Trades Union Congress, and co-operative societies.
The movement is two parts pressure group and one part
political party. On many political matters, trade-union
and co-operative leaders differ on grounds of political principle rather than group membership. The unions hold 88

[1] See G. Almond, "Introduction," G. Almond and J. S. Coleman,
op. cit., pp. 33-45.

per cent of the votes at Labour Party Annual Conferences, elect 18 of the 28 members of the party's National Executive Committee, and sponsored 93 of the 258 successful Labour candidates for the House of Commons in 1959. The co-operative societies are relatively unimportant, with only one member on the National Executive, less than 1 per cent of the Conference vote directly in their control, and sponsorship of 17 Labour MPs. In some parliamentary constituencies, the local lodge of the National Union of Mineworkers *is* the Labour Party. In others, the party may be the most active and vocal spokesman for the Labour movement. Labour MPs, except in the infrequent circumstance of a Labour government, enjoy complete autonomy only in the election of the party leader. In other matters, they must work in consultation with their allied pressure groups. The trade unions, usually acting through the General Council of the T.U.C. rather than through their delegates to the party's National Executive, exercise a considerable influence on such matters as industrial relations; on many matters, their role in policy formulation is passive. During periods when Labour is in office, the trade unions cannot dictate to the Cabinet by means of their dominance of the extra-parliamentary Labour Party — but they can be sure of a favorable reception in government circles by virtue of their economic importance and their political allegiance.[2]

The Conservative Party antedates the Industrial Revolution; its structure was established independently of the influence of business organizations. The decline of aristocratic influence and the rise of the Labour Party, leaving the Conservatives as the only major anti-Socialist party, has brought the Conservatives and business pressure groups close together in some respects. Business pressure groups fearing the return of a Labour government have no choice but to try to help the Conservative cause. For instance, in the 16 months before the 1959 general election, these groups spent an estimated £1,435,000 ($4,018,000)

[2] Cf. M. Harrison, *op. cit.*, R. T. McKenzie, *British Political Parties*; Saul Rose, "Policy Decision in Opposition," *Political Studies* IV:2 (1956); Leslie Hunter, *The Road to Brighton Pier* (London: Barker, 1959).

in anti-Labour propaganda.[3] Conservative MPs are rarely formally sponsored by pressure groups, but many are ready to identify themselves as parliamentary spokesmen for groups as varied as the Council of British Hotels and Restaurants Association and the Royal Institute of Chartered Surveyors, as well as for the big industrial associations such as the Federation of British Industries. Occasionally, as in the debate within the Conservative Party on whether or not to introduce commercial television, pro-commercial and anti-commercial combinations have formed; in this instance, the commercial pressure group was successful.[4]

The blurring of institutional distinctions between pressure groups and parties is intensified by the blurred distinctions that arise at the boundaries separating the concepts of "principle" and "interest," the reputed bases of parties and pressure groups respectively. In practice, one man may regard as an interest what another regards as a principle. The National Farmers Union, for instance, presents demands for hundreds of millions of pounds in government subsidies, but it justifies these demands by reference to social principles that place a high value on agriculture's contribution to the nation's way of life.[5] Coal-mining communities, especially in Scotland and Wales, lobby government to keep open uneconomic mines not only in order to preserve miners' jobs, but also to preserve a distinctive way of life. Class-conscious demands are thought by some to represent narrow interests, but these interests are also reflected in the principles of the political parties. In a standard work on English pressure groups, Allen Potter distinguishes broadly between groups defending interests and those promoting causes or principles, though noting "the difficulties of drawing a reasonably precise line." [6] The line is further blurred by the tendency of some who promote causes

3 See D. E. Butler and Richard Rose, *op. cit.*, Appendix III.

4 See H. H. Wilson, *Pressure Group: the campaign for commercial television* (London: Secker & Warburg, 1961); S. E. Finer, *Anonymous Empire* (London: Pall Mall, 1958) pp. 135ff.

5 See Peter Self and Herbert Storing, *op. cit.* pp. 213ff.

6 *Organized Groups in British National Politics* (London: Faber, 1961) p. 25.

without financial reward to draw intense psychological grati-
fication, or "psychic income" from their work.[7]

The interpenetration of party principles and pressure-
group interests, with each modifying the other, can be seen in
the resolutions sent by activists to Conservative and Labour
Party conferences. Pressure-group demands, quite unrelated to
party principles, dominate the resolutions in both parties concerning education, pensions, and transportation. This pre-
dominance is particularly striking because there are clear ideological differences between the parties on education and
transportation. In a complementary fashion, the debates at
many trade-union conferences, and elections to national trade-
union offices can turn on questions of left-wing vs. moderate
orientation within the Labour Party, or occasionally, since
Communists may hold trade-union (though not Labour Party)
office, on questions of overt or covert Communist influence.
The Labour Party has sought to counter the pro-Conservative
bias of medical pressure groups by maintaining its own Socialist Medical Association; the Conservatives attempt to counter-
act in a small measure the Labour bias of trade unions by organizing Conservative groups to work within existing trade
unions.[8]

Parties and pressure groups are not independent, as conventional terminology implies. Both are parts of a single political
system.[9] Disputes on particular issues will find pressure groups
and party politicians working together. In economic affairs,
the two will usually be with their natural allies. But in an
instance such as the debate on the country's entry into the
European Common Market, the coalitions seeking to determine

[7] See, *e.g.*, the autobiographical volumes of Fenner Brockway, *Inside the Left* (London: Allen & Unwin, 1942); *Outside the Right* (London: Allen & Unwin, 1963).

[8] On general points, see S. H. Beer, "Pressure Groups and Parties in Britain," *American Political Science Review* L:1 (1956). See also Richard Rose, "The Political Ideas of English Party Activists," p. 367; M. Harrison, *op. cit.*; S. E. Finer, "The Federation of British Industries," pp. 78ff.

[9] And of an international system cf. Morris Davis, "Some Neglected Aspects of British Pressure Groups," *Midwest Journal of Political Science* VII:1 (1963).

policy plainly cut across party lines. A pressure group that consists of organized groups as members, such as the Federation of British Industries or the Trades Union Congress, aggregates demands and decides between competing policies, in a fashion not dissimilar from that of a political party. A party, at times, may present as a point of principle demands arising from the narrow group interests of unemployed railway workers or of cotton manufacturers faced with declining markets.

Although pressure groups and parties are not absolutely separate, one major distinction does exist. Pressure groups do not themselves seek to win control of government by presenting a slate of candidates to the electorate. Parties differ from pressure groups particularly in the degree of their inclusiveness. Parties must include people with all kinds of skills and concerns; they cannot be as narrow as the British Optical Association or the Movement for Colonial Freedom in their membership or in their policies. Furthermore, pressure groups can have extensive nonpolitical activities. Many, such as the Automobile Association or the churches, are primarily nonpolitical in aim, and venture only intermittently into politics in a limited number of areas. Both parties and pressure groups overlap the boundaries of subsystems of society, but in England they perform their boundary-maintaining functions in different, though related ways.

THE CULTURAL CONTEXT

Many demands with which governments must cope are explicit or implicit in the political culture. The relationship between pressure-group demands and cultural norms is of fundamental importance in defining the range, the intensity, and the methods of pressure groups. The relationships include:

1. Harmony between pressure-group demands and cultural norms. Under this heading come groups whose aims are not challenged and whose clients command respect, affection, or other forms of support. For instance, the high regard that Englishmen have for animals places the Royal Society for the

Prevention of Cruelty to Animals in a favored position. It does not need to devote much of its resources to gaining respect or attention from the government or the general public. Its resources can be devoted to the very different (and far from easy) task of negotiating precise details of legislation and administration with government civil servants, and to generating political support ensuring that its demands will be given priority in competition with many other claims upon government.

2. A gradual increase in the acceptance within the political system of norms supporting pressure-group demands. The various groups lobbying on behalf of colonial independence have seen their position gradually change within English politics as belief in and positive evaluation of claims of native nationalist leaders for self government have become accepted first within the Labour Party, and now more widely throughout the political system. Officials of, say, the Fabian Commonwealth Bureau (itself closely linked with the Labour Party) can now concern themselves more with the pace at which demands are granted for colonial self government; twenty years ago, the question that most concerned such groups was whether the demands would be granted peacefully or at all.

3. Bargaining in situations of fluctuating support for relevant cultural norms. Employer and trade-union groups predominate in this category. All have some support for their activities expressed in cultural norms, but the amount fluctuates. In the 1930s, for instance, norms consistent with the views of employer groups were strongly supported in the political system. But in the 1940s, cultural changes worked against employers and in favor of trade unions. In the 1950s, attitudes again were changing, and unions could no longer claim a more favorable position than employers.[10] Leaders of such groups must be prepared to modify tactics, to press claims upon government when support is strong, and to withstand attacks when their demands appear to be inconsistent with the predominant cultural norms.

4. Activity in the face of cultural indifference. Indifference

[10] See especially *Gallup Poll on the Trade Unions* (London: British Institute of Public Opinion, 1959).

is almost a greater handicap than opposition, because a pressure group whose demands are treated as irrelevant to politics will find difficulty in being taken seriously. For instance, smoking is a subject that Englishmen do not expect to be treated as a major political issue. The problem of the National Society of Non-Smokers is, in its own words, that it claims "to represent 15 to 20 millions of non-smokers in this country, the majority of whom have no knowledge of this society." [11]

5. Activity in opposition to long-term cultural changes. A pressure group that finds cultural norms gradually changing to its disadvantage must fight a holding operation. Groups such as the Lords Day Observance Society at one time were strong enough to influence legislation regarding various kinds of Sunday activities. Some of these laws remain on the statute books. The Society, in the face of diminishing cultural support for political enforcement of religious values, now must concentrate on delaying efforts to repeal these laws. It can hardly expect to increase the amount of Sunday observance legislation, given present cultural trends.

6. Conflict between cultural values and pressure-group goals. Since the culture is a gradually evolving set of norms, with shifting emphases upon particular norms, any group may set itself up in conflict with prevailing norms, and may hope that in time the culture will change, and its goals can be realized. This is the position of pacifists, who refuse to fight on behalf of the nation. Groups that have uncompromising positions, however, as the pacifists do, are doubly handicapped, for they cannot bargain with opponents in hopes of partial accommodation: their goal is "all or nothing." Most get nothing, though a few succeed.[12]

The foregoing classification illustrates the different ways in which pressure groups may be influenced by, as well as having influence upon, the political culture of English society. The

[11] Quoted in Allen Potter, *op. cit.*, p. 87.

[12] For a case study of a group that has moved from category 6 to (its supporters hope) category 2, see James Christoph, *Capital Punishment and British Politics* (London: Allen & Unwin, 1962).

relationship is complex. For instance, the rise in standards of morality in late Victorian England appears to have strengthened the United Kingdom Alliance in its crusade for temperance. It won major political victories in the period through the First World War. But since then, perhaps because of the success of the Alliance in reducing the amount of drinking in England, its influence has declined, and temperance values now have no significant place in the political culture. In such ways, as S. H. Beer has written, the political culture "limits and guides what groups will demand of government and provides a commonly accepted standard by which demands of groups can be judged." [13]

THE POLITICAL CONTEXT

Pressure groups can only exert influence within a well-established network of political institutions. Techniques and practices that are effective in England could be quite inappropriate in America, because of the difference between the concentration of governmental authority in Cabinet government, and the opposite in Washington.[14]

Pressure groups concentrate much attention upon the senior civil servants and the ministers who run the departments into which Cabinet government is divided. The departments make the largest number of decisions promulgated in the name of the government; few are made in the Cabinet. The majority of these decisions are not matters of wide interest. For instance, regulations concerning industrial injury claims in the glass industry are hardly a major political issue; they present the sort of problem that can be settled most easily by negotiation between affected organized groups and a government department. Pressure-group spokesmen on many minor matters need "only" convince responsible departmental officials that their requests are reasonable, not contrary to Cabinet

[13] "Pressure Groups and Parties in Britain," p. 17.

[14] See S. H. Beer, "Group Representation in Britain and the United States," *The Annals of the American Academy of Political and Social Science*, CCCXIX (1958) pp. 130-140, and J. Roland Pennock, *op. cit.*

policy, and not likely to cause conflict with other groups. The privacy with which civil servants work and their personal detachment from party politics facilitates bargaining and compromise.[15]

The process of consultation between pressure groups and departments may be given formal recognition by the creation of quasi-governmental advisory committees to which pressure-group spokesmen, or their nominees, may be appointed. The committees deliberate upon many minor and some major problems; their goal is a report that represents a wide measure of agreement. The process of aggregating interests and settling conflicts between groups can begin here. The government then reserves the right to accept or reject the committees' reports. In the case of lengthy deliberations, involving years of negotiations, the government may first set up a Royal Commission, which, rather like a Presidential Commission, sifts evidence from various pressure groups and makes recommendations for public policy. A major study of these bodies rightly concludes that it is "a matter of great convenience if there are many interests and points of view, for compromises to be reached or a general consensus achieved by the outside elements themselves. Committees can minimize the necessary diplomatic to-and-fro by the government without depriving a minister of the last word." [16]

When differences cannot be ironed out at the level of departmental negotiations, or if the problem is *prima facie* important, it will involve a Cabinet decision. A Cabinet decision on a particular issue would be put to the House of Commons as a question involving the whole future of the Cabinet, and of the party forming the majority of the House. In practice, MPs feel compelled to vote in accord with their party in Parliament, in spite of strong ties with affected pressure groups.[17]

15 See S. E. Finer, *Anonymous Empire,* chapter 4; Harry Eckstein, *Pressure Group Politics* (London: Allen & Unwin, 1960), chapter 5, and *Report of the Committee on Intermediaries* (London: H.M.S.O., Cmd. 7904, 1950).

16 P. E. P., *op. cit.,* p. 86. See also K. C. Wheare, *op. cit.,* chapters 3-5, Allen Potter, *op cit,* chapter 11.

17 See J. H. Millett, "The Role of an Interest Group Leader in the House of Commons," *Western Political Quarterly* IX:4 (1956).

This relative freedom from legislative undermining, by comparison with Congressional-executive relationships in America, strengthens the hand of Cabinet ministers in their negotiations with pressure groups. Pressure groups have difficulty in infiltrating the government and creating divisions (though they may play upon existing divisions). Their main strength lies in their influence over extra-governmental resources, such as manpower in trade unions or investment policy in finance.

The existence of strong party discipline and of marked ideological differences between the parties further restricts the maneuverability of pressure groups. Dissatisfied pressure groups rarely can threaten to transfer support from one major party to the other. The Socialist outlook of the Labour Party prevents business groups from joining it, and the Labour and Socialist principles of trade unionists, plus the institutional links between unions and the Labour Party, make a switch in their partisan allegiance difficult to conceive of. Because voting allegiances in England are so deeply rooted in a lifetime of social experience, a pressure group cannot meaningfully threaten to deliver its supporters to one party in return for favors. The Gallup Poll in 1962 found that respondents placed pressure-group support at the bottom of a list of attributes important in judging a party; only one person in nine thought such support important.

Each party's pattern of policy,[18] especially when the policy is made binding by a party in office, further constricts the activities of pressure groups. For instance, the Labour government's nationalization of the coal mines and of the railways after the Second World War eliminated two important private pressure groups. (In a sense, the pressure groups were nationalized, for the National Coal Board and British Railways, state-owned institutions, today lobby the Minister of Power and the Minister of Transport respectively.) By making a political issue of the activities of groups in other parts of the social system, a political party can involve it in pressure-group activities, whether it wishes to be involved or not. The Labour Party usually takes the initiative here. Spokesmen for industries who

[18] See Harry Eckstein, *Pressure Group Politics,* pp. 35-36.

see themselves threatened with nationalization proclaim their desire to get out of politics — that is, not to have ownership of their firms disputed. The decision, in the last resort, does not rest with the pressure groups.

The concentration of authority in government departments and in those who control party discipline greatly reduces the value of ties that pressure groups have with individual Members of Parliament, because of the MP's background, his constituency's interests, or some contractual arrangement. For groups such as trade unions, which have no difficulty in securing direct access to government departments, MPs may be of marginal importance. The National Farmers Union is a conspicuous example of how a pressure group greatly gained in influence by redirecting its efforts from lobbying MPs, restricted by party discipline, to the relevant government departments and party disciplinarians. For groups which have no standing, or which are seeking recognition from departments, MPs may prove helpful, by amplifying their views in contexts that ministers and civil servants cannot avoid noticing. Groups dissatisfied by their treatment at the hands of government can appeal, or threaten to appeal, to Parliament, and can create unpleasantness for a minister there. Occasionally, the Cabinet and the departments may be so divided that members of the majority party in Parliament can provide decisive influence in reaching decisions.[19]

For established groups, appeals for support from the peripheral public can play only a secondary role in their operations, though the threat to put the minister on the spot by making him present publicly his reasons for opposing the group at times may be useful. Through public controversy bargaining groups run the risk of upsetting delicately balanced agreements arranged after lengthy private negotiations. Nonetheless, some public activity is necessary if group members are to feel that their organization is active. At least one group campaigning against nationalization in 1959 did so pri-

[19] Cf. J. D. Stewart, *British Pressure Groups: their role in relation to the House of Commons* (Oxford: Clarendon Press, 1958) pp. 120, 179ff.; Self and Storing, *op. cit.* pp. 45-47; H. H. Wilson, *op. cit.*

marily by directing advertisements to its members and potential members, thereby strengthening its own resolve, though not converting opponents. Appeals to the peripheral public may well be a sign of weakness, resulting from the exclusion of a group from private consultation. It certainly is true of the large-scale marches and demonstrations of the Campaign for Nuclear Disarmament.

The elements of the political system provide a multiplicity of access points for pressure groups — government departments, political parties, Parliament, and the peripheral public. But these access points are not all of equal political weight, and at some points governmental resistance to pressure is great.

PRESSURE GROUPS IN ACTION

The activities of pressure groups are greatly affected by their internal characteristics. Pressure groups vary enormously in size, solidarity, resources, and interests. One authority distinguishes eight different varieties; another, twenty-four. With subcategories, the number of types can be multiplied indefinitely.[20] Solidarity is of special importance. Members of the National Union of Mineworkers, for instance, are knit closely together by common jobs, community ties, class loyalties, and often by regional loyalties, too.[21] By contrast, supporters of world government are widely dispersed geographically and are socially heterogeneous. Members of the Automobile Association are also dispersed and socially heterogeneous, but on the narrow range of matters concerning them as motorists, have a common set of interests. In the case of federations or confederations such as the Trades Union Congress, the members of the pressure group are not individuals at all, but other pressure groups.

Resources vary enormously. Voting strength is of little importance, except for pensioners, who are numerous, and farmers and miners, who are geographically concentrated enough

[20] Cf. S. E. Finer, *Anonymous Empire,* chapter 2; Allen Potter, *op. cit.,* chapters 2, 6.

[21] See Norman Dennis, F. Henriques, and C. Slaughter, *Coal is Our Life* (London: Eyre & Spottiswoode, 1956).

to affect results in a number of constituencies. More typical are limbless ex-servicemen, whose numbers are small and dispersed. More important than votes is a group's strategic position in the social system. Because England imports much of its food, the men who man the docks can quickly create a crisis by going on strike; by contrast, a strike of textile workers would not cause a crisis. Some strategically placed groups, such as teachers and policemen, have norms associated with their roles opposed to striking. In recent years, teachers have talked about striking, but, so strongly internalized are norms against striking in the teaching profession that no large-scale strike has been staged. Money is also an important resource. The wealth of the steel companies by itself could not, however, keep the 1945-51 Labour government from nationalizing these companies. It may well have facilitated the denationalizing of steel by a subsequent Conservative government. Since then, steel companies have been spending large sums on institutional advertising and public relations, hoping to forestall renationalization by another Labour government.

The resources of pressure groups are often employed in counteracting the work of competing pressure groups. The largest number of pressure groups operates in economics and it is here that the largest amount of competition exists, between business and trade unions, and within these two very broad categories. The railway unions press against trucking firms, as well as against the government. The lobby for fuel oil presses against the miners' union as well as against the government. In the debate leading up to the enactment of commercial television, newspaper publishers, fearful of losing advertising revenue, opposed television manufacturers, hopeful of gaining new customers. Trade unions may oppose each other on jurisdiction over employees, or may move far afield and oppose each other in disputes about nuclear weapons. Leaders and members of individual pressure groups may themselves suffer from conflicts arising from a multitude of group loyalties. For instance, a businessman who wishes to see taxes lowered may at the same time, as a parent and motorist, wish more public money spent on roads and schools. In some instances, the government may be able to play competing pressure groups off against one another. In other cases, divisions between pressure groups are also reflected by divisions between government departments and Cabinet ministers. Pressure groups whose demands for increased expenditure in their field of interest are taken up by departments, whether of Health, Education, or Housing, may then find themselves jointly doing battle with the Treasury, which is responsible for approving or rejecting departmental requests for increased expenditure.

Pressure groups lobby the government seeking information about possible changes in public policy; for instance, changes in regulations governing installment credit can very quickly affect production at automobile factories. Governmental consent is needed for matters as different as factory expansion and exporting particular goods. The way in which administrators apply the myriad regulations sanctioned by Acts of Parliament is a matter concerning which groups cannot be disinterested when they are the objects of administrative action. Furthermore, from government, pressure groups can gain status — a knighthood for their general secretary, or the title "Royal" to prefix their name.

From pressure groups, Ministers and civil servants gain information about the impact of projected policies. Through consultations, the government can seek to get support and consent for its policies. Active co-operation is often needed from pressure-group members if a policy is to succeed. For instance, a government policy for exports will not work unless it is framed, after pressure-group consultation, so as to be reasonably sure to supply the incentives that exporters wish. In some cases, extra-governmental bodies may administer services on behalf of the government. For instance, the Marriage Guidance Council receives a public subsidy for its work, and simultaneously lobbies the government on questions affecting family life.

Pressure groups influence government policy (and government influences pressure-group policy) with limited amounts of coercion and no bribery. Each needs the other. The two parts of the political system are interdependent, not antagonistic. As in many relationships, close ties may at times produce harmony and at times, strain. The process of continuous contact and bargaining often results in a dialectical exchange of influence, resulting in policies that are the product of the dialectic, and not specifically of one or the other group.[22]

There is no single or clear set of criteria by which the "pressure" exerted by pressure groups can be judged. The element of uncertainty involved in estimating the weight of pressure groups would make it impossible for a British government to make policy mechanically by weighing pressures for and against given courses of action, assuming that ministers were inclined to such a passive role. At a minimum, government influences policy by deciding what the "natural" balancing point is. At a maximum, this power to strike the balance can change the "weight" of pressure groups concerned with a policy, or even destroy them. For instance, the decision of the Attlee government to establish a free national health service represented an independent assertion of a pattern of policy that not only affected the medical care of millions of Englishmen, but also created a radically new situation within which medical pressure groups have since operated.

The complexities of the political system provide restraints upon all participants in pressure-group activity. Pressure groups can rely upon cultural norms legitimating the claim of each group with a stake in society to have a share in the benefits of government. Usually, this share is most subject to pressure-group influence when a governmental decision is of least general significance. The relative cohesiveness of the machinery of government strengthens its ability to resist permeation by pressure-group spokesmen. Furthermore, the leaders of government know that in any major clash of wills with pressure groups, they can claim superiority within a limited

---

22 For detailed studies see Harry Eckstein, *Pressure Group Politics*, chapters 5, 6, and Self and Storing, *op. cit.*, pp. 75ff. More generally, on the dialectic, see Finer, *Anonymous Empire*, especially chapters 3-6; and W. J. M. Mackenzie, "Pressure Groups in British Government," *British Journal of Sociology* VI:2 (1955).

scope of action. The balance has been aptly described by a director-general of the Federation of British Industries: "Industry may or may not like the policy; and the F.B.I. will say so on its behalf. But when the issue is decided, it may make a world of difference to industry how the policy is implemented and translated through administration into action." [23]

[23] Quoted by S. H. Beer, "Pressure Groups and Parties in Britain," p. 8.

CHAPTER VII

Party Competition and Integration

Party organization is the vital principle of representative government, but that organization is permanently efficient because it is not composed of warm partisans. The body is eager, but the atoms are cool.

P OLITICAL PARTIES, unlike many pressure groups, have a full-time rather than an intermittent involvement in politics; their functions in the political system are numerous and their range of activities is varied. In fact, so varied are the activities of parties, serving governmental, social, national, local, group, and individual demands, that the word "party" cannot be given a simple, brief definition. A party is not just a group of office-seekers, a body of men agreed upon principles, an electoral machine, or a social group; it is all these things in part and simultaneously.

In distinguishing parties from pressure groups, the emphasis is upon the unique role of parties as organizations nominating candidates for elective office. In England, only the Conservative and Labour Parties run national slates of candidates; the Liberal Party contests from one-third to two-thirds of constituencies, depending upon its resources and hopes at a given election. But parties do much more than simply nominate candidates and provide electoral support for competing teams in Parliament. Parties might be described as microcosms of the political system performing, to some extent, all the functions of a national political system. Within both the Conservative and Labour Parties there are small groups whose principles are sufficiently at variance with those of most Englishmen that they form a subculture, and many individuals' cultural attitudes to some extent reflect their party ties. Through youth sections such as the Young Conservatives and Young Socialists, and through adult activities of a political and social kind, the parties seek to socialize potential supporters into lifelong adherence, accepting not only party policy, but also the party's distinctive interpretation of cultural norms at times of political controversy. By stimulating political participation, the parties secure voluntary labor and a pool of potential candidates for local office. The parties confer status (though not wealth) upon their most active supporters, and those in national roles — and in turn, specially welcome support from leaders in certain segments outside politics. The parties are linked to pressure groups, and might claim to act as pressure-group spokesmen on behalf of such imperfectly organized interests as the middle class (Conservative) and the underprivileged (Labour). The parties have within themselves factions and tendencies that sometimes take on the functions of parties. An elaborate communications network exists on paper, and in part in operation, carrying political messages from national headquarters to rank-and-file members and voters. The parties, with permanent constitutions, London offices, and full-time staffs with pensions to look forward to, have many administrative tasks to perform. In addition, committees, cliques, and conferences meet to deliberate on matters of policy. Policy, once made, is then legitimated, especially by the invocation of symbolic principles that are as vague as they are useful in reassuring followers that an abrupt change in policy does not "really" represent a shift in outlook.

In order to understand how parties affect English politics one must first understand what the formal organization is like.[1] Then, the part the parties play in the electoral process,

[1] For a mine of information on party organization, see R. T. McKenzie, *British Political Parties*.

in policy, and in cultural integration can be examined. In this way one can gain an appreciation of how English parties, through a complex variety of activities, simultaneously help to sustain competition within the political system and to maintain the integration of the competing parts.

PARTIES AS ORGANIZATIONS

The Conservative Party organization shows a curious mixture of centralizing and decentralizing features. The constituency associations in which individuals hold membership are formally autonomous and are linked in a federation called the National Union. Parallel with the National Union operates the Conservative Central Office, whose chairman is appointed by the party leader in Parliament. The Central Office handles national publicity and provides many services for the constituency associations. Liaison between Central Office and the constituencies is provided by Central Office area agents. Research is conducted by the separately organized Conservative Research Department; its chairman is also appointed by the party leader in Parliament. The leader is not elected by MPs. Changes have usually taken place while the Conservatives control the government; in these instances, choice of party leader and Prime Minister must be made simultaneously. The party leaves to the Queen, acting on the advice of elder party statesmen, the option of choosing the new Prime Minister and thus the party leader. The Queen is advised to pick the man most likely to command the loyalty of Conservatives in Parliament. But Harold Macmillan's surprise accession in 1957, when it was forecast that politically senior R. A. Butler would succeed Sir Anthony Eden, indicates that this process involves an element of uncertainty. Even more surprising and controversial was the choice of Sir Alec Douglas-Home in 1963, even though he was not necessarily the first preference of a majority of Conservatives. He was selected on the grounds that he was least likely to offend any party group. The method of choosing a leader in Opposition is unclear for lack of precedents. Constituency associations may express, through the National Union, views at variance with some or the majority of their parliamentary leaders. But the separation of the National Union from the Parliamentary Party (*i.e.,* Conservatives in the Commons and the Lords) means that the reverse is also true: parliamentary leaders can make decisions independently of the National Union. In practice, the National Union usually defers to the great political and social prestige of the party leaders — though on major issues, only after a period of discussion within the party.

The process of making Conservative policy within the parliamentary party, and within a Conservative Cabinet, does not involve formal votes. The leader enunciates party policy — but he cannot speak without listening to, or anticipating, the comments that will come from back-bench MPs, from his more senior colleagues on the front benches, from party committees, from rank-and-file party members, and from the electorate. A prerequisite for a successful Conservative leader is to know what is the "sense of the party"; that is, what policies command wide support, which would cause disastrous reactions within the party, and under what circumstances and in what direction modifications may or must be made in policy to increase support. The informality of the process creates areas of uncertainty and doubt, but in most instances the doubts are resolved in favor of the coterie at the top, the party leader and those who share the chief offices under his appointment. One Conservative MP has aptly described this as "leadership by consent." [2]

Of all the features of the Conservative Party, the intense concern with winning elections and holding office is its most notable. So strongly do Conservatives seem to wish to hold office (perhaps as the result of childhood expectations acquired through socialization) that commitment to a particular set of policies is not deep. The party principles are extremely vague, and can be used to legitimate a very wide range of policy alternatives.[3] Since 1885, the Conservatives have succeeded in being in office for 56 years, and in Opposition for

[2] See R. T. McKenzie, *British Political Parties,* pp. 21ff.

[3] Cf. S. P. Huntington, "Conservatism as an Ideology," *American Political Science Review* LI:2 (1957) pp. 454ff.

only 23 years, mostly before the First World War.[4] (In America
in the 80 years between 1884-1964, the Democrats and the
Republicans have each held the Presidency for half the time.)
The concern with winning fosters unity in the face of the
Labour opposition. The Conservative Party is a disciplined
party, and it is perhaps no accident that its active members
often have been accustomed to discipline in public schools
and also in a military career. The unity is also expressed
through the relatively homogeneous social nature of the party
leadership. Conservatives are also a lucky party. When the
World Depression hit England hard in 1931, it was Labour,
not the Conservatives who were in office and suffered blame.
When the Conservative government collapsed in 1940 after the
outbreak of world war, the national leader, Winston Churchill, came from within the party ranks. The party's narrow victory at the 1951 general election placed it in office during a
period of rising prosperity throughout Europe, including England, and allowed it to enjoy and reap the political benefit of
economic prosperity. Given their aversion to planning, Conservatives might claim what could appear to be luck is simply
their just reward for not interfering with the course of events.

The Labour Party is federal in theory and federal in practice. It consists of trade unions, co-operative societies, and
constituency associations of individual party members. Since
the majority of the membership is indirect — e.g., a union
member will be enrolled in the Labour Party by an affiliated
union unless he specifically objects — the relationship of the
Labour Party to most of its members is tenuous. The position
of trade-union leaders who cast votes in the name of their
members is strong. Half-a-dozen trade unions control the
majority of the 6,300,000 votes at the Labour Party Annual
Conference, because, however divided union's leaders are
among themselves, each union casts its Conference vote as a
solid bloc. In other words, if the 50 delegates of the Amalgamated Engineers Union decide by a vote of 28 to 22 to take a
given position, then the whole of the union's approximately

4 See Appendix C.

900,000 votes are cast in support of the views of the 28 delegates.

For most of its period as a major national party, Labour has been in opposition, and its parliamentary wing has been deprived of the added authority of Cabinet office. In opposition there are three different but overlapping centers of policy making, each with a different balance of power. The Parliamentary Labour Party elects the party leader and makes and applies policy in the House of Commons. The long-term programs, involving such issues as nationalization, are drafted by subcommittees of the National Executive Committee, which has a majority of its members elected by trade-union votes. The full-time civil servants of the party work for the NEC. The party leader in Parliament sits on the NEC, where his views have special weight — but these views do not guarantee him command of a majority of NEC votes. The same is true of the Annual Conference, which meets only five days a year, but is nominally the highest source of authority within the party. Except when he is Prime Minister, the leader of the Parliamentary Party must thus control the party with the assistance of trade-union leaders who control the NEC and the Annual Conference. Since these trade unionists will be divided in their views, he can be sure of some independently based support and opposition for most of his initiatives. Loyalty is usually sufficient to give the parliamentary leader victory in intra-party disputes, but not strong enough to prevent frequent disputes from arising.

The structural complexities of the Labour Party have not been the cause of its difficulties; they only intensify them. The chief difficulty arises from the deep concern of many in the party with ideological questions — and the differences in ideological principles and interpretations to be found within the party's scarcely united ranks. (Cf. the late Lord Samuel's remark: "There is only one way to sit still, but there are many ways to go forward.") Many decisions that face the party involve the reassertion of deep cleavages within the party about its ends and means. Some party members are much concerned with ideological purity, in Weber's terms,

with the politics of ultimate ends; electoral defeats do not affect this group. Their viewpoint was aptly expressed in the
following constituency party resolution to the 1955 Annual
Conference:

> This Conference believes that the Labour Party, accepting that
> the preaching of the gospel of Socialism is more important than
> its immediate attainment of parliamentary power, and that
> capturing the crusading spirit of the youth of this country mat-
> ters more than placating the bourgeois nerves of their elders,
> must first decide upon and widely advertise the kind of Great
> Britain it wishes to bring into being.[5]

Those who differ with their fellow party members, following
what Weber called an ethic of responsibility, cannot disprove
the arguments of those who stand for ultimate (or Utopian)
ends, because the two groups employ differing standards of
judgment. For instance, in the intra-party dispute on foreign
policy, which has existed for generations, one group concentrates attention upon plans to change the world, and the
other, upon the less inspiring task of making the best of what
is often a discouraging international situation. Only by gaining control of government can these disputes be contained,
because in opposition the existence of three separate policy
bodies — the Parliamentary Party, the NEC, and the Annual
Conference — provides ample opportunity for groups divided
in principle to demonstrate their divisions in practice. Only
in the Cabinet, where convention requires all members to refrain from public quarrel, can Labour *appear* united.

The Liberal Party has been, for more than a generation,
the third party in an electoral system that favors two. Since
the war it has polled an average of about 6 per cent of the
vote at parliamentary elections, and has won an average of
eight seats. In many respects, the ability of the Liberals, who
last controlled a parliamentary majority in 1909, to survive at
all, in spite of confusion about policy and bitter intra-party

[5] Cf. John Roche and Stephen Sachs, "The Bureaucrat and the Enthu-
siast," *Western Political Quarterly* VIII:2 (1955); H. C. Gerth and C.
Wright Mills, editors, *From Max Weber* (London: Routledge, 1948) pp.
120ff.

quarrels, is remarkable. The party is less well disciplined than the two major parties; some critics say it is the party that looks least like a political party. Sample surveys indicate that approximately half the electorate does not know what attributes to ascribe to the Liberals. The most frequently cited one is "stands for the middle way, moderation." Liberals often present themselves as standing between the working-class Labour Party and the upper-class Conservatives. Some of their electoral advances, most strikingly their victory at a by-election in Orpington in 1962, come in suburbs disproportionately full of people who are socially in the middle. But the Liberal vote is drawn from a cross-section of the population. This broad appeal at present is a liability, for it means that Liberal voters are not sufficiently concentrated, socially or geographically, to ensure it many parliamentary seats.[6]

PARTIES AS ELECTORAL INSTITUTIONS

Elections are the time at which public attention is most concentrated upon political parties. But in England parties function only intermittently and in parts as electoral organizations. The law requires a parliamentary election to be held once every five years, or less, at the choice of the government. Laws regulating campaign expenditure and the conventions of politics limit the active period in which candidates campaign to about four weeks, though increasingly the anticipation of a general election is casting a shadow over events for months ahead. Formally, the election consists of 630 contests in 630 constituencies, each choosing one member of the House of Commons. The candidate with a plurality of votes is declared elected after a single ballot. The office of Prime Minister is awarded to the leader of the party that returns the majority of members in the House of Commons.[7]

[6] See the Gallup Poll report, "Liberal 'Revival' in Fact and Figures," *Daily Telegraph* (London) May 21, 1962.

[7] For a detailed description of a British election, see the Nuffield studies, most recently, D. E. Butler and Richard Rose, *op. cit.* On procedural matters, see D. E. Butler, *The Electoral System in Britain Since 1918* (Oxford: Clarendon Press, 2nd edition, 1963).

Despite their relative infrequency, elections represent the only opportunity at which members of the peripheral public can intervene directly in national politics. (The anticipation of shifts in electoral behavior can, of course, influence some national politicians between campaigns.) Voters do not mandate candidates to support particular policies. Individual MPs cannot be mandated by their constituents, because an MP pledges himself to vote in accord with his parliamentary colleagues; if he refuses to follow the official line, as stated in the party whip, he can be expelled from the party in Parliament. Though retaining his seat in the Commons, an MP without official party support is virtually certain to be defeated at the next general election in his constituency, so great is the electoral importance of the party label.

The effective choice for British voters lies between two parties, and their slates of candidates. If neither slate is satisfactory, an individual can only abstain or "waste" his vote by casting it for a Liberal or independent who has little chance of entering the Commons, and no chance of entering a government. Voters have no say whatever in the nomination of candidates by the parties. In America, the widespread use of primary elections, especially in one-party areas, gives voters a say in the nomination of candidates. In England, parliamentary candidates are never chosen by party members or electors through a public primary. Instead, the constituency party association in each constituency is responsible for nomination. In practice, this responsibility is delegated to committees of the associations, with memberships ranging from a handful to one-hundred or more persons. They interview individuals whose names are put forward by party members, and choose between the candidates after subjecting each prospective parliamentarian to a short cross-examination. The parliamentary candidate is not required to live in the constituency, or even to have visited it prior to his nomination. Especially in the Conservative Party, local men can be at a disadvantage. The constituency parties choose a large proportion of candidates from a pool of those who have been socialized in youth for national political roles.

Although divisions on policy exist within many constituency associations, these appear to have little influence in the selection of candidates, when the resolutions of parties to Annual Party Conferences are compared with the views of MPs and candidates. The opportunity for a national caucus to attempt to organize the nomination of candidates exists, but has not been seized. The choice of candidates is not entirely random. First of all, there is the bias introduced through political socialization; some people acquire the expectation of becoming MPs, or at least expect that they could be MPs if it took their fancy. The relative unfamiliarity of would-be MPs to those who nominate candidates means that superficial personal judgments will be made, with social characteristics, such as class or manner of speech, serving to type an individual favorably or unfavorably. From two-thirds to three-quarters of the seats in Parliament are "safe"; that is, unlikely to be lost by a sitting member, who, once nominated and elected, is rarely likely to have to fight to regain nomination.[8] In most parts of Britain, "nomination is tantamount to election" to a degree unknown outside the American South.

In addition to nominating candidates, local party organizations are expected to provide the manpower for fighting elections, by canvassing from door to door, by holding meetings, and by otherwise bringing the party name and candidate favorably before the electorate. Until the 1880s, organization was important because the ballot was not secret and the buying of votes was tolerated, and in some places, even expected. The local party machine could claim to be of use in manufacturing parliamentary majorities. But today, the machine seems to operate with little effect. The series of election studies carried out at Nuffield College, Oxford, have provided evidence against the effectiveness of the volunteer and paid workers who man the party organization. The fortunes of the major parties fluctuate in spite of the permanent superior-

[8] Cf. Richard Rose, "Political Ideas of English Party Activists"; Leon Epstein, "British MPs and their Local Parties: the Suez Cases," *American Political Science Review* LIV:2 (1960); Nigel Nicolson, *People and Parliament* (London: Weidenfeld and Nicolson, 1958).

ity that the Conservatives have over Labour in organization. The Liberals have almost no national organization — yet at times they can make substantial inroads into the vote of the major parties. The electoral machine today no longer smacks of corruption; it smacks if anything of futility.[9]

The rise and fall in electoral fortunes is often described by a metaphor — the swing of the pendulum. If the phrase means, as Sir Ivor Jennings states,[10] that "majorities are unstable, and the opposition of today is the government of tomorrow," then the phrase is not very illuminating. The major questions of party politics concern when and how majorities become minorities, and what difference, if any, the substitution of one party for another makes to national life. As applied to history, the idea of a steadily swinging pendulum is false, because it suggests a fairly regular alternation in office between parties. In the 19th century this alternation often occurred, but the greater differences between parties today reduce the amount of vote-shifting. Since 1900, governments have been dislodged at six general elections, but have retained office after ten elections. The pendulum theory, based upon an assumed tendency of the "Ins" always to lose favor while in office, disregards the very real ability of parties, while in office, to shift ground. For instance, control of government swung from Labour to the Conservatives in 1951, but what was more significant, though less obvious, was that policy did not swing back to the same extent as the change of party might suggest.

Electoral successes and failures are not due to the efficiency of party organization, or to the personal attributes of ephemeral leaders, themselves judged by partisan standards more than as independent personalities.[11] Election results seem pri-

9 Cf. H. J. Hanham, *Elections and Party Management* (London: Longmans, 1959); W. B. Gwyn, *Democracy and the Cost of Politics* (London: Athlone, 1962); D. E. Butler and Richard Rose, *op. cit.,* Appendix II; Richard Rose, "The Professionals of Politics," *New Society,* August 8, 1963.

10 *The British Constitution* (Cambridge: University Press, 4th edition, 1961) p. 30.

11 On this point, see the evidence in "People Behind the Party Masks," *New Society,* January 17, 1963.

marily to be determined by the course of national events, and the capacity of the government to deal with changing national problems. The parties have followings that are relatively stable. Public-opinion surveys taken in postwar England show a striking degree of persistence in the attributes that respondents use to describe the parties. The Conservatives are perceived as providing superior leadership and more skill in foreign affairs, and as best at looking out for the nation. Labour is perceived as the party of the working class, of the underprivileged, and of those in need of welfare benefits. The ups and downs of the parties are not related so much to changes in the parties as to changes in the salience of what the parties stand for and against. In 1947, for instance, the economic difficulties of the nation led to widespread disillusionment with Socialist economics; the Conservatives gained on the Gallup Poll as a consequence. In 1962-63, the economic difficulties of the Conservative Party created rising fears of economic difficulties, and the Labour Party, the party of the worker in trouble, gained on the Gallup Poll. In both instances events, more than the electoral activities of the party organizations, appear to have accounted for the shifts in opinion.[12]

PARTIES AND POLICY

The unity that the British electoral system encourages in political parties is pre-eminent at election time. But in between elections, when policy decisions are made, the differences *within* parties become as important as, or more important than the differences between them. In the policy process the apparently monolithic parties divide into factions, tendencies, and nonaligned partisans.[13] Factions are self-consciously organized groups within electoral parties, persist-

[12] See M. Abrams and R. Rose, *op. cit.;* Joseph Trenaman and Denis McQuail, *Television and the Political Image* (London: Methuen, 1961); R. S. Milne and H. C. Mackenzie, *op. cit.,* chapter 9; and D. E. Butler and J. Freeman, *op. cit.,* pp. 133-135.

[13] What follows condenses ideas set forth in Richard Rose, "Parties, Factions and Tendencies in Britain," *Political Studies* XII:1 (1964).

ing as time passes and collectively advancing a program for possible government adoption. Factionalism gives stability to intra-party disputes, and may even stimulate controversy, insofar as old factional enemies transfer their enmities to new issues for the sake of continuing in conflict.[14] The left-wing Bevanite faction of the Labour Party, often called "a party within a party," is the outstanding postwar example of such a group, operating from 1951 to 1957. A tendency is a stable set of attitudes toward a government program, rather than a stable collection of politicians. The names and the quantities of MPs adhering to right-wing or left-wing tendencies within the parties can vary greatly from issue to issue. Some politicians, on grounds of tactics or principles, will identify with contrasting tendencies on different issues, which makes for instability. Nonalignment represents rejection of concern with intra-party differences on policy, and emphasis upon differences between parties. A Conservative who concentrates on attacking Socialism is aligning himself against one party — but he is refusing to align himself within his electoral party. When factions and tendencies dispute, they make special efforts to convince nonaligned partisans that their own position is most nearly in accord with the "real" principles and interests of the electoral party. For instance, following the defeat of Hugh Gaitskell on defense policy at the 1960 Labour Party Conference, the left-wing faction appealed to nonaligned partisans on the grounds that the constitution of the Party was in danger, and the Gaitskellites appealed to them with the argument that the leadership was in danger of being taken over by pacifists and fellow travelers.

Policy groups lack formal structure. They are fluid collections of individual politicians; in the case of factions, with a stable core. It would be possible to divide and subdivide English politicians until one was left only with individuals — each divided against himself and divided in his sympathies with others. But then a process of building up patterns and aggregating policies would have to be begun again. By intermit-

[14] See James S. Coleman, *Community Conflict* (Glencoe, Ill.: Free Press, 1957) chapter 2.

tent or *ad hoc* activity, party leaders can be reminded of the existence of factions and tendencies within their nominal followings. The anticipation of conflict can itself influence the leadership, which must allow for the expectations of followers and must try to make decisions that will not mobilize a majority against it.

Ideological considerations are of special importance in delineating the divisions within the electoral parties, insofar as acceptance of a common set of values brings politicians together in support of individual policies or a program. Leadership gives a recognized focus to a group, and stature. The presence within a policy group of a leader of senior Cabinet rank changes intra-party struggles from ones between the front bench and a pressure group on the back benches, to one within the front bench itself. Technical knowledge does not seem to be particularly important in these circumstances; instead, discussion is likely to focus on differences of party principles, and on the standards by which technical information from pressure groups or civil servants should be evaluated. (Left-wing members of the Labour Party have always complained that one weakness of moderate Labour leaders was that they listened too much to civil servants.) [15] Communication within a policy group is fairly simple, resulting primarily from face-to-face contacts in and around the House of Commons. Communication through the press may stimulate private conversation and combinations, but is unlikely to be of primary importance in intra-party struggles. Individual politicians with deviant goals or atypical orientations to politics may find the struggle within the party psychologically gratifying, especially if they are identified with a minority cause claiming to testify for "true" party principles.

The Conservative electoral party is pre-eminently a party of tendencies. An analysis of signatures of Conservative MPs to resolutions presented to the House of Commons found that "such disagreements as arise are struggles between *ad hoc* groups of members who may be 'left' or 'right' on specific

[15] See, *e.g.*, Thomas Balogh, "The Apotheosis of the Dilettante" in *The Establishment.*

questions; but as new controversies break out, the coherence of the former groups dissolves, and new alignments appear, uniting former enemies and separating old allies." [16] In exceptional cases, groups advocating a particular tendency may be successful despite strong Cabinet opposition. This, H. H. Wilson argues, was what happened in the introduction of commercial television by a Conservative government a decade ago.[17] The chief tendencies within the party are those toward reaction, defense of the *status quo,* and gradual reform. Factionalism is rarely a threat. Leaders of the Bow Group, a body of young Conservatives of potential national political stature, have carefully refrained from encouraging the Group to become a faction.[18] Aggrieved ex-Cabinet ministers have normally confined complaints against the party leader to a narrow range of issues. In this way, the party's electoral unity is not damaged — and ex-ministers may return to the Cabinet without this return appearing as a sign of the leader's weakness.

Reform, a doctrine of change for its own sake, is a tendency with a great historical tradition in English politics, from Bentham to Beveridge. It is to be distinguished from reform in accord with Socialist ideas, which it antedates.[19] The Liberal electoral party, under the leadership of Jo Grimond, has tried to make itself the chief party for reformers. But its electoral position is too weak to affect policy consistently. Because reform policies often cut across electoral party lines, there are few *ad hoc* reformist groups combining all reformers, except on issues such as capital punishment, which are not the subject of electoral party programs. This does not mean that reform policies and reformers are weak. The dispersion of re-

16 S. E. Finer, Hugh Berrington, and D. J. Bartholomew, *Backbench Opinion in the House of Commons, 1955-59* (Oxford: Pergamon, 1961) p. 106.

17 *Op. cit.,* pp. 14-15.

18 See Richard Rose, "The Bow Group's Role in British Politics," *Western Political Quarterly* XIV:4 (1961).

19 Cf. C. A. R. Crosland, *The Future of Socialism,* pp. 520ff.; A. Bullock and M. Shock, *op. cit.*

formist influences throughout the three parties is also an indication of persisting strength.

The Labour Party has a long history of factionalism. From 1951 until the death of Hugh Gaitskell in 1963, the left and right were engaged in nearly continuous controversy, only partly suspended during general-election campaigns. The groups of controversialists remained remarkably stable over this period, whether the dispute was about German rearmament, the H-bomb, or nationalization. Only in considering party policy toward the European Common Market in 1962 did Labour politicians divide without regard to these stable factional alignments. Hugh Gaitskell preferred to lead the Labour Party and its moderate Socialist faction simultaneously. His predecessor, Clement Attlee, preferred to "lead" by following the views of the dominant faction or *ad hoc* tendency, and hence was less a symbol of party disunity, though also less influential on policy. Harold Wilson built his whole career, up to his election as party leader in 1963, on a policy of personal nonalignment.[20] The nonaligned group has held the balance of power on some major decisions, deciding to retain the pledge to full Socialism in Clause IV in 1961, and simultaneously supporting Gaitskell in the defense dispute of 1960-61.

The existence of divisions within parties, especially within the majority party in control of government, provides built-in restraints against the concentration of power in the hands of one politician. Traditionally, the power of Her Majesty's government could be checked by a parliamentary vote of "no confidence." But in the past 40 years, this has not been a realistic threat to a Prime Minister with a Parliament controlled by his own party. Today, the downfall of a Cabinet is more likely to come about through internal dissension in the Cabinet than from defeat on the floor of the House of Commons. (Of course, back-bench MPs and ministers may sometimes combine in opposing the Prime Minister.) The Labour gov-

[20] See the interview with Wilson in *The Observer*, June 16, 1963.

ernments of 1931 and 1951 "rotted from within"; that is, they collapsed after much internal dissension in the Cabinet. Another spectacular collapse occurred in the Conservative government of 1900-1905, when ministers divided on the question of tariff reform.

Disagreements do not come often into the open, because a skillful Prime Minister often acts as an arbiter or conciliator for conflicting Cabinet groups, making decisions that will be accepted by the major sections of his Cabinet. The need of the Prime Minister to balance his Cabinet, and to keep a varied group of ministers in line, is particularly important as a restraint upon his authority.

POLITICAL INTEGRATION

Centuries ago, the very existence of political parties was often deplored by English writers. The first Marquis of Halifax, writing after the English Civil War in the 17th century, described parties as "a kind of a conspiracy against the rest of the nation," dividing society into warring camps, instead of uniting people for the sake of the common good. Today, political parties are not regarded as un-English, and two-party competition is regarded as one of the hallmarks of British politics. But the question posed by early writers remains — how can party competition exist without resulting in the development of sharp cleavages within the political system?

One answer is that the homogeneity of the electorate leads the parties to resemble each other in a process of competition much like that in some forms of retailing. In pursuit of the marginal or floating voter, the parties tend to offer similar programs designed to appeal to the same group. During the 1950s, the existence of similarities between certain tendencies in the Conservative Party associated with R. A. Butler, and a faction in the Labour Party, associated with Hugh Gaitskell, led to the coining of the term "Butskellism," to describe the existence of agreement across party lines.[21] This cross-party policy group, however, did not contain all national politicians. If, as has sometimes been argued, the majority of

21 See *The Economist,* February 13, 1954, p. 440.

the voters are in a middle-of-the-road "Butskellite" position, then competition would tend to produce one party with an almost uninterrupted tenure of office, as in Sweden for the past 30 years.[22] In practice, however, the parties do not agree upon all major issues, though agreement — in a particular instance, if not always on principles — can always be found in some areas. Nor is there any reason why consensus on the political community and the parliamentary regime should result in agreement upon particular items of policy. By contrast with America, there are relatively marked differences between parties. By contrast with France or Weimar Germany, none is so deep as to threaten the maintenance of the political system.

The historical evolution of the English political system has provided a basis for restraining competition within limits. Major differences have usually emerged one by one in the system, and happen to have been solved in good time.[23] The practice of settling political differences peacefully has existed for so long that it has come to be expressed in basic cultural norms concerning compromise, self-restraint, and national duty before party duty. Of particular importance is the positive value placed upon assimilating new ideas — and the negative evaluation of ideological consistency, which deepens and intensifies disputes between parties.

The survival of the Conservative Party through the centuries is in large measure due to its adherence to a set of ideas that are themselves either indeterminate or conglomerate.[24] The expectation of party leaders that they should govern has made them, from Sir Robert Peel's time in the mid-19th century until today, ready to make a virtue of shifting policies quickly. The strands of thinking found under the heading "Conservatism" in England are sufficiently numerous so that in changing circumstances some relevant and constructive principle can usually be found to serve as a basis for policy

[22] See Anthony Downs, *An Economic Theory of Democracy* (New York: Harper, 1957) especially Part Two.

[23] See Leslie Lipson, "The Two-Party System in British Politics," *American Political Science Review* XLVII:2 (1953).

[24] Cf. S. P. Huntington, *op. cit.*

rethinking, or for legitimating policy.[25] In extreme cases, Conservatives will not hesitate, in the words of Lord Hailsham, "to make use of the true lessons taught by their opponents. They see nothing immoral or even eccentric in 'catching the Whigs bathing and walking away with their clothes.' There is no copyright in truth and what is controversial politics at one moment may after experience and reflection easily become common ground." [26]

The Labour Party too has assimilated influences from its opponents. Many of the principles of English Socialism, in the past and today, are shared with Liberals, with reformers of all sorts, with non-Socialist sections of American political parties, and even with a few Conservatives.[27] From its period of foundation the Labour Party, unlike some Continental Socialist parties, did not seek to cut itself off from the other parties in the political system. The first Labour MPs were elected with Liberal support. In the 1920s, Labour governments were formed with Liberal support, and much of the outlook of the 1945-51 Labour government was forged during experiences of wartime coalition with the Conservatives. The repeated protests of the Labour left during the past 40 years concerning the alleged desertion of Socialism by Labour leaders only emphasizes the right-ward rather than the left-ward orientation of the party leadership.[28]

Members of the electorate, in spite of showing a remarkable stability in their party voting, also show a readiness to assimilate values of both parties — or to lump the two together. For instance, in a survey in November, 1962, the Gallup Poll found that 47 per cent of those interviewed thought the parties were "all of a muchness" and only 45 per cent thought there were "really important differences." Even more striking

25 For an historical analysis, see J. S. Saloma, *op. cit.*

26 *Op. cit.*, p. 16.

27 Cf. D. E. Butler, "The Paradox of Party Differences," *American Behavioral Scientist* IV:3 (1960).

28 Cf. Egon Wertheimer, *op. cit.*, pp. 91ff.; R. O. Bassett, *The Essentials of Parliamentary Democracy* (London: Macmillan, 1935) Part II, and, for a contrasting left-wing view, Ralph Miliband, *Parliamentary Socialism* (London: Allen & Unwin, 1961).

is the persisting sentiment in favor of coalition and an end to party disputes. For instance, the Gallup Poll found in a survey in October, 1961 that 31 per cent of those interviewed thought the Opposition party should support rather than criticize the work of the governing Conservative Party. Among intending Labour voters, 21 per cent expressed such views, and only 41 per cent replied that Labour should do all it could to turn the government out. This indifference to party labels with regard to policy (though not with regard to voting) also shows itself when survey respondents are asked to state which of a series of characteristics applies more to either of the two nominally competing parties. In a list of sixteen such statements, Mark Abrams found that up to 63 per cent attributed particular characteristics to both parties.[29] In other words, party supporters do not reject one party when they vote, and they certainly do not reject the ideas, the motives, or the integrity of the party they vote against. Changes in party control of government are not perceived as shifting power from one monolithic party to a mutually exclusive alternative. Even political party activists, despite their involvement in electoral competition between parties, share many views. In fact, 45 per cent of the resolutions submitted to the two parties' annual conferences can be classified as non-partisan.[30]

The existence of agreement across party lines has also shown itself at the level of party leadership. Many of the most important of England's political leaders in the past century have switched from one party to another during their careers. The names include Sir Robert Peel, William Gladstone, Lloyd George, Ramsay MacDonald, and Winston Churchill. The post-1945 period has been exceptional in the absence of such changes. But policies, if not men, have moved across the aisle dividing the parties in the House of Commons. The foreign policy of the 1945-51 Labour government, for instance, was more in accord with pre-1914 Conservative

[29] "Social Trends and Electoral Behaviour," p. 236. See also Jean Blondel, *op. cit.*, pp. 75-79.

[30] Richard Rose, "The Political Ideas of English Party Activists," p. 371.

thinking than with earlier Labour proclamations, and it received stronger support from Conservative than from Labour MPs. The domestic welfare policies of the Conservatives in the 1950s similarly showed the influence of values and beliefs of Labour.

Coalition in government is the extreme expression of the integration of nominally competing parties. In a sense, all British Cabinets are coalitions, because of the existence of so many differing policy groups within the electoral parties, most of which must be represented in the Cabinet. In the formal sense of a government either depending upon votes of a second party to secure a parliamentary majority, or making up a Cabinet with leaders of more than one party, coalition government is a recurring feature of modern English politics. The two-party system is an ideal, not an accurate generalization about events since 1885. Since that time, seven parties have shared in the making of government majorities — Conservatives, Liberals, Liberal Unionists, Irish Nationalists, Labour, National Labour, and National Liberal. Three historical periods are fairly clearly defined: 1885-1914, a period of four-party politics (Conservative, Liberal, Liberal Unionist, and Irish Nationalist) with Labour as a fifth wheel in the latter half; 1914-45, a time of coalition and minority governments, twice interrupted by Conservative majority governments; 1945-63, a time of two-party electoral competition, with the existence of a third party preventing either major party from securing a majority of popular votes, but not preventing single-party parliamentary majorities. In the 78-year period from 1885 to 1963, single parties governed with a clear parliamentary majority for only 44 years.

Coalitions and minority governments involve a burying of old differences and a recognition of common cause along new lines. In times of political crisis in France, political parties have subdivided and new fissures have been added to old ones. In England, subdivision has been followed by the joining together of former enemies along new lines. For instance, when Joseph Chamberlain and his radical supporters broke with the Liberal Party on Irish Home Rule in 1886, the group went into alliance with the Conservatives, previously Chamberlain's enemies; the Chamberlain wing of the Liberal Party did not become a new party perpetuating old disagreements at a time of crisis. But the amalgamation of the Chamberlainite Liberals with the Conservatives made of the Conservative Party something different from what it had been before.

Coalition, rather than change of government, is the usual reaction of English politicians to a crisis. Coalition governments saw the nation through two world wars, and also through the impact of the World Depression in 1931. In all three cases, the party system was radically altered subsequently. The period after 1945 was unusual in that the Conservatives, though greatly changed internally, did not emerge as a party with a new name, thus masking rather than calling attention to the extent of the party's internal transformation. The success of the Liberal Party at by-elections in 1962 indicates that the *possibility* of three-party politics, with a minority or coalition government, is always present, just as the *possibility* of party realignments is present, because the parties are not divided by the sort of unbridgeable gulfs that separate, say, Catholic and Communist parties in France and Italy.

The electorate in England is not presented with a choice between two mutually exclusive parties, or one set of policies presented under competing labels. The choice is between parties that differ from each other on a number of specific short-term issues and in principle on a number of long-term emphases, although they share common outlooks on other issues and principles. Furthermore, the parties contain groups that differ from each other about the program of their electoral combination. The outcome of a particular election is likely to influence public policy in a limited number of policy areas without threatening a total change of policy, as in the case of a country in which Communists or Fascists are one of the two major parties. Activists can commit themselves to party work knowing that the instabilities of alignment within a party make it meaningful to attempt to influence the balance of power within a party. The single-member electoral system and the conventions of parliamentary government, together with the basic distribution of attitudes within the population, limit the extent of competition; a high premium is placed upon differing groups sinking some differences in order to have a chance to share in the advantages of controlling government.

CHAPTER VIII

Communication and
Noncommunication

*A parliamentary minister is a man trained by elaborate
practice not to blurt out crude things.*

THE POLITICAL system of England requires an elaborate
apparatus for the communication of information. A
steady flow of information from the peripheral public to
the government is necessary if the latter is to be able to
respond to mass concerns and preferences. This communication can take place through a variety of informal channels, as well as through parties, pressure groups, and
elections. A steady flow of information from government
to the peripheral public is necessary if the directives of
government are to be understood and obeyed.

The communications network can be stratified horizontally in the same manner as that applied to political roles.
For instance, when one Cabinet minister talks to another
during a crisis, it is communication at the level of national leaders; when one man in a pub talks to another
about the crisis, it is horizontal communication at the
level of the peripheral public. Because so many different
kinds of people operate at a given level of politics, horizontal communication cannot take place easily, as has

163

been evidenced by efforts to collect and coordinate information in such fields as economic planning. The more intensively a man is involved in his own specific political task, the greater the possibility that he will be ignorant of the activities of others whose work is not only at the same level, but also relevant to his own.[1]

The network of communication is also divided vertically. Individuals and groups at different horizontal levels are linked vertically by channels such as political parties, the civil service of government departments, and the branch and regional offices of pressure groups. Institutions such as elections and public-opinion polls bring the views of unorganized members of the peripheral public to the attention of national politicians, and the mass media carry the views of national politicians to readers and viewers. Messages often have to move both horizontally and vertically. For instance, pressures for wage increases at the shop-floor level of a nationalized industry first move vertically up to the national officials of a trade union and to the national director of the industry, and then horizontally to the government departments concerned. The greater the number of levels and channels involved, the greater the opportunity for distortion. The risks of distortion are increased by the inability of national politicians to verify the accuracy of many messages. For instance, the claims of pressure groups to "speak for" their members are conjectural rather than easily ascertained statements of fact. Insofar as a message moves simultaneously through a variety of channels of communication, chances of losing it are reduced, and distortion can be guarded against by comparing the findings of disparate channels.

Government requires a continuous two-way flow of information, horizontally and vertically; this feedback is necessary if governors and governed are to take into account each other's behavior and adjust their future actions accordingly.[2]

---

[1] Cf. C. P. Snow, *op. cit.*

[2] Cf. L. S. Amery, *op. cit.*, chapter 1; more generally, V. O. Key, *Public Opinion and American Democracy* (New York: Knopf, 1961) chapter 16, and Kenneth Boulding, *The Image* (Ann Arbor: Michigan, 1956) chapter 7.

For centuries the work of English government was conducted on the basis of a horizontal flow of messages between the Crown and Parliament. This predemocratic experience still finds support in norms of the political culture: the value given deference and leadership contrasts with the liberal value of government by public opinion, involving intensive vertical feedback. Both of these norms find expression in the communications network, which transmits and short-circuits messages.

THE PROCESS

Political communication is simple in its outline form. Communication involves a sender, a message, a channel, and a receiver. The sender or receiver may be an individual or a group. Communication between the Prime Minister and the Foreign Secretary is very different from that between the Conservative Party and the electorate, because the former are individuals, the latter themselves complex groups of people. The position of the sender and the receiver is integrally related to the message and its channel of communication. For instance, MPs and party workers usually listen carefully to messages from their party leader. Conversely, if the recipients have a position higher than that of the sender, messages may be ignored, as in the case, say, of a letter from a local activist to the Foreign Secretary. The high status need not be political to command attention. Those of high status in any field — economics, religion, or cafe society — enjoy special opportunities to communicate messages to some in high political positions. Memoirs of politicians suggest that statements that would be of no account if presented by inconsequential strangers may be treated respectfully if transmitted by those of high social status.[3]

The patterns of political communication are affected by the norms of the political culture. Since almost the whole population shares a common attitude of respect for the Queen, communication does not need to take place. When

[3] See, *e.g.*, Thomas Jones, *A Diary With Letters, 1931-1950* (London: Oxford University Press, 1954).

the Prime Minister congratulates the Queen upon a birth in the Royal Family, he is almost certainly communicating accurately the views of the vast majority of the public, though he has not sampled their sentiments by survey techniques. Communication is legitimately avoided insofar as individuals do not expect to state their opinions on politics, or to have them solicited. The process of political socialization in England involves inculcating in a relative few a concern with national politics and an expectation that their views are worth communicating; the majority are socialized for passive political roles, involving the avoidance of much political communication.

Of special importance are the cultural norms concerning political representation, since it is only through representatives — local activists and auxiliaries — that members of the peripheral public can ordinarily communicate with national politicians. When, for instance, belief in the King as the efficient representative of the whole population was widespread, there was little need for communication from the peripheral public insofar as the monarch seemed to embody the views of everyone. In the 18th century, Parliament, rather than the monarch, came to be valued as the embodiment of public opinion. At that time Edmund Burke developed the classic statement of the duty of the MP to vote in Parliament on the basis of his own independent judgment, and not simply in accord with the views communicated by his constituents. This norm is still supported by many in English politics today, and is strikingly in contrast with American ideas of a legislator as a delegate of his constituency.[4] In the 19th century the spread of Liberal values concerning Parliament as an assembly representative of individual constituents gave emphasis to vertical communication from the peripheral public to national politicians. In this century the most significant development has been that of Radical doctrines concerning government by the majority. The norm of "majority rule" on the one hand gives special importance to the views of those in the peripheral public; on the other, it can be used to ignore criticism from

4 See especially Nigel Nicolson, *op. cit.*

minorities. Consider, for instance, the disregard for some 15,-
000,000 middle-class people shown by the remark of Frank
Cousins, a leading trade unionist and Labour politician: "We
represent Britain, we represent the working class of Britain
and they are Britain!" [5]

Today, Whig, Liberal, and Radical attitudes toward national political representation can all be found. The Whig
and Radical orientations, both of which give much leeway to
elected representatives and relieve them of constantly communicating with their constituents, appear to have the strongest support. S. H. Beer argues that much communication is
made unnecessary by the identification of party and class; the
party represents class interests without continuous feedback.
When specific problems arise, individuals may invoke pressure groups rather than parties as their channel of communication and representation. National politicians are freed from
constant communication with the peripheral public yet,
through pressure group, party, and class ties, individuals may
still communicate with national politicians.[6]

Many conventions of British government have as a consequence the reduction of the flow of political information,
both vertically and horizontally; this increases the privacy of
government. The doctrine of ministerial responsibility is of
special importance. All Cabinet ministers are supposed to
share joint responsibility for policies of any one; hence, they
are not allowed to differ publicly from their colleagues without first resigning from office; differences can only be expressed privately within the Cabinet. Hence, in 1963, seven
years after the Suez War, politicians, in particular those at
lower levels, do not know definitely which Cabinet ministers
supported the war and which opposed it, because of a doctrine
of secrecy. Within a government department, the minister is

[5] *Report of the Sixty-First Annual Conference of the Labour Party*
(1962) p. 182.

[6] See S. H. Beer, "The Representation of Interests in British Govern-
ment," pp. 645-650; A. L. Lowell, *Public Opinion and Popular Government*
(New York: Longmans, 1914) pp. 113ff., A. H. Birch, *Representative and
Responsible Government* (London: Allen and Unwin, 1964).

personally responsible for all that is done in the department by his civil servants, as well as by his express instructions. The views which civil servants put to the minister, and which may in fact prove crucial to his decision, are by convention strictly private. Critics of a government department are thus prevented from reading memoranda that influence the formation of departmental policy.[7] The blanket of privacy covers past as well as present deliberations. Cabinet documents may not be published without special government permission if they are less than 50 years old. Channels nominally meant to provide information can be used to reduce the flow of information, and most important, as D. C. Watt notes, "control of what is said remains in the hands of the authorities." [8]

Members of Parliament, whether government supporters or in opposition, lack the specialized and powerful committees in which Congressmen interrogate politicians and civil servants in Washington. The chief means of interrogation is through the parliamentary question, which any MP may put to any government minister, as long as it concerns a problem within his jurisdiction. But ministers may consciously try to withold information by careful phrasing of replies. In the opinion of a former civil servant concerned with drafting answers, "the perfect reply to an embarrassing question in the House of Commons is one that is brief, appears to answer the question completely, if challenged can be proved to be accurate in every word, gives no opening for awkward 'supplementaries' and discloses really nothing." [9] The government always reserves the right to refuse to communicate information on grounds of national interest. For instance, at the beginning of the Suez War, Sir Anthony Eden refused to answer a question in the House as to whether or not the country was at war with

[7] See especially S. E. Finer, "The Individual Responsibility of Ministers," *Public Administration* XXXIV (Winter, 1956).

[8] "Foreign Affairs, the Public Interest and the Right to Know," *Political Quarterly* XXXIV:2 (1963) p. 127.

[9] H. E. Dale, *The Higher Civil Service of Great Britain* (London: Oxford University Press, 1941) p. 105. Cf. D. N. Chester and N. Bowring, *Questions in Parliament* (Oxford: Clarendon Press, 1962).

Egypt.[10] The conventions governing parliamentary parties further inhibit communication outside the restricted circle of MPs
and their close associates. Major decisions of parliamentary
parties are more likely to be taken in private party meetings
than publicly during a parliamentary debate or vote. These
meetings are private, and only very limited accounts are leaked
to the press. Thus, discussions of Conservative back-benchers
about the Suez War remained almost as private as discussions
in the Cabinet, though in the Profumo scandal of 1963 this
secrecy began to be breached. Similarly, the deliberations by
which the Parliamentary Labour Party chose Harold Wilson as
Leader (and potential Prime Minister) in 1963 were conducted in private; Labour MPs agreed to refrain from discussing the matter on television. The contrast with an American presidential nominating convention is extreme.[11]

The press, the chief means for making political information public, suffers under a variety of constraints in reporting
news. Press conferences are not held regularly by government
ministers, nor do ministers or senior civil servants regularly
leak news to the extent it is done in Washington. Journalists
may find themselves embarrassed and treated as social in-
feriors in their contacts with upper- and upper-middle class
ministers and civil servants, since many journalists come from
humble backgrounds and left school at 14 or 16 to serve a
newspaper apprenticeship. Journalists who are the social
equals of national politicians and dine with them may find
themselves inhibited by diffuse social obligations; gentlemen
in England are not expected to make public all that they
learn in private social gatherings. For instance, in the inter-
war years, Geoffrey Dawson, editor of *The Times,* the country's leading serious newspaper, suppressed news unfavorable

---

10 See *House of Commons Debates* Vol. 558, Cols. 1452-54 (October 31,
1956) and Cols. 1620ff. (November 1, 1956).

11 For a case study of an MP's private communications, see Nigel Nicolson, *op. cit.* On the privacy of party meetings, see *Report from the Committee of Privileges* (London: House of Commons Paper, No. 138, 1947)
especially paragraphs 17, 20. Cf. "No Closed Shop for Political Hostesses,"
The Times, July 1, 1963.

to Nazi Germany for the sake of his political and social associates in the government.[12] The Official Secrets Act, which places severe penalties upon those who leak information to the press, and libel laws far more stringent than those in America further restrict press comment on current affairs. Cecil King, publisher of the mass-circulation *Daily Mirror* has charged: "The press is so hedged about by legal restrictions and penalties that it can no longer be called free. Certainly we have freedom of the press provided what you say is ineffective or unheeded. It collapses like a pack of cards, however, as soon as real issues are at stake." [13] The national press itself is not above criticism. Sensationalism and the competition for exclusive information have brought it often into disrespect. In 1963, its reputation was certainly lowered by the disclosure of irresponsibility in reporting security charges arising from the conviction of an Admiralty clerk, W. J. Vassall, as a Russian spy. Yet within a few months, the press could claim credit for uncovering (though not at first publishing) information leading to the resignation of the Secretary of State for War, John Profumo, in another case involving security.[14]

Communication and noncommunication at the national level includes provision for communication in "code." (The term is borrowed from a veteran parliamentary reporter who employs it in private discussion.) Information may be published if it is coded; *i.e.,* stated so obliquely that only those with private knowledge of public affairs can interpret the actual significance of the message. The majority who read the message will not appreciate its significance. The drafting of an important report, "Control of Public Expenditure," by a

12 See J. E. Wrench, *Geoffrey Dawson and Our Times* (London: Hutchinson, 1955) especially p. 361.

13 "Subtle Censorship is Shackling Britain's Press," in *The Press and the People* (London: Ninth Annual Report of the Press Council, 1962) p. 11. See also D. C. Watt, *op. cit.*

14 Cf. *Report of the Tribunal appointed to Inquire into the Vassall Case* (London: H.M.S.O., Cmnd. 2009, 1963); *The Sunday Mirror* (London) June 9, 1963, and *Lord Denning's Report.*

committee under Lord Plowden, provides an excellent example of how this process of restricted communication operates. The report was entrusted to a committee of men appointed by the government because they could be relied upon not to communicate publicly in a controversial manner what they learned by surveying public expenditure. The report was drafted simultaneously with private memoranda and discussions with senior government officials. Hence, the committee had the option of making specific criticisms in print or privately. It usually chose the latter course. The written report was then submitted to the Treasury, the chief object of criticism, and the decision was left with the Treasury as to whether or not it should be published. Since it was drafted in code, it could be published. Atypically, however, following publication of the coded report, a wartime civil servant now a professor of government, W. J. M. Mackenzie, prepared a "translation" and published it. The first paragraph of the Plowden Report is translated thus: "We proceeded on two principles: no dirty linen in public: outside critics are bores." [15]

The use of code is but one illustration of the fact that the import of political messages varies according to the predispositions and prior knowledge of the sender and receiver. Political messages are not interpreted in isolation. For instance, election speeches are not likely to change an individual's political outlook; rather, they are interpreted in the light of that outlook. When messages have emotional overtones, interpretations may be contradictory. A straightforward factual statement such as "The British government possesses nuclear weapons" can trigger emotional responses to the ambiguous symbol "nuclear weapons." This message can produce emotional pride in Britain's "great power status" in some receivers, and in others an emotional disgust that the nation's government is willing to risk global annihilation for politically unworthy ends. The many different forms and combina-

[15] Cf. "The Plowden Report; a translation," *The Guardian*, May 25, 1963; and the original document, *Control of Public Expenditure* (London: H.M.S.O., Cmnd. 1432, 1961) paragraph 1.

tions that political messages can take must be constantly kept in mind because they influence the meaning that different recipients attach to the same message.[16]

CHANNELS

Important differences exist between channels of communication. One set of differences concerns the relationship of sender and receiver. Television is a channel connecting a few politicians with a heterogeneous mass audience. By contrast, a government report is usually a channel for communicating between government officials and a small audience sharing a common interest. Channels such as newspapers are intrinsically public; others, such as those joining pressure groups with government departments, tend to be private. The channels linking different sections of a political party are both public and private — and a high premium may be placed upon keeping from the public some private communications.

Some theories of democracy place special emphasis upon the exchange of messages between the peripheral public and national politicians. These theories mistakenly presuppose that most citizens actively seek to communicate with their governors, and have some political sophistication. Yet American survey research has found that approximately half the electorate normally does not think about politics in terms of parties, principles, and group benefits, and only one-sixth have a fairly coherent political outlook.[17] Life-history interviews suggest that these findings are relevant to England. Many respondents are completely passive when asked about major political questions; others appear to fix their attention upon a single issue or experience, and not to notice that some of their other views are inconsistent with this response. Surveys suggest that only a minority of Englishmen have interest and information sufficient to maintain a meaningful conversation with a party official or MP about politics.

16 For a classification of characteristics of messages, see Kenneth Boulding, *op. cit.*, pp. 47ff.

17 See Angus Campbell, *et. al., The American Voter* (New York: Wiley, 1960) chapter 10.

Despite the legal freedom of speech that has existed for centuries in England, many people feel psychological inhibitions about talking politics. The Civic Culture survey found that only 29 per cent of Englishmen interviewed felt free to talk about politics with anyone. The majority — 55 per cent — said they felt political topics could be discussed with some people; 12 per cent thought the subject could not be discussed with anyone and 4 per cent were "Don't Knows." Research in America indicates that people avoid political discussion because such talk may threaten friendships or job success, because it seems futile or makes the individual feel inadequate, or simply because it gives no emotional satisfaction.[18] These reasons appear to be relevant in England, too.

The proportion of the population actually seeking to establish personal contact with MPs, a chief intermediary between the peripheral citizen and national politicians, is small. Of 117 persons interviewed in the life-history survey, only 11 had contacted an MP, usually by letter. Most of these communications did not concern matters of public policy, but rather the adjustment of minor administrative decisions that affected individuals personally, such as housing, travel problems, and in one case, burial regulations. A small majority of the rest — 56 out of 106 — could conceive of circumstances in which they might write to their MP. The examples given were either extremely personal or extremely vague; *e.g.,* "to protest against unfairness." Forty respondents could not think of any circumstances in which they might write. The MP appears to his constituents as a court of appeal to whom an individual might in very special circumstances turn for aid. He is not perceived as a man who should and does participate in a continuous feedback of messages between central government and his constituents.

Anthony Downs has shown, by applying the criteria of an economist, that because the ordinary individual can acquire so little influence by constantly receiving and sending politi-

18 Cf. G. Almond and S. Verba, *op. cit.,* chapter 4, and Morris Rosenberg, "Some Determinants of Political Apathy," *Public Opinion Quarterly* XVIII (1954) pp. 349-366.

cal messages, it is economical for him to delegate responsibility for everything but the act of voting to parties, pressure groups, or the mass media. They bear the cost of acquiring, analyzing, and evaluating information. The individual has only to choose between agents.[19] Any Englishman could, if he wanted, spend up to £100 a year on books, papers, and periodicals specializing in political information. He would then have to spend all of his leisure time digesting this information, viewing television, and attending political meetings. Even then, he could only occasionally communicate with those in national auxiliary roles, and very rarely with those acting as national politicians. It is hardly surprising that few people dedicate themselves to acquiring political information in view of the low material return. Englishmen who pursue political information with avidity, like sports fans, may be motivated by psychological rewards.

The majority of Englishmen, when they speak out politically, speak through actions. A general election is the major occasion upon which national politicians turn beseechingly to the peripheral public to "hear" what their verdict will be. Elections, however, are blunt instruments infrequently used. The counting of votes gives a clear indication of which party will govern the country for the next few years. But it does not provide clear indications as to what government policy should be. Studies of voting behavior have shown quite clearly that the electors do not give the government a mandate — a set of instructions on a range of public policies. What is communicated is simply an "on balance" judgment for or against a party, with nothing made clear about particular policies. National politicians and ministers may, for propaganda purposes, talk of a mandate.[20] More important, they may sometimes frame particular policies with special regard to their imputed effect upon a general election. But in England it appears that cultural norms give more sanction to a government judging particular policies without regard to electoral prefer-

19 *Op. cit.*, Part Three.
20 See Wilfrid Harrison, *The Government of Britain* (London: Hutchinson, 5th edition, 1958) pp. 164-165.

ences. The infrequency of elections reinforces such an outlook.

Latent consequences of many social activities can be interpreted by national politicians as political messages. For instance, the shifting consumer preference for motor transport as against railway travel in the 1950s has been interpreted by the Conservatives as a pointer in framing transportation policy. Strikes — of workers against employers or of consumers against high prices for selected goods — may lead to adjustments in government economic policy. In extreme cases, violence may be used to communicate. It was the means by which the Irish Nationalists, frustrated in Parliament, finally secured Home Rule in 1922. But since then, violence has been notably absent from English politics, although it has occasionally erupted in England's overseas colonies. It could be said that the absence of violence on the scale of France or the American South is evidence of the harmony between national politicians and the peripheral public.

The growing awareness of public-opinion polls in England in the past decade has introduced a new element into the process of political communication. Prior to the development of polls, individual national politicians could not have their assertions to speak for the peripheral public properly evaluated. The polls can now provide evidence to support or refute such claims. For instance, in the debate on revising Labour Party policy following its 1959 election defeat, an opinion poll was commissioned by Hugh Gaitskell's supporters because they were confident that its findings would show a lack of popular support for their factional opponents. The involvement of polls in partisan and factional politics has led to attacks on the validity of their findings and also on the ethical propriety of adjusting policies — in substance or in appearance — to agree with information gained by market-research techniques. The opposition is aroused by cultural norms that sanction strong leadership, and also by left-wing Socialists, who are opposed to the findings of polls. The contrast with America is marked. Many English politicians still retain a distrust of statistical and psychological analysis. Pollsters

176 *Communication and Noncommunication*

have sometimes misunderstood the inelasticity of political parties, which cannot change policies quickly even if leaders or pollsters wish them to do so. Polls are occasionally used tactically to assist in framing propaganda messages to sections of the electorate, but hardly ever in policy making.[21]

The press, radio, and television — collectively, the mass media, though parts are only for the few — daily diffuse throughout England accounts of the workings of government. It is largely through the media that the peripheral public is kept informed of national public affairs.

TABLE VIII.1   *National Daily Newspaper Readership*

	Paid circulation	Readership (% adult population)	Politics
(*Popular papers*)			
Mirror	4,610,000	38%	Labour
Express	4,288,000	33%	Conservative
Mail	2,548,000	19%	Conservative
Herald	1,348,000	13%	Labour
Sketch	954,000	10%	Conservative
(*Serious papers*)			
Telegraph	1,261,000	8%	Conservative
Guardian	263,000	2%	Labour-Liberal
Times	254,000	3%	Conservative

Source: National Readership Survey, January-December, 1962 (London: Institute of Practitioners of Advertising, 1963)

The media in England differ from their American counterparts in the extent of their centralization and specialized readerships. The small size of the country permits eight daily morning newspapers edited in London to circulate throughout England, and also in parts of Scotland (Table VIII.1).

21 Cf. Mark Abrams, "Public Opinion Polls and Political Parties," *Public Opinion Quarterly* XXVII (Spring, 1963); and his "Why the Parties Advertise," with Ralph Samuel, "Dr. Abrams and the End of Politics," *New Left Review* (No. 5) September-October, 1960. See also Richard Rose, "Political Decision-Making and the Polls," *Parliamentary Affairs* XV:2 (1962); D. E. G. Plowman, "Public Opinion and the Polls," *British Journal of Sociology* XIII:4 (1962).

The popular papers emphasize features and human-interest stories; they are primarily vehicles of entertainment; the limited amount of news reporting is sometimes heavily biased. The serious papers give broad news coverage, and contain articles of a degree of sophistication unlikely to be found in the news columns of a paper such as *The New York Times*. About 10 per cent of the population read at least one serious paper daily; the readership of *The Times* and *Guardian* gives the best indication of the demand for serious political information. Quality weeklies with political commentary, such as *The Economist,* enjoy readerships of a fraction of 1 per cent of the electorate; there are no weekly periodicals such as *Time, Life,* and *Look* that bridge the gap between the small weeklies and the mass audience. To some extent, the serious Sunday papers fill this gap.

The British Broadcasting Corporation provides radio and television programs without commercials. It is primarily financed by an annual license fee paid by all with radio and television sets. Its board of governors is appointed by the government; in general producers are free from political influence. The BBC runs in competition with commercial companies broadcasting on the network of the Independent Television Authority. These companies finance themselves by advertisements, and are free from governmental interference with program content except on technical points. The BBC has a monopoly of radio broadcasting, offering a Light Service of popular entertainment and a Home Service, which mixes drama, talks, and current affairs with entertainment. The Third Program broadcasts "highbrow" listening nightly for audiences of about 50,000, and Network Three provides a small ration of programs for those with specialist and minority interests. By comparison with America, British broadcasting offers fewer stations but greater variety in program content and more programs for those with more education.

Insofar as popular journalists and television programs attempt to transmit messages from the peripheral public to national politicians, their efforts involve a short-circuiting of communication. Journalists normally are local activists or in auxiliary political roles. Their contacts with the peripheral public do not provide them with a cross-section sample. For instance, when a journalist covers a general election, he tours the country talking primarily to politicians, local activists, and fellow journalists. The published reports do not provide a basis, before or after the event, for accounting for national swings in voting. Editorial writers are even more likely to be removed from the peripheral public, though some on the national quality papers may be in close touch with those in national political roles. In this case, they may serve to facilitate horizontal communication at the national level of politics.[22]

The enormous cost of producing popular papers and television programs, and the pressure from advertisers to maintain or increase circulation or viewership provide strong economic incentives for publishers and programmers to maintain feedback with their readers and viewers. Without extremely large audiences, the popular media collapse. The *News Chronicle* (the only national Liberal newspaper) was closed down in 1960 because its circulation of more than 1,000,000 was insufficient to sustain advertising revenue.[23] Editors of the popular papers are conscious of the relatively low interest in politics of many of their readers, and scale down the amount of space given to the subject. It is almost impossible by reading the popular press to keep fully informed about public affairs, especially international affairs. In some cases, political coverage may be modified in order to please what are perceived as shifting political preferences among readers. This shift occurred notably in the *Daily Mirror*'s reaction to Labour's defeat in 1959; after that election, the paper began to devote less space to Labour politics. The most important innovator in contemporary British journalism, Roy Thomson, a Canadian, has made a point of refusing to meddle in the politics of his pa-

22 See Donald McLachlan, "The Press and Public Opinion," *British Journal of Sociology* VI:2 (1955).

23 On the economics of the press, see Francis Williams, *Dangerous Estate* (London: Grey Arrow, 1959); *Report of the Royal Commission on the Press, 1961-62* (London: H.M.S.O., Cmnd. 1811, 1962).

pers, for fear that he would distract his staff from their primary aim — making money.[24]

The quality daily papers and the political weekly magazines regard themselves as facilitating horizontal communication among national politicians and those in auxiliary roles, though the majority of their readers are likely to be local activists or members of the peripheral public specially interested in public affairs. (By reading the same publications read by those in national political roles, individuals can enhance their own status — a point that some of the periodicals emphasize in appealing for new readers with slogans such as "Top People Take *The Times*" or "Lively Minds Like the *Guardian*.") Employees and editors of the quality papers have access to Cabinet ministers and to many others in national political roles. But access should not be confused with influence. Journalists usually use their contacts to gain information that will make stories, and not to construct private memos aimed at influencing policy. Reciprocally, politicians use their contacts in an attempt to secure public reports that will aid them in advancing policies. For instance, when the Chancellor of the Exchequer in 1957 decided that he would dramatically raise the interest rate for banks, he carefully prepared editors and publishers of the quality papers. Later, at a public inquiry into the change in bank rate, the journalists testified that they had not sought to argue with the Chancellor to change his policy, though many disagreed with what they thought he intended to do.[25] In other words, these prominent journalists enjoy private access to ministers by virtue of their status, but they need not have influence.

Television, like the press, transmits political messages with great speed and comprehensiveness from those in national political roles to the peripheral public. Because television,

[24] Cf. his interview with John Freeman in *The Listener*, February 15, 1962; Raymond Williams, *Communications* (Harmondsworth: Penguin, 1962) especially pp. 28ff.; and Hugh Cudlipp, *At Your Peril* (London: Weidenfeld and Nicholson, 1962).

[25] See *The Bank Rate Tribunal*, pp. 8ff.; p. 279.

like radio, is subject to government control of its quasi-monop-
oly license, broadcasters have a much greater inducement
to report news impartially than do newspaper editors. In programs involving comment upon the news, the broadcasting
companies are compelled by Act of Parliament to maintain
a fair balance between points of view. Commercial television
is primarily concerned with viewer ratings, and hence interprets
the feedback from audience research as a sign that entertainment programs are more important than those concerning
politics. The BBC, however, is less concerned with audience
sizes. It still shows the influence of Lord Reith, its director general during the formative years of radio before the
war. Lord Reith believed in shaping the tastes of his audiences to conform to his own ideas of what was best. He once
wrote, "It is occasionally indicated to us that we are apparently setting out to give the public what we think they
need — and not what they want — but few know what they
want and very few what they need." [26] The BBC still retains
in some measure the belief that it should not only transmit
information, but also, change the outlook of its audience.

The influence of the press and of television upon political
behavior, whether sought for its own sake or as a by-product
of its everyday business, is very limited. Newspapers in England, like their American counterparts, cannot deliver the
votes of their readers, who rarely subscribe on the grounds of
editorial policy. Graphs of newspaper circulation show no relationship to voting behavior. The intensive series of political
television programs that were an innovation of the 1959 general election appear to have had very little effect upon voting.
Instead, judgments of the programs were primarily a reflection of the viewers' prior partisan commitments.[27] It is possible to speculate that over a long period of time, television
and the press may have a significant impact upon political

[26] *Broadcast Over Britain* (London: Hodder & Stoughton, c. 1924) p. 34.
See also the *BBC Handbook* (London: BBC, annually), and, for criticism,
Henry Fairlie, "The BBC," in *The Establishment*.

[27] See J. Trenaman and D. McQuail, *op. cit.*, and Robert Silvey, "Election Broadcasting and the Public," *The Listener*, November 26, 1959.

attitudes. The major English study to date, concerned with television's influence upon children, came up with generally negative conclusions.[28]

Unlike the mass media, pressure groups can claim to represent a collection of people who share a common set of opinions on aspects of public policy. But the structure of pressure groups, separating full-time officials from rank-and-file members, means that at times the national leaders of pressure groups may be manufacturing opinions rather than transmitting the views of rank-and-file members. For example, the position on nuclear weapons of the Transport & General Workers Union, with a million members, was very abruptly changed when a politically moderate general secretary died and was succeeded by Frank Cousins, a man of the Labour left. In another instance the leaders of the British Medical Association conducted an opinion survey among doctors during its campaign against the National Health Service. They found to their surprise that the leadership policy was rejected. The national and auxiliary leaders of the B.M.A. then proceeded to reject the findings of their rank-and-file survey at the annual meeting of symbolically named "representatives" of the rank and file.[29] Pressure-group leaders are less likely to distort or invent messages purporting to come from their rank and file if the latter can repudiate such statements by their own actions — *e.g.*, a strike called for political purposes can be defeated if union members report to work. Leaders, however, retain much leeway in communicating their own opinions as the views of their membership in areas unimportant to most members.

Political parties, like pressure groups, play an important part in the feedback of political messages. The ambiguity involved in party membership has created controversy. On the

[28] See Hilde T. Himmelweit, *et. al., Television and the Child* (London: Oxford University Press, 1958). See also Joseph T. Klapper, *The Effects of Mass Communication* (Glencoe, Ill.: Free Press, 1960).

[29] See Harry Eckstein, "The Politics of the B.M.A.," *Political Quarterly* XXVI:4 (1955) pp. 352ff. Note also B. C. Roberts, *Trade Union Government and Administration in Great Britain,* pp. 95ff.

one hand, national party leaders are interested in communicating with all who belong to the party simply by voting for it. On the other hand, the organization of the party provides a means of communication for the small fraction of voters who pay dues and attend party meetings. Some writers have argued, largely on a priori grounds, that active party members will inevitably be extremist in their outlook, and in conflict with the many who only vote for the party.[30] Studies of the opinions of active party members have found that they have a variety of outlooks, as do those who only vote for the party. The messages from active party members may differ in language, in sophistication, and in emphasis from those of voters, but they are not in contradiction to them.[31]

MPs can sometimes be an important channel of communication from the peripheral public to national politicians. They are the only group of men within the national government who are formally linked with the peripheral public by election. But the norms concerning the MP's role do not emphasize the function of messenger for a constituency. Furthermore, few MPs are concerned with verifying the representativeness of the persons with whom they come into contact in their constituency. In the course of holding "surgeries"; that is, open house for constituents wishing to state problems of grievances, MPs can gain some insight into views of electors.[32] This information may affect occasional speeches in the Commons or private discussions in the club rooms of Parliament, but the party whip prevents constituents' communications from affecting MPs' votes.

Government departments differ enormously in their channels of communication with the peripheral public. The two chief departments, the Treasury and the Foreign Office, have

[30] See especially Nigel Nicolson, *op. cit.*, and R. T. McKenzie, *British Political Parties, passim.*

[31] See Richard Rose, "The Political Ideas of English Party Activists," and A. H. Birch, *Small-Town Politics,* chapter 5.

[32] See Robert Dowse, "The M.P. and His Surgery," *Political Studies* XI:3 (1963).

virtually no means of ensuring a continuous feedback of vertical communication. Only indirectly, through its economic policies and the marketplace reactions of those in the economy, can the public and Treasury officials "speak" to each other. A department such as the Ministry of Pensions has elaborate channels of communication, because it is applying government policy to thousands of individuals in local and regional offices. The problem of such a ministry is a surplus of information. It is necessary to have fixed procedures in order to handle multitudes of individual communications. But routine, essential in a bureaucracy, can sometimes frustrate the attainment of policy goals. Eckstein found in his study of the National Health Service that routine procedures meant that unanticipated factors of substantial consequence in individual cases tended to be ignored in order that the flow of messages could continue to move smoothly.[33]

The great bulk of messages flowing within the government are kept from publication by the restrictions referred to above. At times, the government consciously encourages public deliberation by establishing on an *ad hoc* basis Royal Commissions or Committees to hold hearings and report recommendations for action within a specified area of public policy. The reports of these bodies thus afford insight into governmental channels of communication with those outside government. Particularly worthy of examination is the Pilkington Committee on Broadcasting, which published a report in 1962 on the future of radio and television, after holding 120 meetings over a two-year period, and spending £45,000.

The Pilkington Committee explicitly stated that it was evaluating broadcasting on behalf of viewers and listeners, primarily members of the peripheral public. Its members thought that it was communicating with this public by inviting comments from national officials of pressure groups, many of which had no continuing concern with broadcasting (4-5).[34] Organ-

---

[33] "Planning: A Case Study," *Political Studies* IV:1 (1956).
[34] Numbers in brackets refer to paragraphs in the *Pilkington Report*

izations such as the Association of Municipal Corporations were assumed to speak "as viewers," though the Association has no individual members, and its primary purpose is to lobby concerning local government legislation and administration (81, 209). The Committee treated "the strong feeling, amounting often to a conviction" of some pressure groups that television was harmful to society as conclusive evidence of allegations against television (39 *et seq*.). Significantly, among the few pressure groups that had their views rejected were the two that claimed explicitly to speak for the broadcasting audience (66, 425-26).

Although the Committee criticized the Independent Television Authority for failing to do research into the impact of television upon English society, it too failed to do so (162). It asserted that television is "of profound social significance," without any empirical evidence to support so controversial a hypothesis (21, 42). (Less than a year after this report, the government established a committee to investigate whether or not the assertion was true.) The Committee assumed that it could, by introspection, arrive at the "attitudes and values . . . held by most people to be good" (248). The easy arrogance of the Committee in projecting the views of its high-status personnel upon the peripheral public is indicated by its casual unsubstantiated assertion, "We have no hesitation in saying that the BBC command public confidence" (149) .[35]

The Pilkington Committee provided a dignified façade of vertical communication; efficient communication was carried out within a small stratum of the population. The unrepresentativeness of the stratum was clearly revealed in a national sample survey conducted by the *Sunday Times* following publication of the report. This survey found that only 18 per cent of those interviewed shared the acute dissatisfaction and anxiety of the Committee. A major Pilkington proposal — that broadcasting authorities should devote more time to raising the level

---

(London: H.M.S.O., Cmnd. 1753, 1962). See also House of Commons *Debates*, Vol. 664, Cols. 421-541, July 31, 1962.

[35] Independently conducted surveys support this assertion.

of public taste — was supported by about two-thirds of those with education beyond the age of 18; it was opposed by about two-thirds of those with less education. The significance of this division is that the pro-Pilkington stratum in this instance constituted about 5 per cent of the nation's population, and the anti-Pilkington strata contained 95 per cent of the population.[36]

Many of the problems facing a government are heavily technical, and vertical communication with the peripheral public is not of the same significance as it is in an evaluation of television. Public-opinion polls can make clear that the peripheral public wants peace and prosperity — but the public can provide very litle useful and specific guidance concerning means to these ends.[37] In dealing with technical problems, horizontal communication at the national level is important. For instance, L. W. Martin has shown how defense policy involves a feedback of information and values between government ministers, senior military officers, defense correspondents of serious papers, members of the Institute for Strategic Studies, a few Opposition MPs specially interested in defense, and spokesmen (sometimes ex-military officers), for firms producing armaments.[38] This network has few vertical contacts with the majority of the population. But within its horizontal levels it is open to a wide variety of ideas and kinds of influence. In other words, strictly limited communication does not necessarily result in the circulation of identical ideas.

"THE INNER CIRCLE" [39]

British government operates in a way that gives each individual an equal vote, but hardly an equal voice in government.

[36] See Harry Henry, *Public Opinion and the Pilkington Committee* (London: *Sunday Times*, 1962). The financial interest of the *Sunday Times* in television does not appear to have biased the survey in any significant way. Cf. the Gallup Poll findings in the *Daily Telegraph*, April 6, 1962.

[37] See Richard Rose, "Political Decision-Making and the Polls," pp. 197ff.

[38] "The Market for Strategic Ideas," *American Political Science Review* LVI:1 (1962).

[39] See Ely Devons, "Government on the Inner Circle," *The Listener*, March 27, 1958.

Representatives often fail to reflect accurately the divided opinions of those in whose name they claim to speak. National politicians may confuse their own voice with the "voice" of the peripheral public. Institutions such as Royal Commissions and newspapers provide an appearance of vertical communication belying the reality.

Non-communication is not explicitly valued in English politics; rather, it is the by-product of other cultural values, institutions, and conventions. Englishmen are socialized for differing political roles from an early age. The majority of persons in national political roles are drawn from a fairly homogeneous social class, facilitating horizontal communication and impeding vertical communication. Under Labour governments, the balance is shifted. But even a leading Labour minister such as Herbert Morrison can easily mistake horizontal for vertical communication, saying of a plan to build a gasworks in Oxford that it caused "extensive controversy and reached the correspondence columns of *The Times*." [40] The unification of executive and legislative responsibility in the Cabinet, and the convention of ministerial responsibility is primarily intended to fix responsibility for government; it is only incidentally that it shields the process of deliberation from the public prior to the announcement of decisions. So accepted are the limitations upon political communication that even a critic will not plead for full national publicity for political communication, but only for increasing the small numbers kept fully informed in "that curious inner circle of journalists, academics, men of affairs, civil servants and public commentators." [41]

Political communication between the peripheral public and national politicians does take place indirectly. Many national politicians, in the course of communicating with others at the same horizontal level, will refer to, or present as their own, views gained through vertical communications links. This

[40] *Government and Parliament* (London: Oxford University Press, 1954) p. 317. *The Times* correspondence columns are a favorite channel of communication among those in national roles. Cf. Table VIII.1

[41] See D. C. Watt, *op. cit.*, p. 134.

practice is much more likely to be used by pressure-group spokesmen, whose roles involve the obligation to represent a specific vertical section of society, than by civil servants. (Civil servants can, of course, claim to "speak on behalf of the national interest.") National politicians concerned with electoral victory will go out of their way to gather clues, sometimes by methods of dubious validity, as to the preferences of the peripheral public. Constant concern with electoral preferences sometimes reflects personal insecurity; it need not be a prime characteristic of those in the leadership stratum. Horizontal and vertical links are often enough combined by individuals so that messages from the peripheral public are not often suppressed, though they may be misinterpreted. The great stability of the regime is strong indirect evidence of the general satisfaction with existing patterns of communication and of noncommunication.

It would be misleading to say that English government fails to represent with mathematical accuracy each member of the population, or to listen with equal attention to each voice raised on a public issue. The standard of judgment implied by such a statement is impossible to achieve — in America or in England.[42] English politics is notable for the *degree* to which political communication is centralized in London, among those who occupy roles as national politicians. Furthermore, it is notable for the degree to which the emphasis on horizontal communication is sanctioned by the norms of the political culture. The feedback of political information, by means of which problems can be identified, policies formulated, and acceptance sought, can be carried out more efficiently and more easily. Government gains in cohesion because of the relative ease of horizontal communication. But this gain is not without risks. D. N. Chester, in his brilliant description of government in wartime, has described how the process that draws national politicians together tends to isolate them from the peripheral public and local activists. "What can come to be important, if one is not careful, is not how decisions affect

[42] Cf. V. O. Key, *op. cit.,* and Robert Dahl, *Who Governs?* pp. 223ff.

people, but how they are thought to operate by people in the Whitehall circle. The leader or letter in *The Times* or *Economist* can become the reality by which one's actions are judged." [43]

[43] "The Central Machinery for Economic Policy," in *Lessons of the British War Economy*, edited by D. N. Chester (Cambridge: University Press, 1951) p. 30.

CHAPTER IX

Policy Processes

> *If we think what a vast information, what a nice discretion, what a consistent will ought to mark the rulers of that empire, we shall be surprised when we see them. We see a changing body of miscellaneous persons, sometimes few, sometimes many, never the same for an hour.*

POLICY IS MADE when uncertainties arise within the political system and these uncertainties are resolved by government action or inaction. Sometimes policies are consciously made: a Chancellor of the Exchequer may decide on a particular day to cut income tax, and this action follows. Sometimes policy just happens, without conscious government influence. For instance, Conservative governments in the 1950s made no decision concerning university expansion; the increasing number of qualified young people seeking university places forced an expansionist policy on the government. Sometimes the consequences of a policy are very different from those intended: Neville Chamberlain signed an agreement with Hitler at Munich in 1938 intending to secure peace. Instead, war followed.

Administration is important if policies are to be regularly and efficiently maintained throughout the country. British government could go on for months without new legislation, but it would collapse if hundreds of thousands

189

of civil servants were to stop administering prosaic laws dealing with taxes, pensions, health, and national defense. Adaptations can be introduced into English politics only because,
away from the conflict and the drama that attend the making
of new policy, thousands of administrators are quietly maintaining in operation the policies effectively settled by past
conflicts.

The line between making and administering policy is a
shadowy one. Senior administrators are often confronted with
situations in which they must exercise some discretion on
questions of policy, as in town and country planning. They
must also be sophisticated enough politically to recognize
when the application of fixed rules in unusual situations may
have policy repercussions. Constantly, they are engaged in di-
alogues with other civil servants or with ministers about
changes in particular policies or administrative practices. Administrators are closely involved in policy making because the
effectiveness and even the desirability of policy innovations
may hinge upon the administrative implications involved in
attempting to reach goals such as economic growth. Civil servants who effectively demolish proposed policies on the
grounds that they are administratively impractical are making
as great a contribution to British government as those, whether
ministers or civil servants, who force through policy and administrative innovations. The difference between ministers and
senior civil servants is not that between policy makers and
administrators. It is a distinction between those who are primarily partisan and those who are primarily nonpartisan. Both
are deeply involved in politics.

The people making and administering policy are numerous.
The assumption that making policy is solely the job of the
Cabinet, Parliament, and the civil service is misleading. It
results from identifying governmental institutions with the
whole of the policy process. But individuals with many different positions and roles outside government can also be involved in making and administering policies. In addition to
ministers, civil servants, and MPs, the policy process involves

leaders of pressure groups, party politicians, academic experts, and sometimes members of foreign pressure groups, and leaders of other nations.

The very gradual and often unintended development of policies makes it difficult to describe the process simply by relating what a ubiquitous observer might hear and see in Westminster over a period of months. For instance, educational policy in England today incorporates institutions and practices dating back to medieval times. The momentum of history must be allowed for, difficult though it is to observe or to measure. Cultural norms of policy makers are often developed decades before they reach positions of influence. These values, beliefs, and emotions are of great importance in affecting the recognition (or avoidance) of policy problems, how they are studied, and how they are disposed of. For instance, an account of the Labour government's decision to nationalize steel in the late 1940s would have to deal with the long-matured attitudes of actors toward the values, beliefs, and emotions represented by "nationalization," as well as with day-to-day discussions and memoranda.

Three aspects of the policy process are especially important to understand. First, how the formal machinery of government works, since it is usually involved in some, if not all aspects of policy. Of particular importance is understanding how the Cabinet, the civil service, and Parliament are related to one another. Second, one must consider the processes of identifying problems and deliberating about policy. Third, a tentative answer must be given to the fundamental question — is there one policy process or many in this political system?

THE CABINET AND CIVIL SERVICE

Bagehot described the efficient secret of the English Constitution as "the close union, the nearly complete fusion of the executive and legislative powers."[1] Fusion is the result, he said, of the Cabinet. It is the committee that controls the legislature through its majority party, while simultaneously its

[1] *Op. cit.*, p. 9.

members are the executive directors of the civil servants who administer the various departments of government. The formal machinery is thus fundamentally different from American government, with its separation of the presidential executive from the legislature. At one time in English history it was argued that the independence of the legislature from an executive dominated by an hereditary monarch was desirable. The decline in the efficient powers of the monarch has increasingly led to support for the belief that the fusion of powers is the most efficient and the most desirable form of government.[2] British government is still often referred to as parliamentary government; in fact, it is more accurately described as Cabinet government.

The head of the Cabinet is the Prime Minister. Selection of the Prime Minister is the last important power nominally remaining in the hands of the Queen. (Efforts of left-wing writers to find instances in which a monarch has used the power of choice, or the periodic consultations with an existing Prime Minster, to influence policy, only illustrate how rarely a suspicion of monarchical influence exists in contemporary conditions.[3]) In practice, the monarch's choice is usually dictated by circumstances. In 1945, Clement Attlee became Prime Minister following his party's overwhelming electoral victory. In 1951, Winston Churchill was chosen after his party won a narrow majority in Parliament at a general election. The choice of Anthony Eden to succeed Churchill in 1955 was simple, for the Conservatives recognized Eden as the heir apparent. In 1957, and again in 1963, there was no clear heir when a new Conservative Prime Minister had to be chosen. In both instances, the Queen remained passive until the Conservative leaders could decide among themselves who would least divide the party. Once this decision was taken within the party, the Queen was given the name of the man to choose.

2 The evolution is traced in J. P. Mackintosh, *op. cit.*

3 See Kingsley Martin, *The Crown and the Establishment* (Harmondsworth: Penguin, 1963) chapters 3, 4. Cf. Herbert Morrison, *op. cit.*, chapter 5.

The Prime Minister's position is sometimes compared to that of the President's, but the comparison is misleading. Unlike the President, the Prime Minister retains office only as long as he can command majority support in Parliament, in his party and in Cabinet. If an issue is made a vote of confidence in the Commons and the result is a vote of no confidence, the Prime Minister must resign. In practice, a Prime Minister need not fear losing a vote because, unlike the President, he is leader of the legislature as well as of the executive, and also the leader of the majority party in Parliament. By combining in his person the three chief political offices, the Prime Minister can make decisions without the need that the President has for constant consultations with Congressional and party leaders.

The Cabinet is important because it is composed of a collection of departmental ministers and because it is superior to them. Decisions made within a department must be supported by the Cabinet, for the Cabinet is held collectively responsible for all the activities of government, in addition to individual ministers being responsible for the work of their departments. The convention of collective responsibility requires all ministers to give public support to the policy of the Cabinet, and to refrain from public criticism of their colleagues. It does not require them to refrain from private criticism, or pressing disagreements in the Cabinet itself. If a minister wishes to make his disagreement with colleagues public, then he must resign from office. Failure to resign makes him responsible along with his colleagues for a policy he may privately oppose.

The existence of a formally united Cabinet ensures a large measure of public harmony, and gives British government the appearance of monolithic unity that American government lacks. But the exigencies of choosing Cabinet ministers ensure that the Cabinet will rarely be all of one mind in private. A Prime Minister, in distributing Cabinet offices, usually includes individuals representing varying factions and tendencies within his parliamentary party, even though they may be known to disagree upon several of the major questions of policy. By doing this, he broadens the support for his government within the party, and increases the size of the pool of talent from which he chooses. In addition, potential critics are publicly silenced, because they become jointly responsible for all that the Cabinet does. Many accept muzzling on some points of policy in return for the prestige and influence that comes from being in charge of a department. However, the policy views and personal ambitions that lead men into the Cabinet can also lead to disputes within Cabinet. For instance, in 1951, Aneurin Bevan, a left-wing Socialist, was frustrated in his ambitions for promotion and in conflict with colleagues on policy; he resigned from the Labour Cabinet and led a violent public attack upon the program of his recent colleagues. The Prime Minister, Clement Attlee, wishing to avoid public controversy, had sought in vain to restrain him from resigning. Bevan was so prominent within the party that he could not easily be threatened with political isolation if he resigned. A resigning minister always runs the risk that his colleagues may find that they can dispense with him. A badly timed resignation thus led to political oblivion for Lord Randolph Churchill, father of Winston Churchill. In many instances, the threat of a minister to resign can lead to his getting concessions from Cabinet colleagues, and the threat is sometimes made for this purpose.

Notwithstanding its central position in government, the Cabinet meets only two or three times a week for a total of six to eight hours. Part of the time is regularly taken up with discussion of parliamentary debates and of foreign affairs. Some items on the agenda will not come before the full Cabinet until after they have been threshed out in the departments, and between affected departments, sometimes in Cabinet committees. In such instances, the full Cabinet is presented with complex background documents and asked to give formal approval to what has been informally agreed upon by the groups most directly affected. In some instances, however, major questions of principle will be involved, and a minister may initiate, or be compelled to listen to, a Cabinet discussion of the work of his department, and cannot begin to draft a policy for later presentation to his colleagues until after they have discussed fully and clearly its general outline, and agreed upon a directive that he must follow. In most instances, decisions are announced by the Prime Minister following his evaluation of the comments of ministers. Discussion is intended to lead to a consensus, and voting is avoided, if at all possible, because it emphasizes differences among men who will then have to unite in publicly endorsing whatever is decided.[4] The Cabinet has a small administrative Secretariat, to assist in coordinating Cabinet activities. But these civil servants are not a large group, nor do they provide the Prime Minister with a staff of advisors comparable in size or variety with that possessed by an American President. In times of crisis, Cabinet meetings cannot keep pace with events, and this gives considerable leeway to the Prime Minister and his closest ministerial associates.

Much of the importance of the Cabinet derives from the fact that its members are simultaneously heads of major administrative departments of state. A few Cabinet members, including the Prime Minister, are usually free from specific departmental responsibilities, and are free to chair interdepartmental committees and handle many *ad hoc* problems. Three-quarters of the twenty or so men who form a Cabinet have large and specific responsibilities for formulating and administering policy in a given subject area, whether it be Foreign Affairs or Agriculture. If a department's work is not of great public concern or involves routine operations, then a minister may be put in charge without being made a member of the Cabinet. Hence, the MP appointed Postmaster-General is a minister of Cabinet rank, but not a Cabinet member.

Individual departments are the administrative instruments through which collective decisions of the Cabinet are most often put into effect. The vastness of the operations of government makes it necessary for large measures of Cabinet authority to be delegated without question or with little supervision to individual ministers. A minister who knows well the work

4 See Herbert Morrison, *op. cit.*, chapters 1-3, for an excellent description of what goes on in Cabinet meetings.

of his department will have a ready answer to questions and criticisms of his colleagues. Within his department, he is un-challenged — as long as his decisions do not result in public controversy, or bring him into conflict with another minister. To a considerable extent, an individual minister's reputation rests upon his skill in handling the work of his own depart-ment. Because of such specialization, from time to time ex-ministers and political scientists can be heard to argue that the Cabinet is not a body suitable for planning broad policies that cut across departmental lines, and coordinating the work of departments, because most of its members are burdened with heavy responsibilities in one problem area. Men such as L. S. Amery have praised the peacetime utility of forming a small Cabinet of about half-a-dozen men charged with gen-eral oversight of government policy. But no Prime Minister has followed this view except in wartime. The majority have held with Herbert Morrison that "a cabinet without depart-mental ministers would be deficient in that day-to-day admin-istrative experience which makes a real contribution to col-lective decisions." [5]

The internal organization of a government department var-ies enormously, depending upon the subjects it is concerned with.[6] The Ministry of Pensions and National Insurance pro-vides a convenient illustration of departmental structure be-cause it is comparatively simple. The head is the Minister, a political appointee who retains his seat in Parliament while serving as a minister. He is assisted by two junior ministers called parliamentary secretaries, also drawn from the majority party in Parliament. In addition, the minister has an unpaid parliamentary private secretary, a junior MP serving as a per-sonal assistant in order to gain experience that may lead to his promotion to the job of parliamentary secretary in another department. (All political appointees shuffle from department to department every few years; very few spend their whole ministerial career dealing with one subject.) The Permanent

[5] *Op. cit.*, p. 34. Cf. L. S. Amery, *op. cit.*, pp. 77ff.

[6] See the list of departments in Appendix B, and W. J. M. Mackenzie and J. W. Grove, *op. cit.*, Part Two.

Secretary is the chief civil-service advisor to the minister, and receives a salary 40 per cent higher than his. By virtue of his ability and detailed knowledge of the department, the Permanent Secretary often influences the administration and formulation of policy. The Ministry of Pensions is divided into a number of functional units, dealing with legal, medical, and other problems; it is also divided into regional units covering the country. Each unit is normally headed by a senior civil servant. In addition, the ministry works with six statutory boards and advisory committees. Some services that directly affect its principal clients, pensioners, are handled by other departments, such as the Ministry of Health. The Ministry of Pensions has about 37,000 employees. The formal responsibility for this department rests upon one Member of Parliament, the minister.

The work of a government department is now so wide-ranging and complex that a single minister cannot be responsible in fact as well as theory for all that is done in his name. But the doctrine of ministerial responsibility still plays an important part in government. A minister is formally responsible for what goes on in his department, he must answer to Parliament for what is done, and he may be regarded as the object of blame for whatever mistakes his subordinates make. This doctrine is meant to apply whether or not the individual minister has personal knowledge of what his subordinates do. Insofar as the admission of individual ministerial error casts blame upon the whole of a Cabinet, a minister at fault may, however, be saved from resigning when he has made a major error, since this action would reflect against the whole government and the governing party.[7]

A by-product of this doctrine is that civil servants are freed from political responsibility for their actions. Their private advice to ministers is not published, for that would detract from the dignified appearance of ministerial responsibility. The efficient relationship may take many forms. A minister

[7] See S. E. Finer, "The Individual Responsibility of Ministers" and Geoffrey Marshall and Graeme Moodie, *Some Problems of the Constitution* (London: Hutchinson, 2nd edition, 1961) pp. 67ff.

may know what he wants to do and simply require civil servants to put into practical legislative and administrative form
policies already decided. Or, a minister may have a desire to
advance himself politically by improving the work of his department, and he may canvass his civil servants for ideas. In
some instances, a minister may have little interest or involvement in his work, and may thrust upon his civil servants the
power to make decisions.

Ministers and civil servants are joined closely together by
complementary needs. The minister has the formal authority
and responsibility for the work of a department; to exercise
this authority intelligently, he needs the advice and assistance
of his civil servants. Civil servants need from their minister
the formal authority to act, and they need political support for
the department in negotiations with civil servants from other
departments, and in pressing departmental policies that are
discussed in Cabinet. In order to carry his views and departmental views in Cabinet, a minister needs information and arguments to be carefully drafted by civil servants. The civil
servants instruct a minister in the intricacies of departmental
activities, just as he is expected to instruct them in the intricacies of party politics and public opinion. As ministers become
experienced in office, they begin to acquire administrative expertise, and in complementary fashion, experienced administrative civil servants acquire expertise in political tactics. A
frequent relationship between a minister and his senior civil
servants is one of an informal exchange of opinions and ideas.

In thinking about departmental policy, both ministers and
civil servants may identify with a wide variety of interested
parties. For instance, a minister may be so impressed by the
value of existing departmental practices and values that he ac-
cepts them wholeheartedly and argues the department's point
of view even when it conflicts with that of his party or Cabinet
colleagues. Reciprocally, a civil servant may closely identify
himself with a particular policy, whether it is a subject of
partisan controversy or controversy between pressure groups.
In departments such as Agriculture or the Board of Trade,
both ministers and civil servants may identify themselves with

the pressure-group clients of these departments, the farmers and businessmen respectively. Civil servants may identify themselves with professional experts outside government, be they economists in the Treasury or traffic engineers in the Ministry of Transport. A variety of such loyalties can exist in addition to the conventional identification of the minister with his party colleagues and the civil servant with his fellow administrators and with the code of conduct of his corps.

These two groups of men work well together because they share a common experience of government and often, a common social background. Both have entered government service as amateurs. They have been subjected to an intensive process of socialization in the norms appropriate to their political roles. Before a civil servant or an MP receives promotion to an important post, he will have been tested for his ability to get along with both ministers and civil servants. Occasionally, an individual minister or civil servant will gain fame in government circles for his ability to break down conventional practices and produce major innovations. But the backbone of British government are the politicians and civil servants capable of adjusting their personal views to take into account the expectations and demands of others in the majority party and in other departments.

So heavy are the strains of high office that nearly all the time of an important official is taken by official duties. Lord Strang has described in detail this strain, when as Permanent Under-Secretary at the Foreign Office he was working up to fourteen hours a day for long periods, though allowing "some easing up on Saturday afternoons and Sundays." [8] This concentration of effort inevitably tends to isolate senior civil servants and ministers from the peripheral public. Occasionally, instances come to public light in which individual rights have been abused for the sake of administrative convenience. Lack of respect for nonbureaucratic values can arise from the isola-

[8] *Home and Abroad* (London: Deutsch, 1956) p. 274. Cf. the genteel prewar pace described in H. E. Dale, *op. cit.*, chapter 2. Note also P. C. Gordon Walker "On Being a Cabinet Minister," *Encounter* (London) No. 31 (1956).

tion of administrators.[9] More important, perhaps, for general policy making, is the tendency for ministers and officials to be isolated from expert criticism and thinking of politically alert persons outside public office. Of particular importance in maintaining an intellectual closed circle is the fact that there is little provision for the introduction of individuals without previous experience as junior ministers or civil servants at the top of departments. In America, by contrast, many government executives bring with them to a job a team of experts and personal friends who provide, within the department, comments very different from those matured by officials inside it. In British government, a minister will have only about three assistants who are drawn from his party in Parliament; these men are junior in the hierarchy.

The departments form the backbone of the machinery of British government, but they are not the only channel for the exercise of governmental authority. Many agencies of government exist without ministerial directors, yet enjoy the authority of Acts of Parliament and the support of the Cabinet. The variety of these agencies in part arises from historical accidents, and in part it represents an accumulation of *ad hoc* decisions made to meet the requirements of particular situations. For instance, the British Broadcasting Corporation is an agency that is free from governmental interference except with regard to the periodic renewal of its broadcasting charter. British Railways, by contrast, is subject to governmental influence at all times, and its work is directly related to that of the Minister of Transport, though British Railways has its own chairman. Agencies that do not have a minister as their chief executive include public corporations, such as the National Coal Board, regulatory bodies such as the Independent Television Authority, professional bodies with recognized public functions, such as the Royal Colleges of Physicians and Surgeons, and advisory bodies such as the National Food Sur-

[9] See especially the *Report of the Committee on Administrative Tribunals and Enquiries* (London: H.M.S.O., Cmnd. 218, 1957) and D. N. Chester, "The Crichel Down Case," *Public Administration* XXXII (Winter, 1954).

vey Committee. Decentralized administrative agencies exist to a varying extent for Scotland and Wales, though usually linked to the Cabinet. (Northern Ireland is part of the United Kingdom but is exceptional in having its own Parliament and Cabinet as well as returning representatives to Westminster.) These agencies enjoy varying degrees of autonomy from the Cabinet. They may resemble government departments, may be subordinated to them, or may act as pressure groups upon them — or do all these things.[10]

Chief among the extra-departmental agencies are local government authorities. In England and Wales these are of two principal types — the 83 county boroughs, which govern larger cities subject only to central government controls, and the 61 county councils, which share local authority powers with subordinate units termed non-county boroughs, urban district councils, rural district councils, and parish councils. London is governed by special institutions, reorganized in 1964. Control of local authority policy is vested in the hands of a local council, consisting of councillors elected by wards, and a number of aldermen chosen by councillors. Usually, elections take place along party lines. In large cities, the size of the council results in many decisions being made by specialized committees. Committee chairmen are unpaid, and much of the actual work of administration is in the hands of administrators appointed primarily on the grounds of merit and experience, rather than patronage.[11]

Unlike American federal government, in the United Kingdom the central government has the formal authority to direct local authorities. This direction exists not only with regard to such national matters as roads, but also in respect to education, town and country planning, and fire and police. Although local authorities are involved in a wide range of ac-

[10] For an idea of the variety of nondepartmental agencies, see *Whitaker's Almanack* (London: Whitaker, 1964) pp. 355-478. Note also "The Growth of Government," *Planning* (London) XXIII:417 (1957).

[11] See, *e.g.*, J. H. Warren, *The English Local Government System* (London: Allen & Unwin, 5th edition, 1957); J. G. Bulpitt, "Party Systems in Local Government," *Political Studies* XI:1 (1963) and the special supplement of *The Economist,* January 30, 1960.

tivities, ranging from antenatal clinics to crematoria, they are often administering and executing policies whose broad lines have been determined by Acts of Parliament or ministerial directives. Furthermore, central-government financial grants are about as large a source of local authority revenue as are the rates, the tax on property and land that is its chief independent source of revenue. The placing of immediate control of education, health, town and country planning, and other services in the hands of local authorities makes their work significant. But the retention, in the hands of the central government, of overriding authority for local-government tasks leaves the central government in a stronger position in dealing with local government than is the case in America.[12]

The complicated structure of British government is often under-emphasized, and great emphasis is given to the position of the Prime Minister, who stands at the apex of a structure that reaches down to the level of parish council and parish pump activities. The Prime Minister, by presiding over the Cabinet, by informal interviews with departmental ministers, and on his own initiative, can intervene in the affairs of any government department, and in extra-departmental agencies. But it is impossible for one man simultaneously to remain abreast of the complexities of foreign affairs, economics, defense, colonial affairs, depressed areas, education, housing, internal security, etc. Without remaining abreast of these policy areas, potential influence cannot be converted into actual influence when major decisions are made in some of these fields. For instance, the then Prime Minister, Harold Macmillan, was in an awkward position after the Profumo scandal because he had delegated his formal responsibility for internal security to others.[13] A Prime Minister, like a President, must carefully ration his time, and choose only a few fields at a time in which he personally intervenes in making policy. Meanwhile, the making of other major decisions must go forward. (One can avoid this conclusion only by adopting a

[12] For an account sympathetic to local-government discretion, see D. N. Chester, *Central and Local Government* (London: Macmillan, 1951).

[13] See *Lord Denning's Report*, Chapter 18.

tautological criterion of a major decision: one made by the Prime Minister on the basis of his own evaluation of a problem.) The extensive extra-departmental duties of the Prime Minister give him added opportunities for enhancing his personal prestige, but they represent additional demands upon his time. Yet only by building up prestige can he dominate his senior colleagues (and potential successors) in the Cabinet. Occasionally, he may fail to do so, as in the case of Ramsay MacDonald, Prime Minister in a Coalition from 1931 to 1935. A Prime Minister may be anything from a clerk to a commanding leader, depending upon his personality, his political preferences, and his position within the party. In appearance he is an autocrat. But no man can rule a nation of 52,000,000 people by himself. In the effective exercise of authority, a Prime Minister is inevitably something less.[14]

The difficulties inherent in a Prime Minister guiding, or even coordinating the major activities of government have increased enormously in the past century because of the growth of the work of government. In 1870, the supply expenditure of the national budget equaled only 4 per cent of the gross national product; in 1961, it was 22 per cent. When all forms of public expenditure are reckoned, the government in 1962 was responsible for 44.4 per cent of the gross national product.[15] This expansion has taken place in conjunction with improvements in transportation, communications, and office equipment that have greatly increased the administrative capacity of central government, but the increase in capacity does not appear to have been proportionate to the increase in burdens.

The widened impact of government has also led to the growth in the number of ministers of Cabinet rank. In this century, new departments such as Education, Labour, Pensions, Transport, Fuel and Power, Aviation, and Commonwealth Relations have been started. The work of established

[14] See Richard Rose, "Complexities of Party Leadership." Cf. Richard Neustadt, *Presidential Power* (New York: Wiley, 1960).

[15] See *Control of Public Expenditure*, p. 6, and Treasury *Bulletin for Industry* (London) No. 167 (October, 1963) pp. 3-4.

departments such as the Treasury and the Foreign Office has greatly expanded. Only a few departments, such as the India Office and Ireland, have disappeared.[16] The greater the number of departments and the more complex their internal organization, the more difficult it is for the Prime Minister, the Cabinet, or even individual department heads, to maintain continuous oversight of policy. For instance, the Foreign Office is for many purposes divided into units dealing with geographical areas, yet the Foreign Office must also deal with problems such as disarmament, which have a global impact that varies from area to area. Any international policy with economic implications concerns not only several units of the Office, but also the Treasury and the Board of Trade. Both intradepartmental and interdepartmental coordination become necessary. So numerous are the groups within the government that require consultation that a former senior minister has referred to the process of gaining clearance as running "the Whitehall obstacle race." [17] By maintaining *status quo* policies, departments avoid the difficulties of running this race — but may turn themselves into obstacles.

Once Cabinet decisions are made, they appear to reflect governmental unanimity and are treated as binding upon administrators and individual ministers. But in the deliberations leading up to Cabinet decisions, individual ministers often find themselves disagreeing with colleagues because of inherent conflicts in the interests of the various departments. Of special importance is the conflict between departments whose proposals involve large-scale expenditure and the Treasury, which has the administrative responsibility for controlling the whole of government expenditure.[18] In contrast to Amer-

16 See D. N. Chester and F. M. G. Willson, *The Organization of British Central Government, 1914-1956* (London: Allen & Unwin, 1957); F. M. G. Willson, "The Organization of British Central Government, 1955-1961," *Public Administration* XL (Summer, 1962).

17 Hugh Dalton, *Call Back Yesterday* (London: Muller, 1953) p. 237. See also W. J. M. Mackenzie, "The Structure of Central Administration" in *British Government Since 1918* (London: Allen & Unwin, 1950).

18 As an introduction, see S. H. Beer, *Treasury Control* (Oxford: Claren-

ican practice, ministers frustrated in their request for Treasury approval of extra expenditure cannot appeal to the legislature to increase their appropriation, for appropriation bills in Parliament must be approved by the Cabinet before they can be debated. The Treasury is aided in controlling expenditure by the existence of interdepartmental conflicts concerning the allocation of scarce economic resources. For instance, the Ministry of Defence takes a large share of the budget, and thus threatens the claims of civilian departments; in turn, it is subject to having these departments gang up to call for cuts in defense expenditure in order to provide for increases in civilian expenditure. Because control of appropriations is so important in making policy, the Treasury's responsibilities make it pre-eminent among the home departments; its prestige in Whitehall is matched only by the Foreign Office. Yet because Treasury control inevitably involves broad questions of policy, the Treasury cannot be allowed to exercise this authority by itself. Much of the most important work of the Cabinet and its committees consists in adjudicating between the competing claims of ministers for limited financial resources, and reviewing Treasury decisions. In 1951, the then Chancellor of the Exchequer, Hugh Gaitskell, succeeded in carrying the Cabinet with him, and Aneurin Bevan resigned because of economies forced on the Ministry of Health. But in 1958, Peter Thorneycroft quit as Conservative Chancellor because he was unable to force economies upon other government departments, and the Prime Minister.

Repeated attempts by British governments to devise peacetime methods of economic planning illustrate just how difficult is the problem of combining broad policy decisions with effective administrative control. At present, economic growth is the target of planners in all parties. This target can most easily be reached if government planners define it cautiously in terms of expected annual increases in production, given

don Press, 1956). Cf. W. J. M. Mackenzie, "The Plowden Report: a translation."

existing institutional arrangements. Setting the target higher involves making assumptions and predictions about future international economic trends, because the British economy is integrally a part of the international economy. Unanticipated shifts in trade or the demand for sterling or for exports can put any plan awry. Not all of these difficulties can be foreseen. As a leading banker in The City said during an investigation into changes in government fiscal policy: "We talked for a long time, and at the end of it all I came to the conclusion that we were beating our head against the wall. We were trying to be too precise. We did not know what was going to happen." [19] The closer the central planning agency is to day-to-day administrative problems, the more readily it can appreciate the detailed problems of planning, and control policy through administration. Yet a Treasury-based planning body loses detachment and time to look ahead. At present, the government has taken planning responsibilities from the Treasury and entrusted them to the National Economic Development Council. The Council can advise the government contrary to certain traditional and economically restrictionist policies of the Treasury.

The checkered history[20] of economic planning by British government illustrates the extent to which the appearance of unanimity, efficiency, and clarity obtained by the fusion of legislative and executive authority in the Cabinet can be belied in fact. To emphasize this is not to deny the fact that decisions within a British Cabinet are far more important than decisions in the American Cabinet. A British Cabinet can be virtually certain that Parliament will accept whatever it decides. But Cabinet decisions are very rarely the result of complete agreement among dozens of men. Nor are they necessarily the result of compromise and bargains, as is much Congressional legislation. Compromise is not inevitable, given the "winner-take-all" convention of collective responsibility, which compels a minister in the minority to vote for the majority's decision. Instead, the decisions of the Cabinet are best de-

19 Testimony of A. D. Marris, *Bank Rate Tribunal*, p. 162.
20 See D. N. Chester and F. M. G. Willson, *op. cit., passim.*

scribed as the outcome of deliberations in which differing combinations of men, departments, and events impose themselves upon the whole membership of the Cabinet. In this process the Prime Minister is pre-eminent, though the complexities of government in relation to the time at his disposal compel him to limit the areas in which he makes his potential influence actual. Furthermore, the process itself is not static but dynamic; the individual, be he Prime Minister or Secretary of State for War, can never be sure when circumstances will combine to upset the equilibrium of the moment and make him a loser rather than a winner in the struggle to command the collective support of the Cabinet.

PARLIAMENT

In its dignified aspect, Parliament can be extremely impressive. The House of Commons and the House of Lords both meet inside the Palace of Westminster, a massive Victorian Gothic building that is a landmark of central London, and a familiar symbol throughout the Commonwealth. Parts of the building date back to the 11th century, and on this site have taken place many dramatic scenes in the nation's history. Some Officers of the House emphasize its dignity by wearing elaborate formal dress, including wigs, even today. In spite of this dignity, the actual conduct of parliamentary business emphasizes informality, within a traditional, formal framework. A visitor to the House of Commons can see resting on the center table, not only the Royal Mace, a symbol of authority, but also the feet of many Cabinet ministers, who slump down on the front benches, while listening to debates, and put their feet up to rest better. During the course of debate, members may shout out interjections, heckle the MP, or break into fits of laughter or loud protest.

In terms of power, Parliament is not so impressive, because its role in policy making is strictly limited. The Cabinet is effectively in control of its proceedings. The choice of topics to be debated and the timing of the debates is in the hands of the Cabinet; by convention, the Leader of the Opposition is also allowed to fix topics for debate on a limited number of days. Thus the Prime Minister, unlike an American President, can always be sure that any proposal his government puts forward will be promptly voted upon in Parliament, and voted on in the form desired by the executive, for it handles most of the drafting of legislation and also controls amendments. Furthermore, the Cabinet enjoys the powers of the purse. In England, as in America, the executive annually prepares a budget concerning government income and expenditure, and submits it to the legislature. In America, the budget must run the gauntlet of Congressional committees, which can alter it and reject appropriations considered important by the executive. In England, the budget prepared by the executive is debated at length in Parliament, but it is not altered in this process, for votes in the House of Commons are almost always foregone conclusions. Party discipline ensures the subordination of MPs in the majority party to party leaders — and party leaders gather in the Cabinet.

The strength of party discipline in the House of Commons is very great. Not since 1940 has a Cabinet collapsed because of a setback in a House of Commons vote. Even then, the governing party was not defeated; its margin of victory fell from more than 200 to 81, which was regarded as tantamount to defeat. This setback occurred during a wartime crisis. Since the Second World War, there have been many major crises of confidence in the government, but in each instance, Labour and then Conservative cabinets have succeeded in carrying into the division lobbies nearly all their party members — including many who privately and publicly opposed the policy causing the vote of confidence. Party discipline is so strong because, for all practical purposes, there are only two parties in the House of Commons, and the difference between the Labour and Conservative parties is such that dissidents in the governing party, no matter how dissatisfied they are with their leaders in Cabinet, are not so dissatisfied that they would act so as to put the Opposition in office and split their own party. Conversely, in times of crisis Cabinets can be repudiated by the House of Commons, but when that happens, as in the debate over Ireland in 1886, the controversy over directing the

First World War in 1916, and the economic crisis of 1931, parties have split.[21]

Although the majority party controls voting, it does not monopolize the use of parliamentary time. A typical House of Commons day proceeds as follows. At 2:30 P.M. the House assembles for prayers and deals with routine, minor matters. By 2:45 P.M. ministers are answering questions put, on short notice, by MPs of both parties; this continues until 3:30 P.M. At this point, ministers, opposition leaders, or backbenchers may raise exceptional and often urgent items for brief discussion. For instance, the Prime Minister may make a statement concerning an international crisis, and may answer questions concerning his statement. Usually, by 3:45 P.M. the House is dealing with its ordinary business — discussing pending legislation or debating general policy questions. At 10 P.M. major debate ends, unless the rules are suspended, or a debate is continued for a second day. The last half hour of each parliamentary day is reserved for an individual back-bencher to air a grievance, and receive a reply from a junior minister.

In the course of a parliamentary year, about half of the days are spent in the discussion of government business, a quarter in discussions initiated by the Opposition, about a sixth in private members' business, and the rest in a miscellaneous variety of proceedings.[22] The Opposition time is spent in criticizing government policy. Whatever the cumulative impact of such criticism upon the electorate and the governing party, the immediate result is certain — this criticism will not be endorsed in a parliamentary vote. Private members have the right to initiate legislation and to initiate debates on policy questions, but private members can only hope to succeed

---

21 See Richard Rose, "Parties, Tendencies and Factions in Britain," and Leslie Lipson, *op. cit.*

22 See *Sir Thomas Erskine May's Treatise on the Law, Privileges, Proceedings and Usage of Parliament* (London: Butterworth, 16th edition, 1957) pp. 312-315, and Eric Taylor, *The House of Commons at Work* (Harmondsworth: Penguin, 1951) chapter 3. The former book is the definitive description of parliamentary procedure, and the latter an excellent introduction. Note also Sir Ivor Jennings, *Parliament* (Cambridge: University Press, 2nd edition, 1957).

when their motions and bills deal with nonparty matters of little general significance. If an individual member raises a general point, it inevitably involves existing government policy, and a private member cannot change this policy without government approval.[23] In that half of the parliamentary calendar directly controlled by the government, nearly all the major legislation of the government is discussed and approved.

The procedure of the House of Commons for enacting legislation ensures that the government of the day must submit any legislation to a lengthy scrutiny, even though Parliament cannot block legislation. Prior to its introduction in Parliament, the principles and details of a bill will have been thoroughly discussed in the relevant government department, and with pressure groups and other interested parties. Furthermore, the relative importance of the bill will have been assessed by the Cabinet, in deciding whether it is to have a high priority, or whether it may be delayed for a year or two until time can be found for it in a usually crowded legislative calendar. When the minister first announces the bill to the House, he does so very briefly, without debate, in what is called the first reading.[24] The bill is then published and amendments are considered. The bill next comes before the House for a general debate on the principles, initiated by the minister in charge, and replied to by a leading Opposition figure. This is called the second reading of a bill, and is the point at which questions of principle are thrashed out. Then the bill goes to a committee for discussion about details, and possible amendments. Major bills are usually debated by the Committee of the Whole House (the same 630 MPs meeting under slightly different rules of procedure); lesser legislation, by standing committees containing only a fraction of the

23 See P. G. Richards, *op. cit.*, chapter 10, and J. B. Cristoph, *op. cit.*

24 In addition to public bills introduced by ministers, a few public bills are introduced by back-bench MPs, and local, private, and personal bills can also be introduced on behalf of private persons, companies, and corporations. Only government public bills are discussed above. See Eric Taylor, *op. cit.*, pp. 131ff., 226ff.

House. These committees do not specialize in particular topics, as do Congressional committees, and party discipline is effective there. If a bill has been to a standing committee, then the House debates the report containing its decisions. If a bill has already been debated by the Committee of the Whole House, this is not necessary. The Report stage is the last one at which amendments of substance can be added in a bill's progress through the House of Commons. There follows a third reading debate, and, once carried, the bill is sent to the House of Lords. It goes through similar stages in the Lords, and if passed there becomes an Act of Parliament. If amended, it returns to the Commons, where the amendments are quickly considered. In practice, Conservative governments are little troubled by the Lords because they enjoy a *de facto* majority there. If the Lords refuse to pass a bill certified by the impartial Speaker of the House of Commons as a money bill, it becomes a law within a month after it leaves the Commons, whether or not the Lords assent. Less urgent but often more important bills can be enacted into law if approved by the Commons after the Lords reject them twice in successive annual sessions. The House of Lords thus retains the power to delay the passage of a bill, but not to defeat it outright. A bill does not finally become law until it receives the royal assent, but that is now a mere formality. A major piece of government legislation can be sure of approval by Parliament within twelve months of its introduction, or slightly less. But the process of securing approval from Parliament is a lengthy and tiring one, involving the discussion and justification of many matters of technical detail and of principle. Hence, ministers do not seek to introduce major legislation lightly, because of the effort involved in taking a bill through all these stages.

The business of carrying government legislation through Parliament is the responsibility of about 100 ministers and junior ministers in the majority party. More than three-quarters of MPs are back-benchers, sitting behind the ministers on the majority side, and behind the potential ministers, the "shadow" Cabinet, on the minority side. Traditionally, the position of a back-bench MP was not considered a full-time job, but rather an honor that gentlemen should have. Even today, the MP's salary of £1750 a year is not sufficient to support him and his family without private means, a pressure-group subsidy, or a part-time job. (Some MPs argue that part-time employment is helpful in keeping an MP in touch with affairs outside politics.) A back-bench MP has no office, no secretary, no telephone, no research assistants, and must pay his own postage. The absence of offices makes it less easy for constituents to contact their members, and some MPs argue that they should be spared the task of running errands for constituents. The absence of research assistants means that MPs cannot rely upon ghost writers to give their speeches an air of authority; they must do their own research. The provision of many dining rooms and smoking rooms gives the Palace of Westminster the atmosphere of a club; MPs like to boast it is the finest club in Europe. Life in Parliament, as in a London club or an Oxbridge common room, is intended to create strong group loyalties while permitting individual idiosyncrasies to be expressed. It also tends to isolate members of a select group from the general public, in a way that a Congressman's office does not.[25]

As an MP, a politician has a recognized role and status in policy making that is not evident in considering public debates on legislation. Part of the reason is that much of the work of government does not require legislation, as in the making of foreign policy. When policy rests upon the judgment of ministers, MPs can hope to influence this judgment more readily, though less measurably, than they can influence legislation. The same conditions apply to the formulation of ministerial judgments concerning the discretionary use of administrative powers granted by existing legislation. Furthermore, the MP's standing gives him the right to participate in many private

---

25 Cf. P. G. Richards, *op. cit.;* Roland Young, *The British Parliament* (London: Faber, 1962); Earl (Clement) Attlee, "The Role of the Member of Parliament," *Fabian Journal* (London) No. 26 (November, 1958); Robert E. Dowse, *op. cit.*

deliberations that take place on the periphery of the government.

The customary and often the most efficient means by which a back-bencher can exercise influence is by private lobbying in advance of public debates. The intimate social arrangements of the Palace of Westminster facilitate informal contacts between ministers and back-benchers over a drink or a meal. Because ministers are often difficult to approach, every minister has at least one parliamentary private secretary, a junior MP whose job it is to collect views and grievances about departmental policy from back-benchers. Both parliamentary parties have specialist committees that meet privately. Ministers usually seek to keep on good terms with their members in order to gauge party sentiment about proposals from civil servants, and to avoid public controversy. Because these informal committees have none of the powers of Congressional committees, ministers can be relaxed in dealings with them. Occasionally, as in the introduction of commercial television, such a committee may instigate a major piece of legislation.[26] Back-bench MPs dissatisfied with party leaders may raise their views privately at periodic meetings of the parliamentary members of their party. On matters of great importance, the Parliamentary Labour Party first votes privately on how its members will vote publicly in the House of Commons. In 1954, for instance, the private party meeting voted 111 to 109 not to oppose German rearmament, and this narrow majority was effective in determining the votes of nearly all the party's members on the floor of the House. At private Conservative party meetings, votes are rarely taken — but the mood of the back-benchers is carefully noted by the leaders, and in times of crisis this mood may be decisive.[27] The party whips provide additional channels of communication between back-benchers and ministers. The whips are responsible for issuing instructions to MPs as to what the party line is. But the party line is usually not fixed by

[26] See H. H. Wilson, *op. cit.* Cf. Hugh Dalton, *High Tide and After* (London: Muller, 1962) pp. 22ff.; P. G. Richards, *op. cit.*, pp. 95-107.

[27] See Leslie Hunter, *op. cit.*, p. 74; R. T. McKenzie, *British Political Parties*, chapter 3.

parliamentary party leaders until they have gained some idea of back-bench views by means of a feedback of information through the whips.

Public debates in Parliament complement private discussion; they do not substitute for them. In private discussions, a back-bencher dissatisfied with a minister's policy may threaten to attack him publicly, unless an alteration is made in policy. If refused satisfaction, he can then, at a minimum, make a nuisance of himself on the floor of the House — though if he is only pursuing a vendetta, he is likely to damage himself more than the minister. A minister who often occasions attacks from back-benchers, and who fails to answer criticisms convincingly, may find himself dropped from the Cabinet. Furthermore, if a back-bench MP can in public debate make a startling disclosure, or give good grounds to believe he has uncovered an urgent and serious public problem, a minister will usually be compelled to give detailed consideration to the MP's statement, even if not to the satisfaction of the latter. Ministers can use parliamentary debate as a sounding board for opinion, before committing themselves on a policy question. By taking views without commitment, potential sources of criticism can be evaluated, and critics may be conciliated if necessary. In the committee stage of a bill, a minister may decide to accept some amendments to a major piece of legislation, if he judges from debate that this will make the bill work better and significantly diminish opposition. However, if a minister is publicly challenged on a matter of principle, then both he and his challengers know that he cannot back down without loss of face, and that he need not back down because of ministerial control over parliamentary votes.

In exercising oversight on administration, MPs again combine private with public communication. MPs, sometimes on behalf of an aggrieved constituent or a pressure group, can call to the attention of a minister decisions, usually made by civil servants enjoying delegated authority, which seem anomalous, unfair, or unreasonable. These queries from back-benchers are given special attention within the minister's private office, and the grounds of the decision under question are carefully reviewed.

If the MP is not satisfied with the results of this review, he can then raise the issue at question time in the House of Commons, or at the end-of-the-day adjournment debate. The knowledge that dissatisfaction can be made public affects ministerial decisions. Of course, the minister can always ride out a brief storm at question time or in an adjournment debate if he chooses. Thus, the threat of a parliamentary question may be more effective in influencing administration than the asking of a question, which may be a sign that the asker has been privately rebuffed by a minister.[28]

By the use of committees, the House of Commons is able to strengthen its oversight of administration. The Standing Committees consider the detailed clauses of new legislation thoroughly and their particular administrative implications. Because the Standing Committees meet without publicity and without the power of delaying or frustrating pending legislation, MPs have a strong incentive to concentrate upon administrative details, and save criticisms on principle for the second reading and final debates in the full House. Select Committees have specific terms of reference relating to particular aspects of government, such as Estimates, Public Accounts, Nationalized Industries, and Statutory Instruments. (In addition, Select Committees can be established to investigate and report upon unusual affairs that concern the working of the House itself.) The committees respectively scrutinize selected categories of public expenditure, review the national accounts, review the work of nationalized industries, and examine the administrative regulations made by departments with broad legislative authorization. They may make a point of questioning ministers and civil servants, and can examine the detailed workings of selected aspects of government. But there are also narrow limits set on the influence of such committees. The Select Committee on the Estimates can be effective in revealing administrative inefficiency in preparing an estimate of a department's expenditure. But it will dissipate its potential influence if it broadens its criticism to attack policies that have them-

[28] On parliamentary questions generally, see D. N. Chester and N. Bowring, *op. cit.*, especially chapters 9-11.

selves resulted in wasted expenditure since this would question the government's confidence, a question with a predetermined answer.

Ministers and aspiring ministers cannot treat back-benchers cavalierly since the vote of confidence that they occasionally require at a private party meeting or on the floor of the House is a vote of personal trust in men, as much as it is of trust in policies. Most back-benchers cannot hope to know the details of policy as well as a departmental minister does. A minister with a reputation for ability, integrity, and sincerity can appeal for justification on these grounds. The disclosure that the Secretary of State for War, John Profumo, had lied in a statement to the House in March, 1963 greatly shocked MPs because they are accustomed to trust ministers when they give their word of honor, and Profumo had, atypically, betrayed this trust. The trust is founded upon the intimate knowledge of men that MPs can develop by close association over a period of years or decades in the clublike atmosphere of the Commons. Through the years, back-benchers and ministers weigh up each other, and failures can be winnowed out and men with good reputations promoted. Both the Cabinet and the Commons must weigh men as well as measures. For the Commons, the task of assessing the qualities of potential Cabinet ministers is probably as important as assessing the legislation they introduce.

The House of Lords, composed primarily of hereditary peers of the realm, is an historical anachronism. In form, it is the second chamber of Parliament. In practice, it is an institution that facilitates the making of policy, and survives because it has not interfered sufficiently strenuously in the past forty years to make its opponents wish to take the trouble to abolish it. Occasionally the Lords may delay a Labour bill, as in the case of the Attlee government's proposal to nationalize steel; it may even defeat a bill of a nonparty character, such as the 1956 bill proposing the abolition of the death penalty. Under the terms of the Parliament Acts of 1911 and 1949, however, a bill may become law without the approval of the Lords if twice approved by the Commons with a year intervening between its first and second endorsement. In addition to this delaying power, the Lords has the power to amend legislation, and spokesmen of both parties have emphasized the utility of using the Lords to revise bills that contain weaknesses not always noticed as such in the course of drafting, or pushing through the Commons. Minor bills can originate in the Lords, thus relieving pressures on the House of Commons timetable. The Lords hold occasional debates on broad public issues, ranging from foreign affairs to the publication of *Lady Chatterley's Lover.*

Although the membership of the Lords is primarily hereditary, many hereditary peers never attend. Much of the everyday work is done by a few dozen peers, many of whom had been active in the House of Commons before receiving a peerage. Because of the Lords' hereditary basis, the Conservative Party enjoys a permanent majority. Under the Life Peerages Act of 1958, nonhereditary peerages have been conferred on several dozen prominent men and women, but their membership has yet to affect the activities of the Lords. (Certain bishops and judges also enjoy nonhereditary positions in the Lords.) In 1963 the passage of a bill allowing peers to renounce their titles immediately and dramatically affected the Conservative Party, by making the 14th Earl of Home eligible to enter the House of Commons and assume the leadership of the Conservative Party. At present, the hereditary bias in the Lords helps it to survive, by keeping it politically weak. Hereditary peers do not wish to jeopardize their titles and position by precipitating a head-on clash with a government, particularly a Labour government. The Labour Party, though opposed to hereditary privileges on principle, has never agreed upon a formula for reforming the Lords, and prefers to ignore it as much as possible.[29]

The influence of Parliament upon the executive is both intermittent and intangible; it cannot be ignored completely, but it can easily be overemphasized — not least by parliamentarians.[30] The greater power of the executive means that, if

[29] See P. A. Bromhead, *op. cit.*, and Herbert Morrison, *op. cit.*, chapter 9.

[30] Cf. the careful discussion of parliamentary influence on African affairs by Roland Young, *op. cit.*, pp. 189-207.

Cabinet and civil service can fix a plan of action, it can be carried out free from legislative interference and restraint. The efficiency thought to result from a lack of strong legislative restraints is positively valued in England.[31]

INFORMAL PROCESSES

The formal institutions of British government do not operate in a vacuum. But many studies of these institutions still follow in the legalistic tradition of A. V. Dicey. The institutions of government are regarded as sufficient as well as supreme, as in Wilfrid Harrison's statement: "If a Cabinet has a stable House of Commons majority, there are no formal limits to its power." [32] The extent to which the formal institutions of government are actually all-powerful can only be determined by examining the informal aspects of policy making. Particularly important in analyzing the policy process (the sum of the interactions between formal institutions and informal ones) are the actors, chief areas of policy, methods of deliberation, strategies, and policy outcomes.

The range of actors involved in the policy process is varied. Some who assume national political roles, such as the spokesmen for the National Sheep Breeders of Great Britain, are concerned with a narrow range of questions, and are involved in politics only intermittently, as a by-product of their business concerns. Others, such as leading trade unionists, businessmen, heads of semi-autonomous government agencies, and technical experts, frequently are involved with a wide range of policy questions. Parliament, the Cabinet, and the civil service constitute a pool of manpower more or less continually involved in policy making. Thus, policy making involves men who are commonly described as politicians, and those who would abjure the description — though not avoiding attempts to exercise political influence.

[31] For an excellent though atypical case study comparing the workings of central government in Britain and America, see J. Roland Pennock, *op. cit.*

[32] *Op. cit.* p. 36. See also pp. 26ff., and A. V. Dicey, *The Law of the Constitution* (London: Macmillan, 9th edition, 1952) pp. 39ff.

The areas of policy with which the political system is concerned are numberless. Five broad areas may be singled out for special emphasis, because of their impact upon the lives of Englishmen and upon the system: foreign affairs, defense, colonial affairs, economics, and social welfare. These problem areas are similar to those important in America, save that in America federal-state relationships, especially those involving racial integration, are more important than colonial problems.

A comparison of Acts of Parliament with contemporary problems in these policy areas illustrates the extent to which policy is not made by Cabinet decisions expressed formally in Acts of Parliament. In the parliamentary year October 31, 1961 to October 25, 1962 parliamentary legislation concerned such things as modifications in rates and methods of taxation, export guarantees, independence for various colonies, road safety, the restriction of immigration from the Commonwealth, and the method of numbering and citing Acts of Parliament.[33] But legislative acts could not cope with what the British government in the year 1961-62 regarded as among its major and immediate policy problems — the Berlin crisis, negotiations to enter the European Common Market, the Cuban crisis, disarmament and defense re-equipment, native unrest in Central Africa, economic growth, wage restraint, inflation, and urban congestion. A century ago, when the expectations of government embodied in the cultural norms were much narrower; an Act of Parliament extending the right to vote could be the primary policy problem of the year. But today, legislative action is largely peripheral to much of the work of government. The policies that a Cabinet frames — in economics and foreign affairs especially — are not legal statutes, but rather statements of intentions that the government will strive to realize (though often failing) through the work of ministers and civil servants in the Treasury, the Foreign Office, and related departments. Parliament debates the expressions of intent and the degree of success government officials have in realizing their intentions.

A major limitation upon the power of British government

[33] For a full list, see *Notes on Current Politics* (London) November 19, 1962, pp. 27-36.

is the fact that most of the major policy areas involve international problems; many key actors are not British. Foreign
affairs is by definition concerned with dealings between formally
sovereign states. At the United Nations, the United Kingdom
is only one among more than one-hundred nations; in NATO,
it is only one among more than a dozen. Defense policy is also
by definition concerned with relationships between nations.
The changes in military technology since the development of
missiles and atomic weapons means that the country cannot
defend itself without allies; its defense policy must be worked
out in alliance with other nations. In colonial affairs the
British government may still claim legal authority over a few
Afro-Asian nations. But it has proven incapable of effectively
maintaining this authority against native political groups de-
manding independence. A measure such as the Uganda Independence Act is not an expression of British power, but a
recognition of the power of nationalist movements. In economic policy, a nation that needs to import and export to eat
is necessarily dependent upon international trade with other
sovereign states. Only in the area of social welfare is the
British government free from much direct concern with international actors — though, indirectly, welfare policy may be influenced by the need to coordinate it with actions in the other
four major areas.

As the focus of attention is shifted from policy area to
policy area, and even within policy areas, the government's
relationships with other actors in the policy process emerges
as a variable. The authority of government is not constant
across all the policy areas. *Hierarchical* deliberation occurs
when individuals confront the government with demands that
the government can accept or reject by unilateral action. This
is the case when a convicted murderer seeks a reprieve from the
Home Secretary, or an aggrieved householder seeks an adjustment in property taxes or local zoning regulations. In deliberating upon many major policy problems, the government is
involved in *bargaining*. It cannot unilaterally determine and
enforce its preferences; its officials recognize that they need the
assent and cooperation of others in order to obtain a more or

less mutually satisfactory outcome. For instance, the development of government housing policy takes place through bargaining between representatives of the Ministry of Housing and Local Government, building societies that lend money on mortgages, contractors and building suppliers, building-trade unions, local-government authorities, and perhaps even homeowners and prospective purchasers and renters. Around the bargaining table, there is no hierarchy with government at the apex; there are only semiautonomous groups, each capable of delaying, vetoing, or complicating the activities of other groups — and in turn, subject to their restrictive actions, too. Sometimes deliberations take place in which the British government is primarily *registering* the consequences of activities that it has not controlled. For instance, it may register the claims of a group of colonial nationalists for independence by an Act of Parliament renouncing formal sovereignty. In some economic situations, the government may be denied a bargaining status and may simply have to register market decisions; for instance, in 1962 the government was forced to register a large wage increase awarded its own civil servants by an arbitration tribunal, even though this action was in contradiction to its announced policy on restraining wages.[34] *Dignified* deliberations convey the appearance of policy being made or administered, but such deliberations are not efficient. For instance, many activities in foreign affairs, such as disarmament conferences and meetings of heads of state seem to have little tangible effect. Only insofar as the appearance of activity is itself important in Cold-War propaganda can such deliberations be said to have instrumental value. In domestic policy, the deliberations of Lord Shawcross's Royal Commission on the Press in 1961-1962 were dignified, involving neither hierarchical influence nor bargaining. The Commission served primarily to give the appearance of government activity in response to a temporary parliamentary concern with monopolistic tendencies in the press. *Popular* deliberation is literally

[34] See reports in *The Guardian,* "Government Regrets Size of Pay Award," June 7, 1962; and also "Dockers Bury the Wages Policy," May 5, 1962.

impossible in a country the size of England; representatives must be used by members of the peripheral public. Occasionally, deliberations take place in circumstances in which awareness of popular preferences (whether or not correctly perceived) dominate the situation. An instance is the decision of the Conservative government to introduce restrictions on Commonwealth immigration in 1961, because it perceived a popular demand to restrict the immigration of colored Commonwealth subjects. *Avoidance* of deliberation can itself have an impact upon public policy. A classic instance is the British government's calculated avoidance of negotiations with Soviet Russia in the 1930s; this avoidance greatly altered the balance of power in Europe. The methods of deliberation outlined above do not exist exclusive of one another. Different methods may be employed consecutively or simultaneously in dealing with a policy area or a political group.

The strategies employed by those seeking to influence policy vary enormously, depending upon the policy area, the position of the actor in the political system, and the methods of deliberation most accessible and favorable to the actor's aims. A group seeking to influence an aspect of foreign policy must accept that any strategy will probably have a low return because of the limited influence of Her Majesty's government upon world affairs. A group seeking to influence an aspect of welfare policy, such as care for retarded children, may achieve a high degree of success because such policy is much more subject to government influence. Groups in the policy process have very different resources to command in pursuing their strategies of influence. For instance, the Campaign for Nuclear Disarmament began as an organization of local activists. Its strategy necessarily involved popular deliberations, even though decisions on national defense are made hierarchically, by the government or by bargaining with allies in NATO. Only in its second phase did the Campaign turn to attempts to capture the Labour Party for its policy, and thus have a chance to control the hierarchically powerful government. It could only do this when the local activists in the Campaign had been augmented by national politicians.

The product of policy deliberations is usually termed a decision. The word "outcome" is perhaps more apt in emphasizing the extent to which the result of policy deliberations is not a particular conclusion determined by a particular group of men at a specified time (that is, a decision). Outcomes may be very different from the intentions expressed in particular decisions, as in the inflationary outcome of various anti-inflation economic policies decided upon since 1945. Furthermore, outcomes are neither clear-cut nor stable. Some outcomes do represent relatively clear-cut once-for-all settlements, such as franchise reform, or the grant of independence to India. But many outcomes are unstable because they involve agreement upon both means and ends. For instance, a policy such as high interest rates may be adopted as a means to the end of stable economic growth. After it has been in operation for a year, growth may not occur. Then an issue arises as to whether high interest rates should be abandoned as inappropriate to a larger end, or whether a high interest rate is in fact an end in itself. Those involved may disagree as to whether a policy is instrumental, to be revised or abandoned as soon as it fails to prove useful, or an ideological policy, which cannot be abandoned because it is expressive of an integrated set of principles believed to be correct, and emotionally appealing.

Making policy is a continuing and dynamic process. In four of the five major policy areas — foreign affairs, defense, colonial policy, and economics — major changes can arise with unexpected and uncontrollable abruptness. In many such situations, difficulties in these areas interact, upsetting momentarily stable arrangements. A classic instance is the crisis that occurred in 1950-51, following the outbreak of the Korean War and American pressure upon England to increase defense expenditure. For months, ministers were abruptly confronted with crises for which they were unprepared — in Korea, in the United Nations, in the Iranian oil fields, in the international commodity market, in exports, in military reorganization, in budgetary priorities, and in the Cabinet itself.[35]

35 See especially Joan Mitchell, *Crisis in Britain, 1951* (London: Secker & Warburg, 1963).

Although the policy process is fluid, one conclusion stands out: In major policy areas Her Majesty's government is rarely able to exercise formal hierarchical power. In foreign affairs, the British government can see a major policy intention such as entry into the European Common Market frustrated by the French government. In economics, establishment of the National Economic Development Council gives overt recognition to the extent to which government economic policy is made by bargaining with industry and trade unions. Even in a welfare area such as higher education, the government has found policy determined by the unanticipated increase in the number of young persons anxious and qualified to enter universities.

It would, however, be false to deduce from these facts that the power of British government is in decline. It is greater today than it was 50 or 150 years ago. However, the involvement of government in an increasing number of aspects of society has led to the diminution of its *independent* power; its power is diffused and shared. In many policy areas the actions of government are conditional upon the agreement and actions of others. There remains a gap between the expectations of those who make demands upon government, and the ability of the government to satisfy these demands. In failing to meet all the demands made upon it, British government is hardly unique.

COMPOSITE GOVERNMENT

A century ago Bagehot described British government as *simple* — "the ultimate power upon all questions is in the hands of the same persons." By contrast, he termed American government *composite* — "the supreme power is divided between many bodies and functionaries." [36] Today, the formal institutions of British government are still simple, concentrating power in the leaders of the majority party assembled in the Cabinet. But this power is not ultimate for many questions. The informal political institutions involved in the policy

[36] *Op. cit.*, p. 201. See also the comparison of monocratic and collegial systems of authority in Max Weber, *op. cit.*, Part Three.

process are so numerous and so strong that the supreme power is, in fact, divided. The processes of policy are plural, and government is a composite of social and political institutions.

The extent to which power is dispersed, even in the government's special field of legislation, is annually demonstrated in *The Times* review of pending parliamentary legislation. This review not only describes pending bills, but also indicates briefly the group or groups in the political system particularly concerned with authorship. In 1963, the review listed twenty-two pending bills. In sixteen cases, the work of government departments was explicitly referred to in describing the genesis of the bills. In eight cases, the recommendations of committees appointed to consider a public problem and recommend legislation were referred to. These committees are an important arena for pressure-group consultation; in two additional instances, pressure groups were mentioned as important without formal committees having been established.[37] In five instances, specific reference was made to the central government negotiating with local government authorities or semiautonomous governmental agencies, and in four instances, bills followed discussions with foreign and Commonwealth nations. In only one instance, a bill concerning major airports, was specific reference made to pressure from MPs as a direct, rather than indirect influence upon legislation. Such a tabulation is not exhaustive, but it is detailed enough to indicate the extent to which *de facto* policy-making activities are dispersed.

The dispersal of political power is accompanied by frequent consultation between governmental and nongovernmental groups, in spite of the formal centralization of authority in the Cabinet. In the process of consultation, ministers can gauge the extent to which political actors and groups will support or hinder alternative policies, and what policy proposals the groups themselves have to make. Those who are involved in

[37] The article did not attempt to describe all groups involved in considering legislation, only the most significant ones. See *The Times,* September 19, 1963, "Many Bills Compete for Priority in Next Parliamentary Session." Note also similar stories in issues of September 25, 1961, and October 8, 1962.

consultations while a policy is under consideration are subject to strong informal pressures to accept the outcome of deliberations in which they share. These pressures can operate against a government that has established a committee to recommend a policy, as well as upon the committee members and those they represent. Because governmental sanction is necessary to make informal agreements legally valid, ministers retain considerable discretionary power in accepting or rejecting the consensus achieved in consultation. Insofar as consultants and the groups they represent cannot be coerced by government policy decisions, then the limits of discretion are narrow rather than wide.

The formal powers of government are thus shared with consultants and those they represent. Consultancy status is possessed by a heterogeneous mixture of individuals scattered throughout English society. Some — for instance, the chairman of the National Coal Board — combine political and extra-political roles almost equally. Many are only secondarily and intermittently political consultants, by virtue of offices and roles in social organizations. Others are full-time participants in the consultative process, by virtue of elective or appointive posts in government; for this category of individuals, political status is their primary status in the social system. At the fringes of the policy process are individuals who have created their own roles, as opinion leaders or even as cronies of leaders. There are also those who demand consultancy status on the grounds that they represent groups of increasing political importance.

The extent to which consultants have a representative function is an important restraint upon their leeway in politics. Representatives operate within limits fixed by the expectations of those represented. For instance, a trade-union negotiator is expected by his members to bargain for higher wages and better working conditions. If he should go against these expectations, his members could repudiate him by a wildcat strike. Similarly, a spokesman for a presssure group against capital punishment cannot bargain to reduce the number of hangings insofar as members expect him to insist uncom-

promisingly upon the complete abolition of the death penalty.[38] Inasmuch as half the population belong to organizations
that can be at least intermittently active as political pressure
groups, they can claim a small share in shaping expectations in
the area of the group's concern. Furthermore, all citizens have
an infinitesimal share in shaping the expectations of the electorate, expectations that affect policy makers in a wide variety
of policy areas.

The fact remains, however, that the majority of the public
have only a slight involvement in shaping political expectations. (Cf. Chapters IV, V.) The distance in England between
the peripheral public and those in national political roles
is aptly expressed in the linguistic distinction between "Us"
(the governed) and "Them" (the governors). From the perspective of the national politicians, however, perhaps the most
striking feature is the conflict at the national level. Individual politicians are subject to conflicting expectations embodied in the various roles they must simultaneously combine
— as pressure-group spokesmen, as party men, and as men
concerned with the welfare of the nation.[39] There can be
added the conflicts between those whose motives, expectations,
and obligations differ greatly from others in the policy process.
These differences are inherent in the diversity of demands and
groups represented in the political system. Those in national
political roles do not form a closely knit and self-conscious
group; they constitute a wide-ranging variety of individuals,
whose apparent unity is an artifact of being categorized together for convenience in analysis.

Similarly, the apparent cohesiveness of the institutions of
Cabinet government are revealed as something else when
policy processes are closely examined. At some stage in policy
making, the Cabinet normally lends its authority — but the
stage at which it does so, and the weight the Cabinet brings
to bear is a variable, not a constant. The structure of govern-

[38] See James Christoph, *op. cit.,* p. 186.

[39] See the discussion of the role conflicts of a Prime Minister in Richard
Rose, "Complexities of Party Leadership," pp. 265ff.

ment concentrates the powers of government enormously, by placing direction of the majority party, the legislature, and the administrative departments in the hands of a few Cabinet ministers. Yet British government is not dictatorial, or unresponsive to those formally subordinate to it. In fact, some critics charge that it is too responsive to pressures from outside government and from semi-autonomous boards, commissions, and councils which it has created.[40] The institutions of British government are simple, but policy making is composite, because of the countervailing strength in English society of individuals, institutions, and cultural attitudes free from government domination, and because of the extent to which decisions of the government are made in reaction to international trends and events over which it has very limited control.

[40] See Brian Chapman, *British Government Observed* (London: Allen & Unwin, 1963). Cf. S. H. Beer, "Pressure Groups and Parties in Britain," p. 1.

CHAPTER X

Legality and Legitimacy

A free government is that which the people subject to it voluntarily choose.

T HE POLITICAL regime in England has been remarkable for the long history of popular acceptance of its authority. The question then arises: What accounts for this longevity? One answer — the constitution — is difficult to accept because England has no written constitution.[1] Another answer — the rule of law — only begs the question; it does not explain why major laws are readily obeyed in England, in a way not always found in European countries or even in the American South. Max Weber provides perhaps the best guide to an answer: the maintenance of a regime, he writes, depends primarily upon a widespread belief in its legitimacy.[2] When members of a society believe that governmental directives are legitimate, they will obey without coercion. When this legitimacy is doubted, then even coercion can fail, as the British government has found in its postwar conflict with colonial independence

---

[1] For a discussion of what constitutes the Constitution in England, see Sir Ivor Jennings, *The Law and the Constitution* (London: University of London Press, 4th edition, 1952) especially chapters 1-3 and the appendices.

[2] *Op. cit.*, pp. 124ff.

parties. Laws themselves play a part in determining what is believed to be legitimate. But what is legal is not necessarily the same as what is legitimate. Legality can be determined in courtrooms; legitimacy is determined, much less certainly, by reference to the norms of the political culture.

The conflict between what is legal and what is legitimate reached its height in modern England around the time of the First World War. Conflict arose with regard to Ireland, economics, women's rights, and the place of the House of Lords in the regime. The opponents of Home Rule for Ireland believed that no government could legitimately place Protestant Ulster under the rule of the Catholic majority in the rest of Ireland. The Irish Home Rulers believed that they had a legitimate right to defy laws that withheld political independence. The pro-Ulster Conservatives countenanced military disaffection and the arming of Ulstermen to resist Acts of Parliament. Bonar Law, the Conservative leader, said of a pro-Home Rule Liberal government that had won three successive elections, that it was "a Revolutionary Committee which has seized upon despotic power by fraud." [3] In the event, the dispute was settled not by parliamentary legislation or by judicial decision, but by the armed rebellion leading to Irish Home Rule in 1922. Industrial unrest continued unabated until 1926, when the trade unions called an "illegal" General Strike in support of economic demands. It was not until this crisis that it became clear that the trade unions, in the last resort, would give greater weight to legal obligations than to socio-economic demands.

Since 1945, the conflict of law and legitimacy has primarily concerned external affairs. The Labour Party has consistently supported the protests of colonial parties against their legal, but "illegitimate" subordination to the British government. The Labour Party has not encouraged violent resistance to the laws — but violence has at times been used by colonial groups. In a complementary fashion, some Conservatives have challenged the legitimacy of proposed legislation that would sub-

[3] Robert Blake, *The Unknown Prime Minister* (London: Eyre & Spottiswoode, 1955) p. 130.

ordinate white settlers to native authority in British colonial Africa.[4] Since 1961, left-wing opposition to the government's reliance upon nuclear weapons has led a militant group, the Committee of 100, to calculated violations of the law, including breaches of military security. The Committee considers that it is illegitimate for any government to risk national annihilation by maintaining nuclear arms, though the policy is undoubtedly legal.

Weber distinguished a variety of modes by which legitimacy could be associated with a regime. One is tradition. A second is the absolute value attached to goals. A third is the absolute value attached to the use of certain procedural processes, such as elections. Fourthly, he showed how instrumental expectations of satisfaction (or avoidance of discomfort) could give legitimacy to actions. Finally, he emphasized the emotional means by which governments legitimated their activities.[5] His approach leaves open the question of the extent to which laws convey legitimacy. It also involves analytical distinctions that may become blurred in particular situations. For instance, a businessman displeased with a contract may initiate a lawsuit against a company for a mixture of reasons — because it is a traditional way to settle such a dispute; because the courts are valued as dispensing "justice"; because the procedure of court action is valued for itself (even if he loses); because it is emotionally satisfying to attack a company with a lawsuit; and because he expects to gain a settlement to his claim by initiating court action.

MECHANISMS OF LEGITIMATION

In contemporary England, absolute value is often given to certain procedural processes, and these values are expressed in the political culture. Governments expect acceptance of their actions as legitimate — regardless of their substantive effect — so long as they are seen to conform to certain highly valued procedures.

---

[4] See the remarks of Major Sir Henry Legge-Bourke, a Conservative MP, quoted in *The Times,* December 12, 1961.

[5] *Op. cit.,* pp. 115ff.

The debates in the House of Commons during the Suez War illustrate clearly the importance given to procedural forms in legitimating government action. The government had involved the country unexpectedly and with much confusion in a war in the Middle East. The Labour Party doubted the practicality and the morality of the war. In Hugh Gaitskell's words, it saw itself "bound by every constitutional means at our disposal to oppose it. I emphasize the word 'constitutional.' We shall, of course, make no attempt to dissuade anybody from carrying out the orders of the government, but we shall seek, through the influence of public opinion, to bring every pressure to bear upon the government to withdraw from the impossible situation into which they have put us." (1462)[6] In other words, although the country was placed in an "impossible situation," the Opposition leader was not proposing to take any actions that would effectively frustrate the government's course; the constitutional means of the Opposition were insufficient for this purpose.

The dispute between the parties while the country was at war was muffled and restricted by the concern with procedural values. Both parties agreed that the government had the legitimate authority to declare war — and that the Opposition had the legitimate right to oppose military action in Parliament. The dispute about the action thus was not presented as a frontal challenge to the government's claim for obedience.[7] At times of tension, the House of Commons often concerned itself with procedural wrangles, rather than with points of substance. For instance, a sitting of the House of Commons was suspended because of noise and disruption caused by the refusal of the Prime Minister to answer what Labour MPs regarded as a legitimate question. (1620-25, November 1, 1956.) The question was whether or not Britain was at war with

[6] House of Commons *Debates,* Vol. 558, October 31, 1956. The numbers in parentheses refer to columns of this volume.

[7] If the war had continued for months, the Opposition might have been under pressure to challenge by "legitimately illegal" means the claims to obedience of the government. Cf. the situation in the Fourth Republic of France during the protracted Algerian War.

Egypt. A debate following a public demonstration in London turned into a dispute about whether or not mounted policemen or policemen on foot should have been used to control the demonstrators.[8] Disputes about procedural questions arose from the deep conflict between the parties concerning the substantive issue of war or peace. But the disputes were also a means for controlling and dissipating tension, by channeling conflict to areas of relatively little significance — and diverting conflict from substantive questions of great gravity. The muffling of inter-party dispute was the more important because public-opinion surveys showed that the peripheral public was also sharply divided along party lines into groups for and against the war.[9]

The legitimacy of governmental activity outside times of crisis is maintained, in part, by the absolute value given to elections. The ubiquity of elections in many societies — whether they are free or manipulated, meaningful or not — indicates the international significance attached to this procedure. In England, elections do not determine policies, as the doctrine of the election mandate has implied, nor do they necessarily affect the balance of power within the governing party. But they do provide, in efficiently symbolic form, an appearance of popular participation in government, an implied consent to the results of the election and to the decisions of the elected government.[10] For example, Conservatives can hardly be expected to support nationalization on the ground that it is good for the country, or Labour voters to approve of higher charges for welfare services if enacted by a Conservative government. The legitimacy of the regime does not depend upon the acceptance of the desirability or the rationality of particular policies; it depends upon individuals accepting as binding the actions of a government, whether the actions are thought to be wise or not. Sections of the population may

8 *Ibid.*, Vol. 560, Cols. 3-15, November 6, 1956.

9 See the detailed evidence cited in Leon Epstein, "Partisan Foreign Policy: Britain in the Suez Crisis," *World Politics* XII:2 (1960) p. 221.

10 See W. J. M. Mackenzie, "The Export of Electoral Systems," *Political Studies* V:3 (1957) pp. 255-256.

thus differ fundamentally about the policies of government, yet unite in accepting them because they accept the authority of a freely elected majority party. Today, there is no sizable political group in England that would challenge the legitimacy of decision of a freshly elected government.

The legitimacy conveyed by certain procedural features of government does not operate independently of the instrumental efficiency of the government's actions and the material benefits it provides. But a government cannot "bribe" the populace to accept them as legitimate simply by maintaining economic prosperity. The history of British colonial rule, which normally raised standards of living in the colonies, contradicts this thesis. The legitimacy of English government antedates high standards of living for the bulk of the population. It could be argued that it was the rise in living standards during the early part of the Industrial Revolution that caused political unrest, and helped to undermine the legitimacy of the pre-1832 system of oligarchic government.

In this century, a striking feature of English politics, particularly by contrast with Continental nations, from Russia to Spain, is the fact that there was no revolutionary challenge to the government between the wars, in spite of economic difficulties. In this period, the level of unemployment among insured workers ranged as high as 22.2 per cent in 1932, and was usually above 10 per cent. The Communist Party nominated only handfuls of candidates in 1931, 1935, and 1945, and at their "strongest," succeeded in returning only two MPs. The Fascists, led by Sir Oswald Mosley, failed to make any impact at the polls.[11] The Conservative governments in this period feared the possibility of civil disobedience, passing such anti-subversive measures as the Police Act, the Emergency Powers Act, the Official Secrets Act, and the Public Order Act. Despite these fears, the economic unrest of the period was marked, by Continental standards at least, by a surprising

[11] Cf. W. H. Beveridge, *Full Employment in a Free Society* (London: Allen & Unwin, 1944); Henry Pelling, *The British Communist Party* (London: Black, 1958); and Colin Cross, *The Fascists in Britain* (London: Barrie and Rockcliff, 1961).

absence of extremist challenges. Today, in the mixed-economy welfare state, only a dedicated believer in "the coming collapse of capitalism" could conceive of a British government having its legitimacy repudiated for failing to meet the economic expectations of the population. Particular governments and parties are repudiated at general elections and by pressure groups withdrawing support, but that kind of rejection is very different from the repudiation of the legitimacy of a regime.

The legal system — the courts and the police — helps to maintain the legitimacy of government as a by-product of enforcing and adjudicating the law.[12] The courts do not by themselves confer legitimacy upon the existing regime. They assist however, in the maintenance of legitimacy, insofar as the behavior of one part of government reflects credit upon the whole. The legal system is maintained in part by a respect for traditions. The English law courts have altered more in substance than in form through the centuries. A courtroom today is a place where traditional symbols of authority and of respect, such as wigs and robes and ritual procedures, are much in evidence. The procedure is traditional, and individuals may find themselves charged with violating laws up to six centuries old — or pleading in their support cases decided centuries ago. The ritual traditions of the courts, and of the lawyers still grouped in medieval Inns of Court, give an emotional aura to the proceedings of the law.

A tradition of nonviolence in English life; in particular, of refraining from the use of firearms against other persons, greatly facilitates the work of the police. Firearms are not widely available or kept in the home, as in America, where frontier habits are formally upheld by the Constitution. Criminals have a tradition of refusing to carry firearms or practicing crimes that involve their use — though this tradition is less strong than in prewar days. The police still go unarmed in the performance of their duties. Only in exceptional circumstances will a policeman carry a gun. The murder rate, even after allowance is made for population differences, is

[12] For an introduction, see R. M. Jackson, *The Machinery of Justice in England* (Cambridge: University Press, 3rd edition, 1960).

fifteen times lower in England than in the United States. Fewer murders are committed in a typical year in England than in New York or Chicago alone. Law enforcement does not involve the continuous risk of life, nor is there present in society a group of people with a tradition of violence that could lead to illegal activity, whether a lynching, a riot, or a political assassination. An English politician, unlike a French politician at the time of the Algerian war, need not fear for his life, nor need any Englishmen regard a policeman as a man ready to shoot his fellow citizens.

Law enforcement gains support for the regime because it is honest, efficient, and free from corruption and political influence to an extent that is outstanding in any comparative analysis. A survey in 1960 found that 82.7 per cent of Englishmen interviewed had great respect for the police, and only 0.5 per cent said that they had little respect. Individual policemen or lawyers may occasionally be found guilty of corruption, but surveys have established that such dishonest law enforcers are social outcastes and deviants, rather than normal figures in the urban landscape.[13]

Because there is neither a written Constitution nor a convention of judicial review of the constitutionality of government legislation, the position of the legal system in England is fundamentally different from that of America's system. The highest court of appeal, the Law Lords, does not have the power of the United States Supreme Court to declare legislation unconstitutional. The English courts concentrate upon interpreting the meaning of statute law and of precedents derived from common law, rather than upon validating or invalidating laws. The courts may void actions of the government only insofar as they are outside the jurisdiction granted by statutes and precedents. Therefore, opponents of a particu-

---

[13] See *Royal Commission on the Police:* Appendix IV to the Minutes of Evidence (London: H.M.S.O., 1962) especially p. 6. See also G. Almond and S. Verba, *op. cit.*, chapter 4. Cf. the views of Barbara Wootton, *Social Science and Social Pathology* (London: Allen & Unwin, 1959) especially pp. 69-70.

lar government policy cannot challenge the constitutionality of the policy in the courts, as happens in America. As a result, the courts today are rarely involved in the arena of political controversy.[14] On the other hand, the government of the day cannot invoke quasi-priestly symbols to lend legitimacy to its actions. By comparison, an American President pursuing a controversial policy such as racial integration can claim to be acting in the name of the venerated Constitution and the Supreme Court. A British Prime Minister involved in a comparable controversy cannot.

The police and the courts are free from the burden of much "nuisance" enforcement because of the permissive morality underlying legislation. When America and the Scandinavian countries were experimenting with the legal prohibition of alcohol, English police were given the relatively simple task of enforcing the closure of public houses for a specified number of hours each day. The government did not ask the law-enforcement agencies to attempt the impossible — to abolish drinking — but only to reduce the amount of drinking. In 1960, the government legalized off-course cash betting on horse races, and bookmakers now operate openly from neighborhood shops. This legalization has discouraged attempts at police bribery and law violation — by eliminating the need for it. Lotteries on football results and bingo games with cash prizes also operate legally, as do roulette and more expensive forms of gambling. In this way, legal morality and private morality are not brought sharply into conflict, as can sometimes happen in America.

Many hypotheses have been advanced about the place of the monarch in the political system. Bagehot gave the classic description: a monarch is useful in England to disguise the efficient parts of government, to make government intelligible to the ignorant masses, to add to government the sanction of

---

[14] For a historical criticism of the latent political functions of the courts see, *e.g.,* H. J. Laski, *Parliamentary Government in England,* chapter 7. More recently, see Harry Street, *Freedom, the Individual and the Law* (Harmondsworth: Penguin, 1963).

religion and morality, and to provide leadership in society.[15] The monarchy is also the nonpartisan head of state and nominal head of the Commonwealth. The dignified appeal of the monarchy would seem to strengthen the legitimacy of "Her Majesty's" government. But in an area as little documented and as charged with emotion as the monarchy, social scientists should move warily — though some move deferentially or aggressively.[16]

An indication of the ways in which the monarchy assists in legitimating the activities of government is given by responses in life-history interviews to questions about the need for a monarchy. The most significant feature of the responses is that the great majority of those interviewed — 83 of 111 — gave replies that employed emotional criteria; only 28 responded in terms of the instrumental utility or uselessness of the monarchy. Since the majority whose emotions were engaged by the monarchy were in favor of it, it follows that the monarch is of some significance in institutionalizing emotional support for government and segregating it from elective offices. In America, by contrast, the President — as head of state as well as partisan chief executive — must combine both emotional and instrumental qualities of leadership. In England, the Queen may sustain an emotional commitment to the regime, quite independently of the feelings aroused in an individual by the activities of the country's Prime Minister. However, the Queen is not the sole source of emotional attachment to the regime or the political community. An important feature of many responses was that they indicate a shallow, or strictly limited degree of emotional response to the monarchy. The individuals who attract attention by violently assaulting critics of the Queen are *atypical* of the population.

The largest single group of respondents — 45 — said that

15 *Op. cit.*, chapter 2. The authoritative modern discussion of the monarch's role is Dermot Morrah, *The Work of the Queen* (London: Kimber, 1958). For another point of view, see Kingsley Martin, *op. cit.*

16 Cf. Edward Shils and Michael Young, "The Meaning of the Coronation," *Sociological Review* Vol. 1 (1953); Norman Birnbaum, "Monarchs and Sociologists," *ibid.*, Vol. 3 (1955); Lord Altrincham, *et. al., op. cit.;* Henry Fairlie, "On the Monarchy," *Encounter* (No. 97) 1961.

they regarded the monarchy as a means of maintaining traditional ties in society, both ties to the past and ties to each other. Some of these respondents laid special stress upon the Queen as the hierarchical head of the nation. For instance, a widow in Derby explained, "I hold with the royal family. You look to the head of the country. Keeps the country together, having royalty to look up to. They set such a good example." A North of England chemical worker stated, "If there was no monarchy there'd be no England. I look upon the Queen as the head of the family and myself as one of it." Others emphasized the monarchy as a link with past traditions. In the words of a butcher in Stoke, "The monarchy is needed. Always has been one and always should be, because it is tradition to have one." The work of the Queen is so planned as to emphasize these ties. She makes appearances at many different kinds of social functions, and has presented to her representatives of many different social groups — though these representatives usually have, in the words of Dermot Morrah, "a considerable family likeness"; *i.e.,* they are socially conservative middle-class community leaders.[17] With the great advances in the field of mass communications, the Queen is increasingly able to appear before the population as the symbolic head of society.

Few of the respondents — 16 — indicated an interest in the royal family as a family. Typical of this group was an insurance salesman in Liverpool who thought, "We are nominally a Christian country and stand for decency and a good family life. The monarchy give us a lead in this respect." Only three of this group made directly favorable references to Queen Elizabeth and members of her family. In addition, three made direct and unfavorable references to personalities in the royal family. In other words, the official institution is of overwhelming importance; the personal characteristics of members of the current royal family are of little importance in influencing attitudes.

The shallowest form of emotional response came from those twelve who, in Bagehot's words, enjoyed the theatrical function of the monarchy, as exemplified in pageants and proces-

[17] *Op. cit.,* p. 106; see also pp. 69ff., 85ff.

sions, and in ceremonies such as the Trooping the Colour or the Changing of the Guard at Buckingham Palace. Little political importance would seem to be associated with the monarchy in the mind of the Gloucestershire road laborer who responded: "Let's have a Queen by all means. It gives us a lot of pride and something to look forward to, such as royal events and processions."

A small but measurable section of the population (ten in the life-history survey) still confuse the dignified monarchy with the efficient parts of government. For them, the monarchy is not a symbol of government, but rather an important part of its working machinery, emotionally invested with the power to provide restraints against various malevolent social forces. For instance, a Liverpool baker felt: "I'm against handing power to one man. In other countries they'd be better off if they had a King or Queen instead of one man power, which is all dictatorship is." A Glasgow cinema operator declared: "If you hadn't the monarchy, those businessmen and influential people would do what they like with you."

Of those who regarded the monarchy primarily from a pragmatic, rather than an emotional viewpoint, 17 favored the institution and 11 opposed. The unemotional respondents in favor of the monarchy referred to the need for a head of state or a symbol of government. In the words of a housewife in Leeds: "You've got to have somebody at the head. It might as well be her." The 11 who objected to the monarchy on general grounds were objecting to the institution, not the family. This point was made explicit by a housewife in the Potteries, who said: "I don't think there is any need for them. They are outdated and a waste of money. I have nothing against them personally."

Given the present gaps in our knowledge, it is impossible to explain fully the means by which the political regime in England maintains its legitimacy. The foregoing can only serve as an exploration of several diverse mechanisms for legitimation. The very diversity of mechanisms itself seems to be an advantage, providing something for nearly everybody. A political radical may regard the actions of government as legitimate insofar as the government is chosen by the electorate; simultaneously, a traditionally minded Englishman may regard the government as rightfully exercising authority because it is an agent of Her Majesty the Queen.

CHAPTER XI

Continuities and Change

*It is needful to keep the ancient show while we secretly in-
terpolate the new reality.*

IN SPITE OF the great world-wide political changes of this
century, politics in England today reflects many continuities with the past. Traditional, aristocratic, and modern outlooks coexist and sometimes fuse. This point is aptly illustrated by Clement Attlee's characterization of Winston
Churchill: "There was a layer of seventeenth century, a
layer of eighteenth century, a layer of nineteenth century
and possibly even a layer of twentieth century. You were
never sure which layer would be uppermost." [1] Past and
present interpenetrate so easily in part because "modern-
ism" is not a recent phenomenon in England, but in many
ways an integral part of a tradition stretching back through
the 18th century and further. Attempting to date the point
in time at which England became a modern political system, with modern socio-economic characteristics, modern
political institutions, and a modern political culture, illustrates the complex nature of political change in England.[2]

[1] *The Guardian*, April 21, 1963.
[2] This chapter condenses a lengthy analysis of "modernization" in
Richard Rose, "England: a Traditionally Modern Political Culture" in

As the birthplace of the Industrial Revolution in the late 18th century, England has a longer experience of modern socio-economic conditions than any other country in the world. By 1821, the numbers employed in manufacturing, mining, and industry were already greater than the numbers employed in agriculture. Studies by Max Weber, R. H. Tawney, and R. K. Merton have emphasized, moreover, the extent to which there existed in England prior to industrialization predispositions to modern socio-economic activity.[3] For instance, prior to industrialization, transportation was relatively good, due to the early development of shipbuilding and the large amount of coastline in relation to geographical area. The invention of the steamboat did not lead to an increase in the number of ships, for the country had a fleet of 21,000 ships in 1814. It simply led to an increase in the tonnage and the speed of ships, without altering England's leading position as a maritime nation.

Many political institutions — the monarchy, the law courts, Parliament, and others — can trace their origins back to medieval times. Contemporary political institutions have lengthy histories, but the functions of these institutions have changed markedly through the centuries. For instance, in the course of centuries Parliament has functioned as a supporter of royal authority, as a restraint upon royal authority, as a body initiating legislation and making and un-making Cabinets, and as an arena in which the work of the Cabinet can be discussed, but not controlled. If the franchise is regarded as the chief symbol of modernized institutions, then 1885 is a landmark date in the development of political institutions, for at this general election the majority of adult males were enfranchised, and constituencies were for the first time drawn to represent individuals, and not historic and traditional communities. Yet since that time, the traditional influence of a landed

---

Sidney Verba and Lucian Pye, *Comparative Political Culture* (Princeton: University Press, forthcoming).

[3] See Max Weber, *The Protestant Ethic and the Spirit of Capitalism* (London: Allen & Unwin, 1930); R. H. Tawney, *Religion and the Rise of Capitalism* (London: John Murray, 1926) and R. K. Merton, *op. cit.*

aristocracy has not disappeared at the polls — and prior to that date "popular" elections were held in some areas.

Many values, beliefs, and emotions in the political culture — liberty, deference, trust, community, and others — were strongly supported in England even before the Industrial Revolution.[4] In some respects, they were more strongly challenged in the early period of industrialization than they are today. In this century, the growing value given the mixed economy welfare state indicates a return to preindustrial attitudes and a rejection of the outlook of 19th-century laissez-faire thinkers. One cannot, however, describe this movement as involving modernization or retrogression independently of partisan ideological values.

STABILITY AND ADAPTATION

In order to appreciate the dynamics of political development in England, it is necessary to analyze ways in which the political system is stabilized, as well as ways in which it adapts. Furthermore, the successful integration of adaptations in a stable society must itself be explained. The relatively peaceful course of English political history cannot be taken for granted.

Stabilizing influences in English politics are many and strong. The insular geography of the country gives it clearly defined political boundaries, and has separated England from the disruptive sequence of military invasions common to most European nations. Many norms and symbols of the political culture have static implications for society; for instance, much greater stress is placed upon deference to traditional leaders than upon deference to innovators and would-be innovators. The well-developed and cohesive institutions of political socialization give clear-cut cues for political behavior; the continuities in the socialization process and in the political development of England increase the chance of transmitting attitudes successfully from one political generation to the next. Englishmen enjoy a secure political identity. The effectiveness of

4 See Richard Rose, "England: a Traditionally Modern Political Culture," Table I, and Stanley Rothman, *op. cit.*

socialization is reflected too in the remarkably stable patterns of political participation, both among those active in national politics and those on the periphery; today, as prior to democratic franchise reforms, national politicians are disproportionately recruited from a very small stratum of well-bred young men. In a complementary fashion, this process maintains stable trade unions exclusively for manual workers, as well as the recruitment of many talented individuals into leadership positions in sectors of society divorced from politics. The autonomy of the various segments of society, and of their leaders, makes it impossible for the government to exercise authority throughout the social system. Limits on government are recognized in the culture, and a complex network of pressure groups exists to maintain governmental respect for the jurisdictional rights and authority of many social institutions.

Many resulting conflicts of interest are a stabilizing influence, because they complicate the adoption of new government policies that would upset existing bargains. Party loyalties, because they are integrally linked with class and family loyalties, are not readily changed. This stability is illustrated in voting behavior, where the net swing of votes at postwar general elections has averaged only 1.8 per cent, and by inference, gross changes have been proportionately small. The media of communications insulate the great bulk of the population from continuous awareness of political problems, while keeping the small strata of the politically active informed. Because of the convention of communicating in "code," most consumers of the media are further insulated from news of difficulties, and national politicians can act with less disruption from popular pressures.

The importance of collective consultation in the policy process (notwithstanding the existence of hierarchical forms of Cabinet government) is a stabilizing influence, inasmuch as making policy by lengthy consultation with pressure groups, opinion leaders, advisory committees, and civil servants make it difficult for individuals to force through radical proposals offensive to one or more of these composite groups. The high intellectual caliber of the administrative-class civil service is also a stabilizing influence, inasmuch as the talents of these men are usually trained and developed in order to maintain existing administrative arrangements, rather than to innovate. The output of material benefits that citizens receive from government does not appear to be of particular importance in stabilizing the political system, since the system was relatively stable between the wars, in spite of prolonged economic difficulties. More important is the extent to which Englishmen have low expectations of benefits from government. The legitimacy of British government does not depend upon its material economic achievements. The strong sense of legitimacy that government enjoys is important in maintaining support for existing political institutions.

Adaptation arises not only from new political demands of disadvantaged groups, but also from the desire of defenders of the *status quo* to modify the political system sufficiently to maintain its stability notwithstanding changing social conditions. The norms of the political culture support gradual adaptation and assimilation, just as they are in conflict with sudden and radical innovation. The processes of political socialization are sufficiently flexible to assimilate gradually individual political leaders lacking social background; this, in turn, prevents their alienation from the existing political system. In a complementary fashion, the socialization of potential national politicians stresses the importance of continuous adaptation to group norms, and traditional leaders in English politics usually show themselves capable of undergoing extensive adult "re-socialization," adopting new political attitudes and policies. Individuals of talent recruited out of politics at an early age may rise to leadership elsewhere in society, and can later gain political influence on the basis of their extra-political achievements; the leaders of the early Industrial Revolution are an example of recruitment in new ways. Pressure groups are an important mechanism for adapting the political system to extra-political demands, because they help to articulate new demands, and bring to bear upon government influence derived from extra-governmental positions of social strength. Very occasionally, general elections are important in stimulating political adaptation, though since 1885 only three elections, those of 1886, 1906, and 1945 may be associated directly with major governmental adaptation. Sometimes it is the victorious party that adapts to existing policies — as in the case of the Labour governments of the 1920s or the Conservative government of 1951. The Conservative Party and the majority of the leaders of the Labour Party learn from each other, and from non-partisans.

The major media of communication do not appear to be of great significance in generating political adaptation; rather, the media are often manipulated by those promoting adaptations. They publicize new demands, because new demands are news. Events and actions communicate demands for change more clearly and forcefully — whether behavior in the market place, in the polling booth, or in the use of welfare facilities. Because the authority of government is concentrated in the Cabinet, the machinery of government can quickly adopt and administer political changes, once these changes have been fixed by the composite processes of policy making. The existence of many traditional mechanisms of legitimation gives the dignified appearance of stability to government. This dignity can be useful in obscuring major adaptations or innovations. For instance, the end of Empire, a major innovation in the country's external relations, was masked by the retention of the Queen as the dignified head of the Commonwealth, thus making a major change in external relations more acceptable to staunch defenders of the old Empire.

The integration of disparate political groups in England takes place in two major ways. In some instances, groups are joined together by sharing common attitudes. In others, they are joined by complementary attitudes and patterns of behavior. The high degree of social cohesiveness in England greatly facilitates political integration; freedom from the ethnic, racial, and religious divisions that plague many nations is in part due to accidents of geography, and in part to shrewd political compromises in previous generations. The important consequence is that political differences do not represent irreconcilable social differences. The norms and symbols of the political culture emphasize integration, not only in the stress placed upon a common historical inheritance, but also in the importance attached to the reciprocal rights and duties of those in different political positions. The processes of socialization also exemplify these values, by giving young persons an awareness that political roles are hierarchically differentiated, and that leaders and followers have mutually complementary rights and duties. The functional subsystems of society are linked together not only by the complementary functions of economics and politics, but also by the extent to which leaders in different sectors share political outlooks. Conservative Cabinet ministers and businessmen, Labour Party leaders and trade unionists may come into conflict in pressure-group activities, but they can also be drawn together by party loyalties.

Pressure groups, in pressing upon government, recognize the authority of political leaders, and by doing so give implicit support to the system of which they are a part. The competition between political parties emphasizes policy differences, but parties also stress their commitment to political goals shared throughout the population, and compete in regard to the competence of leadership. At times of major national crisis, parties have met problems by merging into coalitions, or splitting and re-forming along lines that join old opponents into new combinations. The public media of political communication appear to be integrative — that is, they immediately disseminate throughout the nation information about political activities. The uses of the media and the stratification of audiences prevents the media from achieving the political impact their coverage and centralization might suggest. The Cabinet is important in integrating in a single body the leadership of the executive, of the legislature, and of the majority party, and this concentration of leadership increases the bargaining power of the government, vis à vis other political actors. At the most abstract level, integration is achieved in common emotional responses to political symbols such as the monarchy.

The factors tending to cause the political system to stabilize, adapt, and integrate are of many different kinds. Sometimes British government is actively shaping change, and sometimes it is passive, simply reacting to external influences. Many major policy developments in the past generation appear to reflect international trends at work in many societies. Not only is this true in the fields of foreign policy, defense, and colonial affairs, but also in certain aspects of domestic policy, such as government intervention in the economy and the increase in the provision of welfare services. Yet seemingly "inevitable" changes involve short-term difficulties and can, if mishandled politically, leave long-term difficulties. Political leaders may be told that the gross national product will "inevitably" be greater in twenty years — but that does not help them to deal with immediate problems concerning the rate, pace, timing, and nature of economic growth. By contrast, a number of important policy developments have resulted from the unique circumstances of war. Both the First and Second World Wars led to major changes in patterns of government, governmental conflict, and political divisions within society.[5] In wartime, too, unique individuals have had a political impact that, though its weight cannot be precisely calculated, is difficult to ignore. One need not subscribe to a "great man" theory of history to see such wartime leaders as David Lloyd George and Winston Churchill as important influences upon the nation. In peacetime too, men as different as William Gladstone and Ramsay MacDonald have influenced politics by acting conservatively while leading nominally radical political parties.

The institutions of government have a momentum that influences the political system. Each year's spate of legislation reflects the role of government departments in drafting and sometimes initiating policy changes. Government departments may not often seize the political initiative, but the cumulative effect of small changes may be great, though not dramatic. Furthermore, the cumulative effect of apparently small initial spending commitments in welfare areas may in the course of time develop great political momentum.[6] The momentum of

[5] See E. M. H. Lloyd, *Experiments in State Control* (Oxford: Clarendon Press, 1924): R. M. Titmuss, *Problems of Social Policy*, and Alan T. Peacock and Jack Wiseman, *The Growth of Public Expenditure in the United Kingdom* (London: Oxford University Press, 1961).

[6] Cf. Oliver MacDonagh, *A Pattern of Government Growth* (London:

the administrative departments can often operate in conjunction with the unanticipated consequences of short-term political decisions. The development of welfare policies financed by insurance types of contributions is a well-documented instance of ad hoc political decisions casting a shadow more than half a century long.[7] Changes in the expectations of government expressed in cultural norms also play a causal part in political activity. A. V. Dicey has provided the classic analysis of the role of attitudes in stimulating legislation in the 19th century — and of legislation in stimulating attitude changes. Less documented, but no less important is the contrasting impact of the First and Second World Wars upon the political system. The impact of the two wars was different because the First World War did not lead to major adjustments in political outlooks, whereas the Second War did.[8]

Because political change is produced by such a wide variety of factors, some reflecting purposeful political activity and some not, it would be rash to extrapolate patterns of political change from existing tensions in English society. The economic system in the past decade has become increasingly adjusted to the production of mass-consumption goods. England is not yet "affluent" by American standards, but its economy is no longer pervaded by a fear of unemployment, shortages, and rationing. Changes in family life are harder to measure, and even more difficult to relate to politics, though the family seems to be changing, both in the relationships of its members to one another, and of the family, as a unit, to society. The system of higher education is undergoing major changes, in response to greater public demand for education and technological needs. Domestic changes in English society take place in conjunction

MacGibbon & Kee, 1961); Henry Parris, "The Nineteenth-Century Revolution in Government: A Reappraisal Reappraised," *The Historical Journal* (Cambridge) III:1 (1961); and J. Stirling, "Social Services Expenditure During the Last 100 Years," *The Advancement of Science* (London) VIII:32 (1952).

[7] See *Lloyd George's Ambulance Wagon*, edited by Sir Henry Bunbury, especially the commentary by R. M. Titmuss (London: Methuen, 1957).

[8] See, as an illustration in the field of economic planning, D. N. Chester and F. M. G. Willson, *op. cit., passim.*

with changes in international society, and to these England cannot remain indifferent. The country has not yet stabilized its position as a second-rank power. Its nuclear deterrent and power of veto in the United Nations are symbols of front-rank status, yet the country's military establishment is insufficient to ensure national defense without the assistance of the United States. The Commonwealth has since the war developed sufficiently to make it clear that England is no longer dominant. Changes in the international economy in the past decade have been sufficient to indicate that England's traditional export industries such as shipbuilding and cotton, developed during its early industrialization, can no longer serve as the basis for its international trade.

One incalculable factor is the extent to which political changes might be stimulated by a change from a Conservative to a Labour government. The Conservatives in the 1950s welcomed and boasted of many alterations in society, but the Labour Party has always claimed that, if in office, it would stimulate changes wider in scope and more fundamental in importance. The return of a Labour government would help to measure the role of parties in effecting change — not only by what a Labour government might achieve, but also by its failures and by what it avoids attempting to change. In England today, party leaders speak glowingly of social change and economic growth. But researchers have been impressed, in studies of such important social groups as well-paid factory workers, how widespread is the preference for everything "as it is." [9] This stability does not preclude the possibility of major political change. It is, however, a reminder that abrupt and sweeping changes would be out of character with the gradual evolution of the English political system.

A COMPARATIVE PERSPECTIVE

Understanding politics in England requires the use of social-science concepts relevant to many political systems. In a complementary fashion, studying politics in England can illuminate

[9] See F. Zweig, *op. cit.,* p. 189. Note also, Peter Willmott, *op. cit.,* pp. 109ff.

the general study of comparative politics, because of England's international importance and its unusual history of political development.

The international importance of British political institutions is indicated by the widespread adoption of parliamentary forms in many countries. Parliaments can be found in India and Canada as well as in England, though the majority of the 64 members of the Inter-Parliamentary Union conduct politics in very "un-British" ways. The well-disciplined two-party system of Britain can be admired not only in countries that have such a system, but also in countries that lack it. The character of the British civil service has served as the model for many developing nations, and its impress has been strengthened by the example set by British administrators in colonial days. Yet nations such as Pakistan and Burma have demonstrated that it is possible to imitate the form of British administration, without capturing its spirit and degree of efficiency.[10] Events in the Union of South Africa in the past decade have clearly demonstrated how institutions of parliamentary government can be used, in certain social contexts, to give a veneer of legality to a totalitarian government. The advantages of the English political system cannot be gained simply by imitating one or more of its institutional parts.

The ways in which British political institutions are altered in foreign countries emphasize the interdependence of political and social institutions. The success of stable, representative government in England owes much to the good fit between politics and other parts of the social system. The majority of nations in the world that rank highest in both socio-economic development and in stable, representative political institutions — America, Canada, Australia, and New Zealand, as well as England — owe much to the influence of England's social institutions, as well as its political institutions.[11]

---

[10] See, *e.g.*, Ralph Braibanti, "The Civil Service of Pakistan," *South Atlantic Quarterly* LVIII:2 (1960); Lucian Pye, *op. cit.*; *Parliaments, a study* (London: Inter-Parliamentary Union, Cassell, 1962); and Leslie Lipson, *op. cit.*

[11] In Phillips Cutright's classification, only Sweden and Switzerland can

The importance of the fit between political and social institutions is illustrated by the history of the political system at a time when England was not a modern society. Like many developing nations today, England was once a feudalistic and agrarian society. Many problems familiar in developing nations today have analogues in earlier stages of English history. For instance, in the 18th century party politics in England lacked discipline, and the parties lacked meaningful programs; control of the government was determined by intrigue within the political elite, with the liberal use of corruption. In the middle of the 19th century, the civil service for which the country today is famed had not begun to develop, and administration was plagued by ritualism, corruption, and anachronisms not unfamiliar in developing nations.[12] Yet socio-economic change by itself was not the cause for England's success in coping with the problems of political development. European countries such as France and Germany have shown how socio-economic development can occur simultaneously with political upheavals.

The history of political modernization in England does not offer a simple solution to problems now besetting developing countries elsewhere in the world. Perhaps the chief cause of England's contemporary political health is the time it has had in which to develop its political system. Politics in England has been developing gradually, without major discontinuities for nearly 300 years. The family tree of the monarchy shows more discontinuities and lopped branches than the pedigree of modern political institutions. The two major and abrupt breaks with the past — the separation from the Roman Catholic

---

compare with these five nations in development. See his "National Political Development," *American Sociological Review* XXVIII:2 (1963) p. 258. Note also Gabriel Almond, "Comparative Political Systems," *Journal of Politics*, XVIII:3 (1956), and Harry Eckstein, *A Theory of Stable Democracy*.

12 See, *e.g.*, Sir Lewis Namier, *The Structure of Politics at the Accession of George III* (London: Macmillan, 2nd edition, 1961); William B. Gwyn, *op. cit.* E. W. Cohen, *The Growth of the British Civil Service, 1780-1939* (London: Allen & Unwin, 1941) chapters 1-9, and Ronald Wraith and Edgar Simpkins, *Corruption in Developing Countries: including Britain until the 1880s* (London: Allen and Unwin, 1963).

Church in the 16th century, and the Civil War and deposition of James II in the 17th century — both ended in compromises, and left no lasting legacy of irreconcilable conflict. England's traditional inheritance is a consensus about basic features of the political system. Today, political differences with deep historical roots do exist in English society, but the differences are not about the nature of basic aspects of the system — the community, the regime, and cultural values. Nor are historically rooted differences anachronistic; they represent the reflection of continuing conflicts of interest, rather than the maintenance today of controversies that have only a traditional and symbolic meaning.

Although England has a history of political development that many nations might envy, modern England has not been free from major political difficulties. Shortly after the achievement of a modern political system in the late 19th century, the political system was disrupted by the outbreak of a dispute in Ireland that was only settled by revolution and guerilla war. This disturbance lasted for 40 years, and in its later phases there were running, concurrently with industrial unrest, constitutional disputes about the place of the House of Lords, and extra-constitutional agitation for women's suffrage. Economic difficulties reached a climax in the General Strike of 1926 and continued to cause concern throughout the inter-war period. In the 1930s, the threat of world war again loomed large, and the government's appeasement policy failed to prevent war, or to prepare the country fully for it. Today, the country probably faces no problem as difficult as that of recent generations. But the stability of the political system in the changing environment of the postwar world has led, some political observers declare, to the failure of the political system to adapt properly to the 1960s.[13]

A broad judgment upon politics in England must combine two contrasting points. First, agreement upon underlying attitudes in the political culture has not produced agreement as to the methods of solving public problems, and the possession

[13] See the files of *The Economist*, 1963, for the most persistent iteration of this theme. Note also Brian Chapman, *op. cit.*

of stable, representative institutions has not ensured the harmonious, prompt, and efficient solution of all the major policy problems that have faced British government in this century. By comparison with the more than 100 countries belonging to the United Nations England has demonstrated for centuries a high degree of success in coping with the major problems of any political system. This achievement is no little thing.

Appendices

A. NOTES ON FURTHER READING

Whitaker's Almanack, an annual publication, is a compendious source of political, economic, and social information about England. It can be supplemented by *Britain: an Official Handbook,* an annual publication of H.M.S.O. The latter contains more explanatory material of use to foreign readers, but less tabulated information. A. M. Carr-Saunders, et. al., *A Survey of Social Conditions in England and Wales* (3rd edition, 1958) contains series of statistics concerning many social topics. More specialized is D. E. Butler and J. Freeman, *British Political Facts, 1900-1960. Who's Who,* published annually in England, gives biographical data for the majority of living persons mentioned in this book; the *Dictionary of National Biography* and its supplements, along with *Who Was Who,* provide details about deceased politicians.

Any standard encyclopedia will provide a brief outline guide to modern English history. Footnotes on pp. 29-36 give more detailed suggestions for reading. Not mentioned there is Henry Pelling's introductory book, *Modern Britain; 1885-1955,* and the more detailed work of K. B. Smellie, *A Hundred Years of English Government.* Constitutional history can conveniently be studied in Sir David Lindsay Keir, *The Constitutional History of Modern Britain Since 1485* (6th edition, 1960) and G. Le May, *British Government, 1914-1953; Select Documents.*

257

258 _Appendices_

The footnotes of this book provide a detailed bibliography. See also John Palmer, _Government and Parliament in Britain,_ a bibliography published by the Hansard Society. The following books are listed topically as especially useful for reference:

CABINET: J. P. Mackintosh, _The British Cabinet;_ Herbert Morrison, _Government and Parliament_ (2nd edition, 1959).

PARLIAMENT: Roland Young, _The British Parliament;_ Eric Taylor, _The House of Commons at Work;_ Hansard Society, _Parliamentary Reform, 1933-1960._

CIVIL SERVICE: W. J. M. Mackenzie and J. W. Grove, _Central Administration in Britain._

POLITICAL PARTIES: R. T. McKenzie, _British Political Parties;_ Martin Harrison, _Trade Unions and the Labour Party Since 1945._

PRESSURE GROUPS: S. E. Finer, _Anonymous Empire;_ Allen Potter, _Organized Groups in British National Politics._

ELECTIONS: D. E. Butler, _The Electoral System in Britain Since 1918;_ D. E. Butler and Richard Rose, _The British General Election of 1959._

In order to get the "feel" of contemporary political discussion, one could begin by reading regularly or randomly in _Hansard,_ the official report of parliamentary debates. _The Times_ provides the most thorough news coverage of daily papers; _The Guardian_ (formerly the _Manchester Guardian_) is less thorough, but its biases largely offset those of _The Times._ Four weekly periodicals — the _Economist,_ the _New Statesman,_ the _Spectator,_ and _New Society_ — all contain political commentary from varying points of view.

The British Information Service, 845 Third Avenue, New York City 22, maintains a large library of English publications, and also publishes special materials for American readers.

B. THE CABINET

The 23 members of the Cabinet, as of February, 1964 were:

The Prime Minister and First Lord of the Treasury
Secretary of State for Foreign Affairs
Lord President of the Council and Minister for Science

Lord Chancellor
Chancellor of the Exchequer
Secretary of State for the Home Department
Secretary of State for Commonwealth Relations and Secretary of
    State for the Colonies
Chancellor of the Duchy of Lancaster
Minister of Defence
Minister of Labour
Lord Privy Seal
Minister of Transport
Minister of Agriculture, Fisheries & Food
Secretary of State for Industry, Trade and Regional Develop-
    ment and President of the Board of Trade
Chief Secretary to the Treasury and Paymaster-General
Secretary of State for Scotland
Minister of Health
Minister of Power
Minister of Education
Minister of Public Building and Works
Minister of Housing and Local Government and Minister for
    Welsh Affairs
Minister Without Portfolio — (two)

The following ministers were not in the Cabinet: the First
Lord of the Admiralty, Secretary of State for War, Secretary
of State for Air, Minister of Aviation, Postmaster General,
Secretary for Technical Co-operation, Minister of Pensions
and National Insurance, Attorney General, Solicitor-General,
Lord Advocate, Solicitor-General for Scotland, and Ministers of
State for Foreign Affairs (two), Welsh Affairs, Scottish Office,
Commonwealth Relations, Colonial Affairs, Home Office, and
Board of Trade (two). The Parliamentary Secretary to the
Treasury (the majority party's chief whip) stands in a special
relationship to the Prime Minister and the Cabinet.

C. PRIME MINISTERS AND GOVERNMENTS

The following is a list of the Prime Ministers of Britain
since the general election of November, 1885. The name of

the party or parties included in the parliamentary majority is given in parentheses; the chief party is *italicized*.

1885	The third Marquess of Salisbury (*Conservative*)
1886	(February-July) W. E. Gladstone (*Liberal* & Irish nationalist)
1886-1892	The third Marquess of Salisbury (*Conservative* & Liberal Unionist)
1892-1894	W. E. Gladstone (*Liberal* & Irish Nationalist)
1894-1895	The fifth Earl of Rosebery (*Liberal* & Irish Nationalist)
1895-1902	The third Marquess of Salisbury (*Conservative*)
1902-1905	A. J. Balfour (*Conservative*)
1906-1908	H. Campbell-Bannerman (*Liberal*)
1908-1916	H. H. Asquith (*Liberal;* then *Liberal* & Irish Nationalist; then in wartime, *Liberal,* Conservative, & Labour coalition)
1916-1922	David Lloyd George (Wartime *Coalition* until 1918, then Coalition Liberal and *Conservative*)
1922-1923	A. Bonar Law (*Conservative*)
1923	Stanley Baldwin (*Conservative*)
1924	J. Ramsay MacDonald (*Labour* & Liberal)
1924-1929	Stanley Baldwin (*Conservative*)
1929-1931	J. Ramsay MacDonald (*Labour* & Liberal)
1931-1935	J. Ramsay MacDonald (National Labour, *Conservative,* & National Liberal)
1935-1937	Stanley Baldwin (*Conservative*)
1937-1940	Neville Chamberlain (*Conservative*)
1940-1945	Winston Churchill (Coalition of *Conservatives,* Labour, & Liberal)
1945-1951	Clement Attlee (*Labour*)
1951-1955	Winston Churchill (*Conservative*)
1955-1956	Anthony Eden (*Conservative*)
1957-1963	Harold Macmillan (*Conservative*)
1963-	Sir Alec Douglas-Home (*Conservative*)

Index